The Charlotte Observer

presents...

DALE EARNHARDT
REAR VIEW MIRROR

www.thatsracin.com

SPORTS
PUBLISHING
INC.

Sports Publishing Inc.
Champaign, Illinois

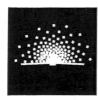

www.thatsracin.com

Supervising Editor: **Michael Persinger**
Coordinating Editor: **Kathy Persinger**
Photo Editor: **John D. Simmons**
Developmental Editors: **Joseph J. Bannon Jr. and Claudia Mitroi**
Interior design and layout: **Michelle R. Dressen and Kenneth J. O'Brien**
Director of Production: **Susan M. McKinney**
Dust jacket design: **Julie L. Denzer and K. Jeffrey Higgerson**
Editorial Assistant: **Lynnette A. Bogard**

Front and back cover photos by
Jeff Siner, *The Charlotte Observer*

All photos courtesy of *The Charlotte Observer*, except where otherwise noted. Credits for photos on page iv go to (clockwise from top left) Ric Feld, AP/Wide World Photos; Layne Bailey/*The Charlotte Observer*; Jeff Siner/*The Charlotte Observer*; Mark Humphery, AP/Wide World Photos; and Christopher A. Record/*The Charlotte Observer*. The photo credit on page v goes to Mark B. Sluder/*The Charlotte Observer*.

Hard cover ISBN 1-58261-426-1
Soft cover ISBN 1-58261-334-6
Leather ISBN 1-58261-428-8

Sports Publishing Inc.
www.SportsPublishingInc.com

Printed in the United States

Acknowledgments

Stock car racing was born in the Carolinas, on Friday nights at little bullrings in places such as Asheville and Hickory and Myrtle Beach. The tradition was begun by bootleggers' sons and other thrill-seekers, sliding through the corners in search of big trophies, small purses and recognition for having the fastest car in town.

From these humble beginnings, stock car racing emerged in the last quarter century as one of sport's most popular and most spectacular attractions. The undisputed leader of this phenomenon was Dale Earnhardt, known to all simply as the "Intimidator." Earnhardt's shocking death at the 2001 Daytona 500 brought the sports world to a sudden stop and took with it a piece of racing history that will never be equaled.

Through it all, *The Charlotte Observer* was there—from the first Strictly Stock race, run with sedans right out of the showroom on June 19, 1949, at a track in Charlotte. That race was the first in what is now the NASCAR Winston Cup circuit, the world's most competitive auto racing series.

For much of the sport's first 50 years, the voice of the sport was *The Observer's* motorsports reporter, Tom Higgins. He was the first newspaper reporter to cover every race on the circuit. He saw the sport rise from those bullrings to national prominence, acting as reporter, critic, advocate and confidant to stock car racing for 38 years, all but the first five of them in Charlotte.

He was among the first to interview Dale Earnhardt, and he remembers a shy, quiet man, scuffing his feet and not looking up when he talked. Higgins broke through by telling Earnhardt he had once interviewed Earnhardt's father, Ralph, at Asheville-Weaverville Speedway. Earnhardt opened up, and Higgins got his story.

But then, Higgins always has a story. Without them, *Rear View Mirror* would not have been possible.

There are others to thank, of course. Reporters such as Bob Myers, who worked for *The Charlotte News* and covered NASCAR's early days. And longtime *Observer* columnist Ron Green, whose career at *The Observer* and *The Charlotte News* started in 1948. He, too, has seen stock car racing's history firsthand.

Their work set the standard for *The Observer's* current motorsports reporters, David Poole and Jim Utter. They carry on the tradition both in print and on the Internet, at www.thatsracin.com.

The photographers who have worked at *The Observer* and *The News* through the years provided the pictures for this book. They watched a career and a life that defined what racing is about—hard work, desire, honesty and achievement—through a camera lens.

Thanks also to Earnhardt himself, for having lived stories worth telling.

And retelling.

THE MAN IN BLACK

Dale Earnhardt loved to race.
No man ever enjoyed his job more. No man ever drove faster or more fearlessly.
No man ever turned left quite as well. Earnhardt was ours.
He was a Kannapolis kid, raised in racing and rooted all his life in North Carolina.
He had an unparalleled career in the No. 3 car, both as the driver
fans loved to hate and, mostly, the one they loved to love.
We lost Dale Earnhardt Sunday, February 18, 2001.
But we will never forget him.

Contents

Chapter One:
Dale and his daddy

June 14, 1972
Like father, like son
by Bob Myers

It was a crisp Saturday night, unseasonal for June. The noise from the old cars shot out through the trees and reverberated sharply, like the train whistle on a cold night.

The good ol' boys, weekend warriors, or what have you, gather at Concord on Saturday to kick up the freshly watered dirt. They've been doing it for ages, and it seems like Ralph Earnhardt was there when they started.

Now, Ralph is oh, 45,46 or so, a granddaddy with a forehead that meets a crew cut about halfway. But they still go there to beat his Camaro. And now they go to beat his son and his brother-in-law.

Ralph has a distinct advantage over the field. He calls on 25 years of experience that date back to some NASCAR Grand National days. Unlike nearly all of his competitors, he's a full-time warrior who works on his cars and that of his adversaries—for a price— in his Kannapolis shop by day. Then on the weekend he hauls his steed out to the area tracks, which is about as far as he wants to go.

"I enjoyed Grand National racing," says Ralph. "But I didn't like the travels. I'm content racing close to home on the weekends." That he's a homebody is evidenced by his five children. That he is content is evidenced by the $20,000 he won at the two tracks last year and the $12,000 he's collected this season.

Dale Earnhardt is 21. He's won five biggies in his old Falcon, has talent and a good attitude after just a year in the ring. "I figure I have a lot to learn," he said. "I guess it took daddy 10 years to know what he was doing. I hope I progress as rapidly as he did."

Dale works in a mill by day, works on the car with owner James Miller by night, splits 50-50, is having his best year with a gross of more than $2,500.

Ralph Earnhardt, father of Dale Earnhardt. (The Charlotte Observer)

September 27, 1973

Ralph Earnhardt, king of short tracks, dies at 45

by Bob Myers

"If they kept records of it, Ralph Earnhardt has probably won more races than any other driver in the country," said Bobby Isaac recently. "He's quite a chauffeur, one of the best short track drivers ever."

Earnhardt, whose driving career spanned 23 years of both Grand National and late model sportsman racing, died Wednesday morning of an apparent heart attack. The Kannapolis native was 45.

While Earnhardt was a major threat in every Grand National race he drove in the late 1950s and early 1960s, it was on the short tracks that he excelled.

No one, including Earnhardt, knew the exact count of his victory total. Like Isaac said, it was an amazing figure.

Earnhardt, who quit the Grand National circuit in 1964, has confined his racing in the past few years to the Fairgrounds Speedway in Charlotte and the Concord Speedway. He captured both track titles last year and his

cars (driven by Stick Elliott and himself) won 10 straight races at Concord earlier this year and have 15 triumphs at the two tracks.

Earnhardt captured the NASCAR sportsman championship in 1956 when he won the track titles at 11 different speedways from Pennsylvania to Florida to Tennessee.

His victory totals have been so impressive in recent years that he said, "I'm making more money now than when I won the sportsman championship."

Earnhardt operated a garage in his backyard and was as talented a mechanic as he was at driving.

Earnhardt, whose last major triumph came in the 1965 sportsman race at Charlotte Motor Speedway, was the father of five.

Son Dale, 22, is regarded as one of the brightest young drivers in the Carolinas. In fact, Ralph felt his son has the ability to be a great Grand National driver in a couple of years.

September 27, 1973

Earnhardt funeral tomorrow

KANNAPOLIS, N.C.—Funeral services for veteran stock car driver Ralph Earnhardt, 45, will be held tomorrow afternoon at 4 o'clock at Center Grove Lutheran Church here.

The family will receive friends from 7-9 o'clock tonight at Lady's Funeral Home here.

Earnhardt died at his home yesterday morning of a heart attack.

Survivors include his wife, Martha Coleman Earnhardt; two daughters, Mrs. Martha Snipes, Concord and Mrs. Kathy Lee Oliver, Kannapolis; three sons, Dale of Kannapolis, Randy of Concord and Danny of the home.

The body will lie in state at the church 30 minutes prior to the service, to be conducted by the Rev. Lonnie Karriker and the Rev. Ralph Brunson.

November 23, 1980

A real father-son racing success story

by Tom Higgins

Although stock-car racing through the years frequently has been a family affair, only two sons have followed fathers to NASCAR national championships.

One duo is the storied Pettys of Level Cross. Papa Lee, patriarch of the clan, sped to Grand National titles in 1954, '58 and '59 before retiring in favor of offspring Richard, the champion in '64, '67, '71, '72, '74, '75 and '79.

The other twosome? Ralph and Dale Earnhardt.

The late Ralph Earnhardt was NASCAR national sportsman division champion in 1956. Son Dale drove to the Winston Cup Grand National championship last week, leading the point standings since the second race of the 31-event season.

Lee Petty's story is well known.

But what of the man who sired Dale Earnhardt, a 29-year-old who in 1979 was rookie of the year and in 1980 won the title?

Ralph Earnhardt, who died at his Kannapolis home of a heart attack on Sept. 27, 1973 at age 45, was a winner from the first time he climbed in a race car.

That was on Easter Sunday in 1949 at the old Concord Speedway, a dirt half-mile track no longer in existence. He won the consolation event, then went on to place third in the late model sportsman feature.

It was the start of a 23-year career that produced more than 500 recorded victories. Undoubtedly, there were many more triumphs that went unlisted in the sport's formative period, when record keeping was shoddy, at best.

"His ability on the short tracks, especially, was amazing," recalls Charlotte Motor Speedway general manager H.A. "Humpy" Wheeler. "Ralph was perhaps the finest dirt track driver who ever lived."

The most intense rivalry I can remember in the sport flared in the summer of 1958. Earnhardt was racing four or five nights per week then, during the era of the short tracks' greatest success, and one of his weekly stops was McCormick Field in Asheville.

The city had lost its minor league baseball franchise, and the park had been transformed into a speedway-of sorts. The track was a quarter-mile around and absolutely flat. Top speed was in the 50 mph range.

Yet every Saturday night the place was packed. A vast majority of the fans came for one reason. To see Earnhardt battle Banjo Matthews, now the sport's top car builder.

Once Earnhardt crashed coming off the fourth turn and his car wedged in the first base dugout. Another time the two tangled in centerfield—er, the backstretch—and Matthews' car flipped and came to rest upside down. It takes some kind of fender-banging competition to flip a car on a quarter-mile track.

With his family—wife Martha and children Kay, Cathy, Dale, Randy and Donny—cheering him on, Earnhardt won the Charlotte fairgrounds and Concord Speedway track titles in 1972.

"Had Ralph lived, I have a feeling he'd still be the best dirt-tracker around," muses Wheeler. "That's the kind of tremendous touch he had."

And that was the man who gave racing its most rousing relative newcomer in many, many years.

May 23, 1981

History lives on Sedan Avenue

by Tom Higgins

The specter of one of stock car racing's most-revered drivers will go along for the ride today when Dale Earnhardt fires the engine of his Pontiac to start the Mello Yello 300 at Charlotte Motor Speedway.

That's because the sleek blue-and yellow machine was built in the backyard garage where the man once engineered his own race cars. The same garage where he suffered a fatal heart attack in 1973 while at work.

That man was Ralph Earnhardt who won NASCAR's national sportsman championship in 1956. In his garage, a 5-year-old towhead of a son named Dale frequently would play with toy cars, proudly mimicking the maneuvers of his pa.

Ah, if only that old garage on Sedan Avenue in a quiet middle-class neighborhood in Kannapolis could talk.

It is a rather ordinary-looking building of cinder blocks, but what extraordinary tales it could tell.

It would tell of first being part of a barn on Ralph Earnhardt's farm, and how one day Ralph put down a square of concrete, moved in some tool boxes and machinery and declared it his racing garage. And then how the cinder blocks were added to form a sturdier exterior.

It would tell of machines humming,

Ralph Earnhardt, father of Dale Earnhardt, in 1972. (The Charlotte Observer)

welding torches spewing flame and engines being revved.

It would tell of matchlessly beautiful Ford coupes, now museum pieces, being painted and shined and hooked to a pickup truck tow rig. The coupes and rig would be taken to places like Columbia Speedway, McCormick Field in Asheville and down the road to Concord for weekly duels with drivers like Banjo Matthews, Ned Jarrett and Dink Widenhouse.

It would tell of hundreds of trophies being brought back and put on the garage shelves by its crew-cut owner.

It would tell of the day the owner died.

It would tell how the distraught family locked the doors for a while, and how the machinery fell silent and dust gathered on the tools—and of an engine its owner never got to use again.

It would tell how Dale Earnhardt, grown to young manhood now, would quit his job at a nearby alignment service in the mid-1970s and reopen those doors, clean the place and start his sportsman racing career from its confines.

It would tell about falling quiet again in '79, when the second-generation racing Earnhardt was given a ride with the bigtime Osterlund Racing organization. That team operated out of a sprawling, glittering shop, and the garage became something of a storage site for Martha, Dale's mom, and the family of his sister, Cathy, both of whom have homes out front.

It would tell of almost bustin' its blocks when Dale first won the Winston Cup Series rookie of the year award in '79 and the Grand National Championship in '80.

And finally, it would tell of a happy day this spring when the doors opened wide again and the machinery came to life and the torches spewed fire and an engine revved powerfully once more.

"Opening my dad's old garage was a have-to case," Earnhardt said.

"But believe me, I didn't mind at all. It's been fun building the car in Kannapolis, and being there brought back a lot of memories that mean a lot to me.

"As we really got into working on the Pontiac, it was almost as if I'd never left the garage. A bunch of mine and dad's old friends who used to volunteer help on the cars came back around again."

Cathy, Dale's sister, looked out the kitchen window of her home toward the garage 50 feet away and sighed.

"It has been like old times having Dale back around," she said.

"We worship him, just like we did Dad all those years he raced out of that old cinder block shop."

Dale Earnhardt takes time out for fishing near his Lake Norman home. (Bill Billings/The Charlotte Observer)

Chapter Two:
The early years, 1975-78

May 29, 1976

Earnhardt's 'going to be a star'

by Tom Higgins

Dale Earnhardt is a 25-year-old Kannapolis resident who walks with perfect posture, shoulders back, head erect. He has the beginnings of an impressive handlebar mustache.

He also has a fire flaming with ferocity somewhere deep within him.

Earnhardt's one ambition in life is to become a driving champion—the equal of Richard Petty, David Pearson, Buddy Baker.

"It has been a long time since I've seen a youngster so determined, so hungry," H.A. "Humpy" Wheeler, Speedway vice president and general manager, said earlier this week. "If nothing happens to sour his attitude, I think he's going to be a star within a few years—and a big one."

"I hope so...I appreciate Humpy saying that," Earnhardt said Friday, with a bit of embarrassment. "Lord knows I've worked hard enough at it and thought about it long enough."

Earnhardt, a rookie who qualified in 25th place in the World 600 lineup, is a second generation driver, the son of sportsman-driving star Ralph Earnhardt, who died in 1973.

"My earliest memory is of watching daddy in a race," said Dale. "Following in his footsteps is all I've ever wanted to do."

Veteran racing observers are amazed at what Earnhardt has done on his own, minus a major sponsor. "He's a threat, right up there with the veterans in every race he enters," said Ned Jarrett, the two-time Grand National champion who now operates Hickory Speedway.

Sunday is important to Earnhardt. "Who knows what a good showing might mean?" he says. "Assurance of a future ride in some more big races at best. Putting my name in some peoples' memory could help later on.

"I'm hepped up about the chance, no sense denying that."

November 8, 1976

Rough and tumble at Atlanta

by Tom Higgins

Hampton, Ga.—Dale Earnhardt, a promising young driver from Kannapolis, flipped and turned an immaculate Chevy racer into a mass of crushed metal Sunday, but walked away with only a slightly cut hand.

His car flipped four or five times—no one was sure which, and Earnhardt didn't remember the crash, which came late in the Dixie 500 at Atlanta International Speedway.

Veteran observers at the track said it was the scariest accident in the super speedway's 17-year history, and there were some anxious moments before Earnhardt was extracted from the mauled machine. It appeared he had to be seriously injured—or worse.

The accident occurred on Lap 271 of the 328-lap race when the steering failed on Dick Brook's Ford. Brook's car blocked the "groove" of the track, leaving Earnhardt helpless to maneuver.

"The last thing I remember is thinking 'I should have gone high' to get around," said Earnhardt, a sportsman division star in the Carolinas. "I don't know what happened after we hit. It's all just a blur. I don't remember flipping."

Meanwhile, many members of the racing fraternity were coming by to tell Earnhardt, making only his second Grand National start not to blame himself. Included was Johnny Ray, the car's owner.

"Hey, don't worry about the car," said Ray. "We can build another one of those. But we can't build another race driver."

But Earnhardt, 25, was not upset about his fate. It was the race car.

"It was just a one-race deal," said Earnhardt, "but it might have been much more if I hadn't torn up the car. Man, that's all Johnny Ray has is that car."

Dale Earnhardt, who lives at Lake Norman, cools it in another form of fast transportation. (Don Hunter/The Charlotte Observer)

Chapter Three:
1979: Rookie of the year

Races	Won	Top 5	Top 10	Poles	Earnings
27	1	11	17	4	$264,086

April 2, 1979

WIN NO. 1: BRISTOL
The future starts now
by Tom Higgins

Bristol, Tenn.—Dale Earnhardt, a rookie for whom stardom had been predicted several years down stock car racing's rocky road, showed Sunday that the future is now, whizzing to victory ahead of veterans Bobby Allison and Darrell Waltrip in the Southeastern 500 at Bristol International Raceway.

Earnhardt, 27, son of the late, legendary short-track star Ralph Earnhardt of Kannapolis, pulled away from his more experienced rivals in a 23-lap dash to the checkered flag, much to the delight of a crowd estimated at 26,000.

"I know that somewhere there's a fellow that's got a big smile and is mighty, mighty proud and even more happy than I am, if that's possible," said Earnhardt, referring to his father, who died of a heart attack in 1973.

His eyes moistened a bit, as did those of crew chief, J.C. "Jake" Elder.

"It's by far the biggest win of my career, no question," Elder said with much emotion, belying his reputation as a tough ol' "kingmaker" who has built winners for such superstar drivers as Fred Lorenzen, David Pearson, Benny Parsons and Waltrip.

"Dale can be as good as anybody I ever worked with, " he said firmly.

Earnhardt, making only his 16th start on the NASCAR Grand National tour, averaged 91.033 mph in earning $19,800 from the record purse of $110,650.

Waltrip was leading when the final, sixth caution flag was waved.

"I knew with so little distance left to go that the key was getting out of the pits first," said Elder. "I'd told the crew we just had to do it..."

The crew did, and Earnhardt rewarded their effort, getting a good jump when flagman Chip Warren unfurled the green and never losing any of that advantage.

When Warren exchanged the green for the checkered, the Osterlund crew embraced and danced jigs while members of other teams came over to offer congratulations.

Earnhardt, the Kannapolis youngster born and bred to racing, went around in unusually slow fashion, savoring the moment and the fact that all those predictions made in his behalf had been realized.

Only difference is, his future is now.

Earnhardt, without his trademark mustache, chats with Bobby Allison at Rockingham. *(Don Hunter/The Charlotte Observer)*

April 2, 1979

He's a winner by any name

by Tom Higgins

Bristol, Tenn.—It was Saturday, sort of a lazy, take-it-easy time for drivers who had qualified Friday for the Southeastern 500 at Bristol International Raceway.

A few members of the media and others involved in racing were kibitzing with Dale Earnhardt, the NASCAR rookie-of-the-year candidate from Kannapolis. There were no heavy or technical exchanges about what gear he and his team, headed by crew chief Jake Elder, were going to run in Sunday's race or anything like that.

In fact, typical of the repartee was an exchange that went like this...

Reporter: "Dale, most everyone in racing has a nickname. What would you like yours to be?"

Earnhardt: "Darrell Waltrip II." He paused, the cogs in his clever mind obviously working. "Naw," he said, "make that Jaws II."

Following Sunday's race, Waltrip, a sporting sort, probably wouldn't have taken offense if someone called him Dale Earnhardt II.

Earnhardt outran Waltrip and the rest of Winston Cup stock car racing's established stars to post his first Grand National victory... The

first of many, estimated Elder.

"I saw how The Boy (Earnhardt) ran at Daytona and I was impressed," he said. "For someone that's been doing this as long as I have, you just have a way of telling (raw talent). Then, back in March, I knew I wasn't gonna be happy without having my own car and I had a chance to go over there and work with The Boy and Roland Wlodyka (the team manager) and the rest. So I quit that team with Herb Nab and (driver) Buddy Baker and went.

"We run our first race together at Atlanta on March 18 and The Boy impressed me even more. I said, 'Hey, we're going to win some races this year the way he can drive.'

"Well there's no limit to what he can do if something doesn't hit us, like The Boy getting hurt. I'll be surprised if we don't win a couple of supers (races on big tracks like Charlotte Motor Speedway) and some more on the short tracks. Darrell Waltrip is a friend of mine; we worked hard together and all that, but right now, at the same stage and the age as when I was with him, I'd have to say The Boy has more potential."

April 7, 1979

Rookie Earnhardt is driving his way to racing's front row

by Bob Myers

"The Osterlund crew couldn't be happier if someone had given them a million dollars," said Earnhardt. "And I think my dad would be proud, too."

It's unusual for a rookie to command a top-flight car. Racing wheel-to-wheel at high speeds and banging fenders on half-mile ovals, it doesn't take long for superstars to get to know a rookie, and they are leery and cautious around inexperienced drivers. But Earnhardt is highly-regarded at this stage of his career.

How good is he? What's his potential?

"Naturally I'm prejudiced," said Elder, instrumental in Darrell Waltrip's rise to stardom over the past six years, "but Dale can be as good as any of them."

Said Cale Yarborough, "Dale's got about as much potential as anybody I've seen in a long time. If he doesn't rush it, he'll make it big."

Earnhardt at Pocono: Hello, wall

by *Tom Higgins*

Long Pond, Pa.—Standout NASCAR Grand National newcomer Dale Earnhardt of Kannapolis suffered a severe setback to his rookie-of-the-year hopes Monday when he suffered broken collarbones in a crash while leading the Coca-Cola 500 at Pocono (Pa.) International Speedway.

The injury is expected to keep Earnhardt, 28, out of action for 6-8 weeks. Earnhardt, winner of the April 1 Southeastern 500 at Bristol, Tenn., led the rookie race entering Monday's event, with 233 points to 216 for Joe Millikan of Randleman.

Earnhardt, driving for a Charlotte-based team owned Californian Rod Osterlund, was fifth in Winston Cup point standings. He had finished sixth or better in six of seven starts, including third-place showings in his past two races.

He was first taken to the track infield hospital, then transported by helicopter to East Stroudsburg Hospital, where his injury was diagnosed as a bilateral fracture of the clavicle (both collarbones).

"Dale was in extreme pain... they put him on the helicopter on a board because the doctors felt there might be some back injuries, and they felt an ambulance ride would be too excruciating for him," a team member said. "The seat and steering wheel were wrenched a good bit to the left. He took quite a lick."

Earnhardt's girlfriend, Teresa Houston of Hickory, talked briefly with Earnhardt, who was sedated heavily. She said all Earnhardt could remember was the tire blowing. He did not remember hitting the wall.

August 11, 1979

Earnhardt's wreck 'a fuzzy dream'

by Bob Myers

is something of a dream walker, and darn glad that he *can* walk and dream.

Earnhardt doesn't remember much about the awful crash of his race car at Pocono, Pa., two weeks ago Sunday. To him, he says, it's like a fuzzy dream.

The physical pain—from two broken collarbones, a concussion and severe bruises of the neck and chest— is subsiding. But the uncertainty of whether he'll be out of action for four to six weeks or longer and unable to defend his current points lead toward rookie of the year honors gnaws at his innards.

Earnhardt, wearing a shoulder harness and still weak from his ordeal, wants to drive in the Aug. 25 race at Bristol, Tenn. He won his first Grand National Winston Cup race there in April. No rookie had won on the circuit in five years.

But a reporter suggested, "That's a tough place on collarbones. You're running over 100 mph on a half-mile track and turning every seven seconds."

"Naw, it wouldn't be that hard," he said Friday, brushing aside any suggestion of potential problems. "I'm the best on short tracks.

"I vaguely remember going down the backstretch and the tire letting go. The next thing I remember was flying (to the hospital) in a helicopter.

"The doctor in charge told me that judging from the way the collarbones were broken, it was an act of God my neck wasn't broken, too," Earnhardt said.

If there is anything Earnhardt has learned from having to face this adversity, it's the concern shown by others.

"I thank God that I have more friends than I ever imagined," he said. "I cannot believe all the calls, messages and remembrances I've received.

"I might have a bruised heart, but it's not broken."

> "The doctor in charge told me that judging from the way the collarbones were broken, it was an act of God my neck wasn't broken, too."
> —Dale Earnhardt

Chapter Four:
1980:
Winston Cup champion

Races	Won	Top 5	Top 10	Poles	Earnings
31	5	19	23	0	$588,926

January 25, 1980

Osterlund issues Earnhardt a 5-year ticket to ride

by Tom Higgins

Charlotte, N.C.—Dale Earnhardt is one young auto racing driver who won't have to worry about where his next "ride" is coming from.

Earnhardt, a 28-year-old Kannapolis native, acknowledged Thursday he has signed a long-term contract with Osterlund Racing, the Derita-based team whose cars Earnhardt drove to NASCAR's 1979 rookie-of-the year championship on the Winston Cup circuit.

"Rod Osterlund and I have agreed on a five-year deal with three option years... and I couldn't be more tickled," Earnhardt said from his Lake Norman home. "Talk about job security, I've got it. It frees me to concentrate on winning races and going for the driving championship, and believe me that's a tremendous plus."

> **"Talk about job security, I've got it."**
>
> **—Dale Earnhardt**

"Rod's as tickled as I am, 'cause now he won't have to listen to rumors all the time about his driver quitting and going to another team.

"We spent last year learning each other and we're ready to go now," continued Earnhardt. "I expect us to make vast improvement over '79 because now we know how to work with each other."

Earnhardt's championship season wasn't without frustration. At the Coca-Cola 600 in May, he finished 20th after a Turn 4 crash on Lap 276. *(Don Hunter/The Charlotte Observer)*

February 11, 1980
Clash victory proves he's a rookie no more
by Bob Myers

Daytona Beach, Fla.—**Dale Earnhardt** doesn't profess to be a Richard Petty, but there is one thing he is not. He is no longer a rookie.

The 28-year-old stock car driver proved Sunday that he is no longer a yearling in the sport's big league by beating 11 of the best in the business in the Busch Clash at Daytona International Speedway.

Earnhardt, a second-generation driver whose late father, Ralph, would have been justly proud, won the 20-lap, 50-mile Busch Clash and earned $50,000 in 15 minutes, 39 seconds.

After the nationally-televised race, Earnhardt was like a kid with a jar full of cookies, absolutely ecstatic, and rightfully so.

"Earnhardt made the right move and Earnhardt won the race and Earnhardt is just tickled to death," said the tall, mustachioed driver for Charlotte-based Osterlund Racing, Inc. "I grew up a little more today.

"This does so much for my confidence and for the team. We really have our act together. Now I feel certain that I can win the Daytona 500 next Sunday."

March 13, 1980
Earnhardt closing in on victory circle
by Bob Myers

Dale Earnhardt is edging closer and closer to a victory, and he could get it as quickly as this Sunday in the Atlanta 500.

The super sophomore of the Osterlund team has finished no worse than fifth in the first four Winston Cup races-second at Riverside, fourth at Daytona, fifth at Richmond and third at Rockingham, all tracks of different dimensions. He won the 50-mile Busch Clash and the $50,000 first prize in the TV special at Daytona International Speedway. He leads Sir Richard Petty by 52 points in the Winston Cup standings and is third in earnings with $76,000.

"What a difference a year makes, said Earnhardt. "Winning the Busch Clash against 11 of the best gave me a lot of confidence. I think that we'll win another race soon. At least I don't feel like I'm a rookie any longer. And I know there were some snickers when I said before the season started we were capable of taking the championship."

The Charlotte Observer

March 17, 1980
WIN NO. 1: ATLANTA
Move over, old guys
by Tom Higgins

Hampton, Ga.—Southern-style stock car racing is supposed to be a sport for the men with the most hair on their chests. But Sunday's Atlanta 500 belonged to a pair of relative youngsters, Dale Earnhardt and Rusty Wallace.

Earnhardt, 28, drove to the first 500-mile victory of his Winston Cup circuit career.

Wallace, 23, finished an impressive second in his very first NASCAR Grand National Division start.

Earnhardt sped a Derita-based Monte Carlo engineered by veteran Jake Elder to victory after a bid by Cale Yarborough was doomed 28 laps from the finish at Atlanta International Raceway by a faulty distributor.

As Yarborough slowed, Earnhardt sped around leader Bobby Allison's sputtering Ford on lap 300 and gambled that his badly worn left side tires would last.

"We took a chance...I left the decision on the tires to Dale," said Elder, never noted for affording his drivers such options. "He asked me back on the radio hookup if we could make it the rest of the way on gas. When I told him we could, then he said...Well, let *him* tell you what he said."

Earnhardt grinned and repeated the line at a post race interview:

"Hell yes, I'm gonna go."

Go he did.

"The win at Bristol was special, but whether I show it or not I'm very excited now. A superspeedway win is so prestigious because all the guys run harder and do their best on the big tracks. I'll probably wake up in the middle of the night and just start whooping."

March 31, 1980
WIN NO. 2: BRISTOL
What sophomore jinx?
By Tom Higgins

Bristol, Tenn. – If there was ever such a thing as a sophomore jinx in stock car racing, forget it.

Dale Earnhardt, the NASCAR Winston Cup circuit rookie of the year in 1979, continued to slash that old superstition to shreds Sunday, speeding to victory by a comfortable 8.7 seconds over Darrell Waltrip in the Valleydale Southeastern 500 at Bristol International Raceway.

Tradition would have the second-year Grand National driver currently in the throes of a terrible season. But Earnhardt, a 28-year-old Kannapolis native who now lives near Terrell on Lake Norman, is speeding along just splendidly.

For example:

• The triumph Sunday in front of an estimated 25,000 fans was Earnhardt's second straight, following the Atlanta 500 March 13. And it's his third of the year, counting the Busch Clash last month at Daytona Beach, Fla.

• He leads the Winston Cup driving championship race with 1,025 points, 80 more than second-place Bobby Allison, who finished third Sunday.

• Earnhardt is the circuit's leading money winner with $132,945 – and that doesn't include the $50,000 Busch Clash winner's purse.

"I love it ... I love it ... I love it!" exclaimed the easygoing son of the late short-track champion Ralph Earnhardt. "Now I could do with making this a habit."

May 27, 1980

A legend turns in his keys

by Tom Higgins

Charlotte, N.C.—Veteran crew chief J.C. "Jake" Elder quit the Osterlund Racing Team on Monday. Osterlund fields cars for Dale Earnhardt, current points leader in the race for the Winston Cup driving championship.

"Jake just came in about 10:30 this morning and turned in his keys to the shop and his credit cards and indicated he was quitting," said Bill Somers, a spokesman for the Derita-based organization owned by Californian Rod Osterlund.

Elder, 42, widely-respected in stock car racing for two decades, could not be reached for comment.

Reliable sources said Elder had been unhappy that the team-managed by Roland Wlodyka entered a car in Saturday's Mello Yello 300 preliminary to Sunday's World 600. Elder, they said, wanted to concentrate on 1979 rookie of the year Earnhardt's Grand National division Chevrolet for the 600.

Earnhardt appeared in excellent position to win both races over the weekend at Charlotte Motor Speedway. However, a broken right front wheel sidelined him as he was pulling away in the 300 and a blown tire foiled his chances in the 600. Elder had contended the Osterlund Team had the fastest car in the 600.

Elder worked feverishly with other team members Sunday, repairing sheet metal damage to the Earnhardt Chevy and getting him back in the race to preserve the points lead.

"I hate to see Jake go," said Earnhardt. "He's tops and has been a key in the development of our team. But if this is his decision, I'm going to respect it."

"I like Jake," said Wlodyka. "Maybe this is best if he needs a break. The sport is so competitive, there is a lot of pressure on everyone involved."

Crew chief Jake Elder talks with Earnhardt at Rockingham in early 1980. Elder, citing differences with team owner Rod Osterlund, resigned in May and was replaced by Doug Richert. (Don Hunter/The Charlotte Observer)

Earnhardt chats with NASCAR great Cale Yarborough before qualifying at Charlotte. Earnhardt's challenge of established drivers like Yarborough made him unpopular with some fans. (Bill Billings/The Charlotte Observer)

July 14, 1980
WIN NO. 3: NASHVILLE
Hot weather, hot car

Nashville, Tenn. — NASCAR points leader Dale Earnhardt practiced while most drivers stayed out of the 101-degree heat. That strategy paid off with a victory Saturday in the Nashville 420 Grand National stock car race.

Earnhardt had pole-winner Cale Yarborough on his back bumper for the final 30 laps, but he held on to win the 420-lap race by 2 car lengths. Earnhardt took home $14,600 and set a race record, averaging 93.811 mph on the .596-mile oval. Bobby Allison, who finished sixth, set the old record of 92.24 in 1972.

"It set the car up for real hot temperatures that we encountered—tires heating up real hot. We got an idea of what the heat was going to be and it helped us."

Saturday's victory was his first since crew chief Jake Elder quit following the World 600 in Charlotte May 25.

September 29, 1980
WIN NO. 4: MARTINSVILLE
Seeing yellow
by Tom Higgins

Martinsville, Va.—Dale Earnhardt escaped an angry fender-banging episode with Dave Marcis and later held off Buddy Baker, winning the Old Dominion stock car race Sunday at Martinsville Speedway.

In keeping with a pattern of peculiar incidents that brought out the caution flag a record 17 times, Earnhardt swept to the lead 13 laps from the finish when seemingly-sure winner Cale Yarborough got a flat tire.

Earnhardt brought his Chevrolet to the checkered flag just 1.35 seconds ahead of Baker's Chevy.

The outcome enabled Earnhardt to pad his lead toward the Winston Cup driving championship to 105 points over Yarborough, who finished third.

On Lap 216, Earnhardt and Marcis, tangled in heavy traffic while battling for the lead in Turn 2. They banged sheet metal two more times entering the backstretch and Earnhardt finally lost control and spun completely around.

Earnhardt, who had replaced Marcis as driver for the Derita-based Rod Osterlund team in 1979, maintained power and kept going.

The "hard racin'" seemed to have the caution flag flying every 20 laps or so —the yellow was out 79 laps total-and held Earnhardt's average speed to a slow 69.728 mph on the .525-mile track.

Crew chief Doug Richert, who replaced Jake Elder during the 1980 season, discusses strategy with Earnhardt. The two youngsters formed NASCAR's top team and produced a Winston Cup title. (Bill Billings The Charlotte Observer)

September 29,1980
Tag, you're hit
by Jody Meacham

No tricky moves or deft fakes-Earnhardt won the Old Dominion 500 Sunday by driving around the people who would get out of the way and over people who wouldn't.

The track was littered with those who tangled with NASCAR's boy wonder and lost-Cale Yarborough and Dave Marcis among others. When it was over, there were few cars on the track without at least a dab of yellow and blue paint.

"I came here to race," he said. "I didn't come here to stroke for points."

If anyone is to take championship honors from Earnhardt now, the leader will have to have a sudden change of fortune. Through 27 races this year, his car has fallen out of only four and has finished fifth or better 16 times.

He cannot lose the championship now by losing races, he can only lose it by not finishing them. But that fact has not made him more cautious.

"I told Roland (Wlodyka, team manager) before the race that I really wanted to win Charlotte," Earnhardt said. "He said, 'Well I want to win Martinsville, too.' So I said, 'OK, we'll win them both."

Earnhardt keeps an eye out while his crew works on his car during practice before the World 600 at Charlotte. (Don Hunter/ The Charlotte Observer)

October 1, 1980

He'd rather do it than talk about it

by Jody Meacham

He said he was scared when the car broke loose down the backstretch at Martinsville Speedway, but he was laughing when he said it.

Dale Earnhardt would not have traded his place in the cockpit at that instant for any safe and stationary armchair.

With his head cocked against the window netting and slumped down until his eyes are nearly at headlight level, Earnhardt is at peace in the noise and tumult of a racing car.

He didn't have to learn how to drive. The touch it takes to keep one of those wild machines under control, the racing instincts, the guts to hang on for the ride-all of those qualities were inherited from his father, Ralph, one of the greatest sportsman drivers ever.

At 29, he seems about to complete the quickest rise to the national championship since Red Byron won NASCAR's first title in 1949.

But Earnhardt inherited the racing genes of a father who, despite his success, never drove in racing's big time. The biggest dilemma Ralph Earnhardt ever faced was which side to pass on. The greatest obstacle he ever had to overcome was making up laps under the green flag. Those were the only skills he could hand down to his son.

Ralph Earnhardt's entire career was witnessed by not many more people than see a single race at Daytona. In all his victories, he was probably interviewed by fewer reporters than will talk to his son in one season. He never won a million dollars, yet his son, at the current rate, will pass that milestone in his third year on the circuit.

He could not prepare his son to handle the success Dale was certain to enjoy.

"I feel at peace out there in a race car, but in here I'm uncomfortable. I have to say the right thing and give you good answers and not say anything that could hurt my team." Dale said.

Earnhardt is a quiet contrast to a sports world full of young stars more than willing to speak their minds.

He didn't have four years on a college team with a coach to protect him while he got acclimated to public attention. It came suddenly last year when he won the Southeastern 500 at Bristol, Tenn., and became the only rookie in history to win a Grand National race.

Any other pro athlete about to accomplish what Earnhardt is on the verge of achieving would probably be demanding to renegotiate the deal. But Earnhardt responded to questions about that subject saying, "Percentage-wise, if the man who owns the car gave me any more, he'd be crazy. He wouldn't be doing the team justice."

Definitely unusual, perhaps naive, but pure Dale Earnhardt.

> "I feel at peace out there in a race car, but in here I'm uncomfortable. I have to say the right thing and give you good answers and not say anything that could hurt my team."
> —Dale Earnhardt

Win No. 5: CHARLOTTE

October 6, 1980

Dream come true

by Tom Higgins

Dale Earnhardt was a 9-year-old growing up in Kannapolis when Bruton Smith and the late Curtis Turner turned the first spade of earth to build nearby Charlotte Motor Speedway.

Since then, the track has seldom strayed far from the thoughts of Earnhardt—son of the late Ralph Earnhardt, a short track star in the 1950s and early '60s.

"I used to come down here to the races with Daddy and Momma," Earnhardt said Sunday. "We'd come to the infield and park over on what used to be a hill between the first and second turn.

"I watched 'em run," he said. And Earnhardt undoubtedly fantasized he'd someday run against—and beat—the stock car racers he mingled with in his youth.

The dream came true Sunday. At 29, he rolled past his own boyhood heroes—Cale Yarborough and Buddy Baker—for victory in the National 500.

"I got a high when I won my first Grand National race at Bristol," said Earnhardt, NASCAR '79 Winston Cup rookie of the year, referring to the Southeastern 500 in Tennessee last year. "I may not show it, but I'm a lot higher now than I was then. This is the best, winning here at home before so many hometown friends and fans."

Earnhardt was pressed at his postrace news conference about whether there was a close encounter when he and Darrell Waltrip and Baker went into the third turn three abreast. "What kind of sensation is that?" someone asked.

"It's a great feeling if you come out of Turn 3," he cracked.

In that case, Earnhardt felt great all day, because he came out of turn three throughout the race, and out of turn four the final time with flagman Harold Kinder waving the checkered flag for him.

So the boy who watched Charlotte Motor Speedway's birth has finally become a winner at the track. In the process, Earnhardt moved closer to the entire Winston Cup circuit championship, now leading Yarborough by 115 points for the title.

"I'm not feeling any pressure," insisted Earnhardt, only three races away from the championship, estimated to be worth $300,000 in bonuses and endorsements. "The pressure as I see it is on Cale and Benny Parsons and Richard Petty, 'cause they're behind.

"And I'm not gonna let up. We're going to win it by racin' all-out."

'Home' is sweet for Earnhardt

At long last Charlotte Motor Speedway is truly home, sweet home for Dale Earnhardt.

Earnhardt, 29, a native of Kannapolis, just 12 miles north of the track on N.C. 29, wheeled to victory in Sunday's National 500 stock car race. The victory delighted most of the chilled crowd of approximately 75,000.

When Earnhardt sped his blue-and-yellow Osterlund Racing Chevrolet under the checkered flag 1.83 seconds ahead of Cale Yarborough, many fans began tossing caps of those same colors (bearing Earnhardt's likeness) into the air.

"No one can know how much I've dreamed and thought about this moment," Earnhardt said upon arrival in victory lane with his jubilant crew, led by Roland Wlodyka and Dough Richert. "It's an even better feeling than I thought it would be."

Earnhardt, in a suit instead of a racing uniform, poses in uptown Charlotte with the new downsized cars NASCAR adopted for the 1981 season. (Tom Franklin/ The Charlotte Observer)

October 6, 1980
One of NASCAR's best
by Jody Meacham

Until recently, what looks to be Dale Earnhardt's first NASCAR Grand National championship was being built of steady, but unspectacular, stuff—a collection of top-five finishes and only an occasional victory.

But in the last two races, the 29-year-old Kannapolis native has begun putting some crown jewels in his championship crown with a pair of victories in the season's stretch run.

First, in Martinsville, Va., a week ago, and then again Sunday in the National 500, Earnhardt out-muscled and outran everyone on the track to add some sizzle to his reputa-tion and take some out of the championship chase.

He now has five victories this year, tying him for the most with Darrell Waltrip.

Earnhardt's victory at Charlotte Motor Speedway, the first at his home track, added 10 more points to his lead over Cale Yarborough, No. 2 in the Winston Cup standings, and put him 115 points ahead with three races left in the season.

It also paid $49,050, which is the most he's ever won in a Winston Cup race. Earnhardt's season winnings now total $432,675, tops in NASCAR.

The temperature never rose above 55 degrees during qualifying for the October race in Charlotte, but Earnhardt was happy. His car was hottest on the track, taking the pole. (Davie Hinshaw/ The Charlotte Observer)

October 18, 1980

Title's in the cards, and Dale's holding aces

by Jody Meacham

Rockingham, N.C.— The NASCAR championship chase has turned into a poker game, with Dale Earnhardt holding most of the high cards.

He has 115 points on Cale Yarborough, the player with the next best hand at the table, and only three more races to run.

But if he's wanting to gamble his winnings to force Yarborough and the rest of his pursuers out of the game, he might choose a better place than North Carolina Motor Speedway to do it.

Sunday's 16th-annual American 500 here at noon is a risky place to bet a championship. Over the years, this track has become a favorite wrecking spot for many drivers, and a wreck is about the only thing that can keep Earnhardt from his first NASCAR title.

One reason, perhaps, is the peculiar nature of this 1.017-mile track-too short, really, to be called a superspeedway, yet too fast to be labeled a short track.

A 500-mile race here takes at least 4 hours to run and that's a long time to suffer ear-piercing noise without flinching.

November 16, 1980
Title help comes from above
by Tom Higgins

Ontario, Calif.— Dale Earnhardt got away with two glaring errors in the L.A. Times 500 Saturday and held off Cale Yarborough to win stock car racing's Winston Cup championship by 19 points.

Earnhardt finished fifth, Yarborough third in their Chevrolets.

For the second straight year, Benny Parsons won at Ontario Motor Speedway. But again, Parson's triumph was overshadowed by the Grand National point competition. In 1979, the NASCAR season finale decided the title in favor of Richard Petty over Darrell Waltrip.

Earnhardt and his Osterlund-Wrangler Racing Team headquartered in Derita made it a cliffhanger with two uncharacteristic goofs.

Earnhardt, a Kannapolis native now living at Doolie on Lake Norman, pitted too early during the first caution period and lost a lap. The deficit loomed as a potential disaster for three-fifths of the $205,000 race, because Yarborough appeared headed to victory as Earnhardt barely made the top 10.

Then, after making up the lap—and actually taking the lead late in the race—Earnhardt and his crewmen crossed signals on his last pit stop, on the 183rd of 200 laps. He drove over the jack and left three lug nuts off the right rear wheel in the process. As a result, NASCAR officials black-flagged Earnhardt onto pit road on Lap 186 for a penalty stop while the lug nuts were put on.

Remaining in the same lap, he rolled away to rejoin a chase dominated by Bobby Allison. More importantly, Earnhardt stayed within enough positions of Yarborough to prevent the three-time champion from Sardis, S.C., from making up the 29-point deficit he had starting the event.

"We were lucky, and I really believe we had some help from a pretty high source," Earnhardt, 29, said after becoming the only second-year driver in the Grand National division's 31-year history to take the title. "You can prepare as carefully as possible and run as hard as you can, but in the end having faith and believing counts for an awful lot."

"Amen to that," said Parsons, who took the $24,385 first prize that seemed almost in Allison's pocket.

> "We were lucky, and I really believe we had some help from a pretty high source."
> **—Dale Earnhardt**

25

November 17, 1980
Lucky in Vegas
by Tom Higgins

Las Vegas, Nev.—Dale Earnhardt's good fortune didn't change when he flew to Las Vegas Saturday night for 18 hours of fun after winning the Winston Cup stock car driving championship via a fifth-place finish in the L.A. Times 500.

First, Earnhardt walked into the room reserved for him by sometime-race driver Mel Larson, whose full-time job is public relations director at the Circus-Circus Hotel and Casino. Dale's eyes bulged, as did those of his younger brothers, Randy and Donny, whom he had brought along from hometown Kannapolis.

They were in an elaborate suite with ceiling-high mirrors, gaudy chandeliers, a fully stocked bar, a spiral staircase, a piano and three bedrooms. One bed, elevated and surrounded by wall and ceiling mirrors, was and must have been 20 feet across.

"Gol-l-l-l-e-e-e!" said 29-year-old Earnhardt, mimicking television character Gomer Pyle. "This is as big as most houses back home."

Then Earnhardt, driver for the Rod Osterlund-Wrangler Team, took to the gaming tables. Within a half-hour or so, Earnhardt won $500 playing blackjack—as if he needed it.

With fifth place at the Ontario (Calif.) track, he pushed his season winnings to $464,860, excluding $50,000 for victory in last February's Busch Clash for 1979 pole winners.

The Winston Cup championship is estimated to be worth another $300,000 in bonuses, personal appearance fees and endorsements.

And it almost didn't happen.

Earnhardt and his crew made two big errors that could have meant losing the championship.

First, there was miscalculation when to pit during the first yellow flag period. That put Earnhardt a lap down, once as far as 11 positions back of point challenger Cale Yarborough of Sardis, S.C. If the race had finished that way, Yarborough and his team would have taken the title easily.

Then, after Earnhardt regained that lap, there was a communication breakdown on what was to be a final gasoline-only pit stop. Three lug nuts were taken off the right rear wheel for a tire change when Earnhardt was told to go and sped off.

"It's embarrassing, but what can you say? It happened," said Earnhardt.

"It's a wonder the wheel didn't come off and put me in the wall. . . We were lucky, but that's part of it."

The Earnhardt-Yarborough showdown—heightened by their Chevrolets starting 1-2—didn't materialize in the early stages. Only once did they vie for the lead, on lap three when Earnhardt challenged but was held off.

After that, Earnhardt retreated, and by Lap 60 was nearly lapped by Darrell Waltrip and Richard Petty, whose Chevys—destined to be sidelined with blown engines—appeared to be the fastest cars. On Lap 69 the yellow flew, seemingly saving Earnhardt, but the hasty pit stop cost a lap anyway.

Then the Earnhardt-Yarborough duel materialized. From Lap 156 to 176 of the 200-lap chase, they maneuvered for the lead in a two-car draft before a crowd generously estimated near 40,000.

Shortly after, Earnhardt and crew made their second mistake and Yarborough began having tire problems. He finished third—behind winner Benny Parsons and Neil Bonnett.

That outcome enabled Earnhardt to become the only second-year driver to be the champ.

There's another important factor that "means about as much to me as anything," Earnhardt said.

"The two years I've been on the Winston Cup circuit many of the veterans have good-naturedly always called me 'Boy.' Now several of 'em, including Junior Johnson, have offered congratulations and called me 'Champ.' "

Chapter Five:
1981: A season in reverse

Races	Won	Top 5	Top 10	Poles	Earnings
31	0	9	17	0	$347,113

February 7, 1981
Big show, no star
by Jody Meacham

Daytona Beach, Fla.—It is the television teaser to stock car racing's biggest event of the year, a 50-mile dash for nearly $160,000, but there's a major flaw in Sunday afternoon's Busch Clash at Daytona International Speedway.

Among the names not in the field is Dale Earnhardt, the sport's reigning driving champion and also the winner of last year's race.

Earnhardt won five of last season's 31 races and nearly $600,000 to claim the Winston Cup title. And what started him on the way to the most successful money-winning season in NASCAR history was his victory in the 1980 Busch Clash.

But about the only accomplishment that eluded Earnhardt in his second full year on the Grand National circuit was qualifying on the pole for any of the races, the sole requirement for making the Busch Clash field.

It doesn't please CBS Sports, which will telecast the race live beginning at 3 p.m., but there seems to be little the network can do about it. TV has come in for a lot of criticism for manipulating the sports it covers and network officials get very touchy if you ask them if they'd rather Earnhardt were in the race.

"Naturally you want the big names in it," said Beano Cook, a CBS spokesman in New York. "If it's a golf tournament, you want Arnold Palmer in the pack on the final round.

"But who's in this thing is none of our business and we don't want any part of making up the rules. We don't get involved in that, I guarantee it."

February 21, 1981

New crew chief . . . no joke

by Tom Higgins

Charlotte, N.C.— Dale Inman's job change started almost three years ago ... as a joke.

During a casual conversation at Atlanta International Raceway, stock car racing team owner Rod Osterlund joshed Inman about becoming his crew chief. Both laughed. Why, the very idea was ludicrous! As the speed sport world knew, Inman had been with his cousin, Richard Petty, the NASCAR Winston Cup circuit's all-time leading winner and most famous figure, since the ascension to the throne began in 1958.

But in the wee hours Tuesday morning, the switch became reality.

After commanding Petty's troops through 839 races, 193 victories and seven Grand National driving championships, Inman resigned from Petty Enterprises to become vice president in charge of racing operations for Osterlund Enterprises, which fields cars for Dale Earnhardt.

"It is the biggest shock wave to hit our sport in many, many years," Benny Parsons said. "It is something that I guess no one in racing ever thought they'd see."

"Rod was just kidding around when he first mentioned it, and I kidded him back," Inman recalled.

Finally the Osterlund overtures, which both the wealthy West Coast real estate developer and Inman had kept Petty aware of all along, became too enticing to turn down.

"I hope I don't have any more decisions in my life to make that are as hard as this one was," said Inman. "I don't know what might come up, but I can't imagine anything else ever being more difficult.

"In this new job, I think I'll have an opportunity to be off more, and that was a very important factor. At times my wife, Mary, has got down on racing because it required me to be gone so much. I was away when our oldest, Tina Dale, who's 14, was born."

Inman chuckled.

"You better know I was there when Jeffrey Todd, who is 11, came along.

"The three of them are my main concern and it was the thought of them that played a great part in my decision as this thing kept building and building."

May 23, 1981
Luck is running a lap behind
by Jody Meacham

Charlotte, N.C.—Dale Earnhardt could hardly keep his name out of the papers a year ago.

But almost as quickly as he climbed to the top of stock car racing in 1980, he dropped out of sight in 1981.

It's not that Earnhardt has done badly by most standards, finishing half of his dozen starts in the top 10, but by now people expect a champion to have at least won a race.

The last time that happened was in October at Charlotte Motor Speedway, and now with the circuit back around to his home track, he stands perhaps in his best position to win again in Sunday's World 600 starting at noon.

He'll start fifth in the field of 40 cars after qualifying in a newly-completed Pontiac at 156.639 mph.

But after accomplishing what was thought to be impossible—winning the national championship in only his second year—the hard times that most drivers expect to precede success have finally struck Earnhardt.

The year began with a new sponsor, Wrangler jeans, which put his team owned by Californian Rod Osterlund in its best financial shape ever.

But instead of the expected success, the luck that seemed to carry Earnhardt through the wrecks and breakdowns of a year ago deserted him. He's managed thirds at Atlanta and Dover since the season opener, but that's been the best.

He's only sixth in the point standings.

A return to victory at Charlotte Motor Speedway is a more important concern.

"I've got a lot of fans who don't get to see me run anywhere else except Charlotte," he said. "But the number of people sitting in that grandstand doesn't affect me.

"I've been racing in front of 10 or 15 people and enjoyed it just as much. But there's a lot more spectacular thrills winning a race in front of a big crowd.

"Didn't Richard Petty go almost two years without winning a race?" he asks.

"I want to win them all. I want to win at every race track and win every race."

May 25, 1981
Problem year continues
by Frank Barrows

Charlotte, N.C.—Dale Earnhardt pushed slowly through Sunday's crowd at Charlotte Motor Speedway, signing autographs for some fans and accepting hugs from others. Just a few idle minutes remained until the World 600 began, and his Pontiac was lined up for the start. A television crew, shouldering a camera and microphone, recorded his every step. He shook hands right and left.

That was just like last year, when he was stock car racing's hottest item. When he freed himself from the crowd, he exchanged a few confident words with his mechanics. That was just like last year, too.

Dale Earnhardt talks with crewmen before climbing out of his car after dropping out early in an October race at Charlotte Motor Speedway. Earnhardt failed to finish 10 races in the 1981 season. (Mark B. Sluder/The Charlotte Observer)

Finally, he slid into his car. From that moment on, nothing was just like last year. Nothing at all.

Dale Earnhardt isn't exactly having a good year, and it got a whole bunch worse when his engine gave out after an hour of the World 600. He coasted into pit row, and his yellow-shirted crew scrambled toward his car.

Two heads popped through the windows asking him for the symptoms. Eight hands went to work beneath the hood. He sat there looking puzzled.

On this particular occasion, the problem happened to lie somewhere in the distributor. "This," said crew chief Doug Richert, "isn't what you'd expect to go wrong, and it took us a long while to figure it out."

People scurried about the pit, grabbing implements from one tool box ör another. The problem did not solve itself. Time ticked by.

The hood went down, then back up for a final check. Earnhardt had slipped off the track in Lap 10. When he returned, the front runners were in Lap 139. He was about a light year behind. He never made up the difference.

June 26, 1981
Team sold; six fired
by Jody Meacham

Charlotte, N.C.—Jim Stacy, a coal mining executive and former racing team owner, has purchased the stock car racing team of defending national champion Dale Earnhardt and fired six team employees, *The Charlotte News* has learned.

The Charlotte-based Osterlund Racing Team, which signed a sponsorship deal with Wrangler jeans this season, was one of the most successful independent teams in stock car racing.

No purchase terms have been disclosed, but *The News* has learned that purchase of the team does not necessarily guarantee that Earnhardt, who won five races and a season record $588,926 for the team last year, will continue as driver.

The question of Wrangler's continued sponsorship was also left hanging. Company officials would not comment.

Dale Earnhardt spent much of 1981 tangled in the web of poor performance. By the time he got to Charlotte in May, without a victory since October of 1980, fans and the media wondered what was wrong. (Jeep Hunter/The Charlotte Observer)

June 28, 1981

Ownership deal . . . firecracker on paper

by Tom Higgins

Daytona Beach, Fla.—The biggest blast related to Saturday's Firecracker 400 at Daytona Beach, Fla., already has been ignited.

It went off Friday in Croft, a Charlotte suburb.

The fuse was lit when papers were signed transferring ownership of the stock car racing team that fields Pontiacs for NASCAR Grand National champion Dale Earnhardt from Rod Osterlund to Jim Stacy.

Osterlund selling out?

The news came, even to Earnhardt, 30, and key team officials, with all the subtlety of a firecracker pitched under the feet. There were calls just after dawn—and at 9 a.m. the transaction was finalized. It happened so suddenly that even the team's seven-month-old sponsor, Wrangler, embarrassingly was caught by surprise.

Earnhardt was not pleased with the midseason change. Osterlund has been more than a car owner to Earnhardt. He gave him his big chance and in the process became a counselor and confidant.

Despite the general impression, Earnhardt never has been under contract to the team.

Earnhardt agreed to stay, but didn't want to talk about it.

Stacy has named long-time employee Robert "Boobie" Harrington as general manager of the new "Racer 2 Corporation."

Harrington is, in racing parlance, a good ol' boy with a friendly demeanor. As crew chief for Stacy cars in selected races the past three seasons, Harrington has done a creditable job.

But he never has fielded a winner.

The biggest question, however, is why did Osterlund get out, and under such surprise circumstances?

He wasn't available to answer.

Osterlund has vast real estate ventures in California and Nevada, and friends suggest he tired of the travel required to run two businesses on opposite coasts.

Whatever, Osterlund and Stacy have exploded a bombshell.

July 2, 1981

Practice quick . . . and swim?

Tom Higgins

Daytona Beach, Fla.—As if there wasn't already enough to talk about with Dale Earnhardt and his racing team, which changed ownership Friday...

Earnhardt, defending Winston Cup driving champion from Lake Norman, posted the fastest practice pace Wednesday at Daytona International Speedway in preparation for today's 10 a.m. time trials leading to Saturday's Firecracker 400.

Afterward, Earnhardt repeated a vow to leap into Lake Lloyd—a 40-acre impoundment in the speedway infield—if he wins Saturday's race, ending an eight-month winless steak.

"If I take the checkered flag first, I'll pull to the backstretch where the lake is located and jump in before going to Victory Lane." Earnhardt remained relatively tight-mouthed about the Friday deal that transferred ownership from Californian Rod Osterlund to Kentuckian Stacy. By one reporter's count, questions about the change elicited seven shakes of the head indicating no comment, five "yeps" and three "nopes" from Earnhardt.

July 22, 1981
The old stuff is new again
by Tom Higgins

Charlotte, N.C.—Dale Earnhardt said Tuesday he plans to become active again in the late-model sportsman competition that spawned his stock car racing career.

During a luncheon at Charlotte Motor Speedway, defending Winston Cup Series driving champion Earnhardt said he would race in the track's Miller 300 in October and "as many major sportsman races as possible" in 1982.

Earnhardt said he'd drive a Robert Gee-owned '77 Pontiac Ventura in the 300. That race will be Oct. 10, the day before the National 500 in which he is defending champion.

August 4, 1981
'Jim . . . I'm going to quit'
by Tom Higgins

Charlotte, N.C.—Defending Winston Cup stock car racing champion Dale Earnhardt said Monday that he has quit the team owned by J.D. Stacy.

Earnhardt announced through spokesman Joe Whitlock that he and his sponsor, Wrangler Jeans, which pulled out with him, are negotiating to become affiliated with another team quickly enough so they will not miss any races.

A change in the team's ownership apparently was the catalyst for the departure of Earnhardt. He left just five weeks after the Croft-based team that fielded his cars was bought by Stacy from founder Rod Osterlund.

Earnhardt resigned shortly after his Pontiac left Sunday's Talladega 500 at Alabama International Motor Speedway on Lap 93 with clutch problems.

"Jim, you're a nice fellow and I haven't got a thing against you. But I've got to do something I should have done when the team changed ownership. I'm going to quit. I wish you well," Earnhardt said.

On Monday morning, Bob O'Dear, a vice president of Blue Bell, Wrangler's parent company, informed Stacy that his firm was exercising an option in its contract with the team to withdraw sponsorship. The package was reportedly worth approximately $400,000 per year.

Childress gets his wheels of fortune
by Tom Higgins

Charlotte, N.C.— Through the years auto racing insiders generally have agreed that all veteran driver Richard Childress, who fields his own cars, needed to win was adequate financial backing.

Childress, a Winston-Salem NASCAR competitor, is going to get it.

Only thing is, he'll just be preparing the cars and serving as team-owner and manager. He'll leave the driving to Dale Earnhardt.

The Observer learned Tuesday night that defending Winston Cup champion Earnhardt, who quit J.D. Stacy's team Sunday and took his big-buck Wrangler Jeans sponsorship with him, has decided to join long-time friend Childress.

The new teammates' first race will be the Champion Spark Plug 400 at Michigan International Speedway on Aug. 16. Doug Richert, 20, the crew chief who helped Earnhardt win the Grand National title last year in his second season on the circuit, will be a crew member.

It was strongly rumored that Earnhardt, considered one of the most promising young drivers, would wind up in the Junior Johnson organization along with another relatively young star, Darrell Waltrip.

Childress was the choice, as he agreed to end his 12-year driving career that has produced no victories, but almost $800,000 in winnings in 284 starts.

August 8, 1981

Team players
by Tom Higgins

Charlotte, N.C.—Defending Winston Cup stock car racing champion Dale Earnhardt and veteran driver Richard Childress made it official Friday night at Charlotte Motor Speedway.

The two showed up arm-in-arm at a news conference and confirmed they will race as a team for the remaining 11 races of this season's NASCAR Grand National schedule.

"I just never thought that I would get a driver of Dale Earnhardt's capabilities and a sponsor like Wrangler," Childress said.

"I'm more determined than ever to prove myself," said Earnhardt, "I'm confident I can."

	Races	Won	Top 5	Top 10	Poles	Earnings
1982	30	1	7	12	1	$ 375,325
1983	30	2	9	14	0	$ 446,272

February 13, 1982
Over the hump
by Tom Higgins

Daytona Beach, Fla.—For most professional athletes, the rise to the top of their professions and the inevitable decline is a process spread over many seasons. Dale Earnhardt, though, has received a condensed dose of the ups and downs.

He went from NASCAR Grand National race winner and rookie of the year in 1979, to Winston Cup season champion in 1980, to an 0-for-31 campaign in 1981 in which he failed to win a pole.

"I don't care who it is," said Earnhardt, 30, during a break in preparations for today's Goody's Sportsman 300 and Sunday's Daytona 500. "When you've been accustomed to winning—winning big—and suddenly you're not anymore, it's going to make you feel down. That's human nature.

"It worries you and bothers you and gnaws at you inside."

There were other things concerning him—both of a business and personal nature.

Yet, Earnhardt insists his confidence remained buoyant all along.

Why?

Earnhardt shrugged and shook his head.

"That's the way I am, I guess."

But what happened to turn Earnhardt's world so topsy-turvy in a matter of months?

"It was the team changing hands. That was the whole thing," said Earnhardt, referring to the surprise June 26, 1981, sale of the organization by founder Rod Osterlund to J.D. Stacy.

"With Rod, I felt I had a personal stake in the team. It was almost like an operation by a big family.

"Then, when Jim (Stacy) came in, he wanted to bring his own people, which is his right and which is understandable. The changing around upset me at the time, so I decided to go, too."

On Aug. 2, Earnhardt dropped out of the Talladega 500 with mechanical problems. When he climbed from the car he told Stacy, "Jim, I've got to quit."

This week, Earnhardt paused for thought, then with carefully measured words, said:

"I absolutely have nothing personal against Jim Stacy. As the months have gone by and I've got to know him better, I like the man. And who knows, someday down the road if he should ask me to drive for him, I might do it."

But last August, Earnhardt left the Stacy team to drive the cars of Winston-Salem independent driver Richard Childress, who gave up the wheel to accommodate Earnhardt.

"Thank goodness for a great guy like Richard Childress," said Earnhardt. "He was

so good to us it's incredible."

Earnhardt and Wrangler have moved on this year, striking a sizable sponsorship deal with veteran car-builder Bud Moore of Spartanburg.

"That's another thing that bothered me," continued Earnhardt. "I didn't think that Wrangler was getting enough out of me for its investment. I wasn't doing them justice, not winning a race and not winning a pole.

"It was frustrating."

But something in Earnhardt's personal life helped keep him going, more than balancing the "blah" turn his career had taken.

In June he received custody of his two children, daughter Kelley, 9, and son Dale Jr., 7.

"It meant so much — means so much now — to see my kids grow," said Earnhardt, who is divorced. "I wasn't getting to do that.

"And I love those hugs and kisses."

(The Charlotte Observer)

Dale Earnhardt confers with friend and rival Neil Bonnett atop a tool box in the garage area at Charlotte. (Bill Billings/ The Charlotte Observer)

March 18, 1982

On the pole . . . finally

by Tom Higgins

For 2½ years Dale Earnhardt has been doubly troubled by droughts.

One was the lack of rain that left the dock high and dry at his Lake Norman home near Doolie in Iredell County.

The other was his long dry spell without winning a pole on NASCAR's Winston Cup stock car racing circuit.

The lingering, troubling North Carolina drought officially was broken earlier this month by the winter's rush of rain, much to the delight of angler Earnhardt, who now has plenty of water and a good population of fish around his pier.

And Thursday, the 30-year-old native of Kannapolis ended the other drought by speeding to the pole for Sunday's Coca-Cola 500 at Atlanta International Raceway.

Earnhardt didn't try to disguise his delight.

"I was beginning to wonder if I'd ever win another pole again," he said. "It's been so long ..."

Earnhardt last won a pole in his 1979 rookie-of-the-year season when he qualified fastest for the CRC Chemicals 500 at Dover, Del.

His last NASCAR triumph was the 1980 National 500 at Charlotte.

"It's been agonizing having to watch the last two Busch Clashes," continued Earnhardt. "Now I'm going to be in it again next February at Daytona. I can't wait."

The pole victory also ended a drought for Bud Moore, who last finished a pole-winning car when Allison won the top spot for his team prior to the Atlanta Journal 500 in November 1980.

"Despite the low water I've had pretty good fishing luck right along," Earnhardt said. "But my racing luck has been lousy. Suppose this means I'm not gonna catch any fish when I get back home?"

March 21, 1982

We get along fine, thanks

by Tom Higgins

The whispers of speculation were spoken often during stock car racing's off-season last winter:

"Dale Earnhardt and Bud Moore teaming up? It'll never work. They're too alike, fiery and aggressive."

"Well, tell anybody who thinks that to wait and see," he said firmly.

The season is young, of course, but going into the fourth event, today's Coca-Cola 500 at Atlanta International Raceway, driver Earnhardt and car builder-team owner Moore are getting along famously.

In fact, with some luck, the Spartanburg-based team could have swept 1982's first three races.

Earnhardt had to exit the Daytona 500 while leading because of a burned piston ... If he'd stayed on the track rather than pitting when the yellow flag came out for rain, he would have won the weather-shortened Richmond 400 ... And he was running away with last weekend's Valleydale 500 at Bristol, Tenn., before a wreck in front of him forced a spin that spoiled the handling on Moore's Thunderbird.

"The way me and Bud—who see eye-to-eye despite what everybody predicted, by the way—are looking at it, we're owed one. A big one. Right now," said Earnhardt.

The team appears in fine position to collect today starting at 1 p.m.

Earnhardt, 30, is to start from the pole after qualifying Thursday at 163.774 mph.

So, where are all the recent winners?

They're starting well back in the 40-car field. But by no means are Darrell Waltrip, Cale Yarborough, Neil Bonnett, Benny Parsons, Bobby Allison and Dave Marcis forgotten.

"We know they're going to be coming strong," said Moore.

"There's some that's up there that aren't going to stay up there, and there are some that's back there that aren't going to stay back there."

So much for those offseason whispers.

April 5, 1982

WIN NO. 1: DARLINGTON
Rollin' in the Rebel

by Tom Higgins

Darlington, S.C.—Dale Earnhardt, a challenger but never a champion in five previous Winston Cup stock car races this season, wasn't to be denied Sunday in a thrilling CRC Rebel 500.

Driving his Ford on the ragged edge of control at Darlington Raceway, Earnhardt held off Cale Yarborough's passing attempt by half a car length at the finish line.

It was Earnhardt's first triumph since the National 500 at Charlotte Motor Speedway in October 1980, the year he won the NASCAR driving championship. That's a stretch of 39 races.

It was the first victory at the 1.366-mile track for Bud Moore of Spartanburg, Earnhardt's car owner and crew chief, since he fielded a winner for Darel Dierlinger in the 1966 Southern 500, 31 events ago at Darlington.

"I knew we had Cale beat when I glanced to the left and didn't see anything at the flagstand," said a beaming Earnhardt, 30. "I figured he was going to swing toward the apron so when I came off the fourth turn going to the checkered flag I started fading."

Fading?

"Yeah. Pulling to the inside where he was going."

> ## "We knew we could win if the car would just stay together."
> ## —Dale Earnhardt

"I knew it was very close, but I also knew I got beat," said Yarborough.

Bill Elliott drove his Ford to third place and Benny Parsons took fourth in a Pontiac. Both finished in the lead lap. Tim Richmond finished fifth in a Buick, a lap down.

Earnhardt had led every race this season. In two of them he earned a bonus for leading the most laps in the race. But mechanical troubles or wrecks not of his making prevented him from winning. His best 1982 showing had been a second in the Valleydale 500 at Bristol, Tenn., the only event in which he was still running at the finish.

The list of potential challengers steadily dwindled from the start. Pole-winner Buddy Baker went out after 2 laps when the flywheel on his car broke ... Harry Gant smacked the fourth turn wall ... Neil Bonnett crashed between Turns 3 and 4 ... Richard Petty and Morgan Shepherd blew engines.

"We knew we could win if the car would just stay together," said Earnhardt.

"Why, I was so close to Neil and Slick (Johnson) in those crashes that I needed a can of Right Guard!"

April 5, 1982

Back by popular demand

by Tom Higgins

Darlington, S.C.— Now there have been two very popular victories on NASCAR's Winston Cup circuit this season.

The first was by Dave Marcis, the hard-working "independent" driver who fields his own car, in February's Richmond 400.

The second came Sunday at Darlington Raceway in the CRC Rebel 500, when Dale Earnhardt dashed to the checkered flag in a dandy duel with Cale Yarborough.

Ever since Earnhardt, 30, flashed brilliantly and suddenly onto the big-time stock car racing scene in 1979, he has ranked high among "the people's choice," enjoying almost as much popularity as all-time victory leader Richard Petty.

Trace it perhaps to his boyhood environment, the textile town of Kannapolis. After all, legions of fans are blue-collar workers like Earnhardt's kinfolks.

Toss in some nostalgia. Many fans saw Earnhardt's father, the late Ralph Earnhardt, race in the sport's short-track heyday in the Carolinas, speeding to NASCAR's national sportsman championship in 1956.

"Ah, I just love it. Ever since I was a little boy going to races with Daddy, I've heard about Darlington. It just means so much to me to win here," Earnhardt said.

An Earnhardt Victory Lane celebration includes wife Teresa and children Kelley (left) and Dale Jr. (right). (Milton Hinnant/The Charlotte Observer)

August 3, 1982

The knee bone's connected to the . . . surgeon

by Tom Higgins

Dale Earnhardt's knee injury is more serious than first thought and he will undergo surgery today in Statesville.

The operation was scheduled even before Earnhardt's crash in Sunday's Talladega 500. He was unhurt in that crash.

Earnhardt sustained a broken left knee on July 25 in the Mountain Dew 500 at Pocono, Pa.

"It's more than a hairline fracture, as first thought," conceded Earnhardt, 31.

"My doctor says we need to put a small wire or two in there ... The knee would heal without wiring, but I might have a slight limp the rest of my life."

Earnhardt said the surgery won't cause him to miss any races, as the next event is the Champion Spark Plug 400 on Aug. 22 in Brooklyn, Mich. "I'll have plenty of time to recover from it," he said.

"I'll be in the hospital a couple of days, that's all. The knee won't require a cast. They'll outfit me with a brace.

"The doctor told me I'd be sore for about three months and unable to put any weight on my left leg for about six. So I'll have to continue to use crutches. But I'll be able to race. I have good mobility and my team (the Bud Moore/Wrangler crew from Spartanburg) has lightened the spring on our clutches for me. The clutch is the only part of the car that requires me to use my left leg and foot."

Earnhardt was injured in a crash with Tim Richmond. Earnhardt flipped several times and skidded for about 250 feet with the car upside down.

"Lots of drivers injured way more seriously than me have drove, like Richard Petty, who has been out there in the past with broken ribs and a broken foot," Earnhardt said.

August 4, 1982

A few screws, and good as new

by Tom Higgins

Former Winston Cup stock car racing champion Dale Earnhardt underwent apparently successful surgery Tuesday in a Statesville hospital for the broken left knee he suffered in a race crash July 25.

Joe Whitlock, an associate of Earnhardt's, said there were no problems in the operation, during which two screws were inserted into Earnhardt's knee.

"The only hitch was that Dale is miffed that Dr. Jim Serene wouldn't follow his suggestion and make the incision in the form of a 'W' like that sewn on the back pockets of Wrangler jeans," said Whitlock, chuckling. "Dale wanted a scar in the shape of the logo (Wrangler sponsors Earnhardt's team)."

The injury to Earnhardt, 31, was described as a depressed lateral tibula plateau fracture. He sustained it when his Ford flipped several times and skidded on its top about 250 yards at Pocono, Pa. Doctors say such a fracture is relatively common among athletes, especially football players and rodeo cowboys.

"The bone was broken on the outside of the left knee," said Whitlock. "Dr. Serene, an orthopedic surgeon, said a piece of bone about the size of a pencil eraser got pushed down during the wreck. This was put back in place and secured by the screws."

"The doctor told us that the operation shouldn't impair Dale's racing ability at all," said Whitlock. "He's not going to be in a cast, and there was no ligament or cartilage damage.

"However, Dale will require the use of a cane or crutches for three to six weeks."

February 16, 1983
Car scrapped; driver rapped
by Tom Higgins

Daytona Beach, Fla.— Bobby Allison lost another race car Tuesday and Dale Earnhardt might have lost $10,000 to the largest fine in NASCAR history.

These were the major developments at Daytona International Speedway as preparations continued for this weekend's Speed Week features, the Goody's 300 on Saturday and Sunday's silver anniversary Daytona 500.

Allison, who crashed his favored Chevrolet Monte Carlo during Monday's 50-mile Busch Clash, destroyed a back-up Buick Regal in a second accident during practice at the 2.5-mile track less than 24 hours later. Officials of his DiGard team ordered yet another Monte Carlo dispatched from their shop in Charlotte for Allison, in hopes he can qualify today.

DiGard president Jim Gardner estimated the loss of the two cars at $160,000.

At mid-afternoon, NASCAR competition director Bill Gazaway announced that Lake Norman's Earnhardt had been fined for ignoring a black flag for 11 of the 20 laps in the Busch Clash.

Earnhardt was ordered in because his Ford Thunderbird, fielded by Spartanburg's Bud Moore, was trailing smoke, obviously from an oil leak.

"We'll refund $5,000 at the rate of $1,000 per race for the next five Grand National events in which Earnhardt competes, so long as he conditions himself to the extent of NASCAR rules," Gazaway said in a statement. "In the event he does not so conduct himself, no further monies will be refunded."

Earnhardt won $10,000 for his team in the Clash, wrecking along with Terry Labonte and Buddy Baker on the last lap. However, Moore's name wasn't mentioned in the fine, indicating that NASCAR expects Earnhardt to pay all of it himself.

"I'm appealing," said Earnhardt. "I appealed the minute they handed me the notification. I'll try to get the money lessened."

Earnhardt was grinning, but said he was highly upset.

"A $10,000 fine! You'd have thought I slapped Bill Gazaway," said Earnhardt.

"I race under NASCAR rules, but the Clash isn't a regular race. It if had been, I would have pitted. The Clash has always been presented to me as sort of a no-holds-barred deal."

February 18, 1983
New math is just fine
by Tom Higgins

Daytona Beach, Fla.— Dale Earnhardt got a clean victory and a split-decision triumph Thursday at Daytona International Speedway.

Before rolling to victory in a 125-mile qualifying race for Sunday's Daytona 500, Earnhardt learned a $10,000 fine imposed on him Monday had essentially been cut in half. NASCAR official Dick Beaty said Earnhardt must pay a $5,000 penalty, $2,000 of which will be refunded "if he adheres to the rules and conducts himself properly on the track during the next 10 Winston Cup Series races."

The original fine called for a $10,000 deposit to NASCAR by Earnhardt, with $5,000 to be returned $1,000 at a time during the next five races if the driver "composed himself properly."

February 19, 1983
'He's the best I've seen'
by Tom Higgins

Move over stock car racing immortals.

Make room-at the very, very top.

Dale Earnhardt is about to join you.

This is the opinion, at least, of Bud Moore, the longtime Spartanburg car builder and crew chief whose team fields the Ford Thunderbird that Earnhardt will drive in Sunday's Daytona 500.

"I'd feel this way and say it even if Dale was driving for someone else," Moore said Friday in the garage area at Daytona International Speedway.

"He can do more things with a car than anyone I've ever seen. I'll put it this way, he's the best I've ever seen, and that includes Fireball Roberts and guys like that."

"He's like a high-strung thoroughbred," Moore said.

Moore is a no-nonsense type, not exactly given to strewing compliments. In fact, it could be said Moore has tended to be stingy with praise.

Then, why such a sudden, lofty acclaim for Earnhardt?

"Because it's true," said Moore. "I've expected Dale has what I guess you'd call a natural touch for some time."

Earnhardt drove his blue and yellow Thunderbird to victory Thursday in one of two 125-mile qualifying races, slingshotting around A.J. Foyt on the last lap and then holding off Buddy Baker at the checkered flag.

"Dale has this urge to run over everything in his way to get to the front. If I can just keep him reined in, if he'll respond to the halter, there's no limit to what he can do. I feel Dale is going to eventually respond all the way," Moore said. "I hope so. If he does, it won't surprise me a bit if he wins 20 out of a season's 30 races in the next three or four years.

"The limit of Dale's ability is out of sight. And on top of this he's got all the courage in the world. It's one thing to have the ability to do something well that's risky; it's quite another to be brave enough to do it time and time again."

Moore knows about courage.

He was a machine gunner in the first wave that went ashore on Omaha Beach during D-Day on June 6, 1944.

Didn't Moore realize he was talking about a driver who has but seven Grand National victories in 178 starts? Granted, Earnhardt was Grand National champion in only his second full year on the circuit in 1980. But he has won once—last spring's Rebel 500—in the past two years.

"I'm aware of all that," said Moore. "But what I said stands.

"The boy...man...has the touch. I don't know which he got it from, heredity or environment, or both. But make no mistake about it, he has got the touch."

Earnhardt, somewhat cocky by nature, was genuinely humbled and touched when told of Moore's statements.

"It takes more than a driver," he said. "You have to have a good team, and they're hard to come by.

"I'm glad Bud feels that way. I can also say I think he's the best.

"It's an honor coming from him, considering what he's seen and the drivers he has seen go by. I hope I can live up to all he said.

"It's for certain the best compliment I've ever been paid."

February 18, 1983
Dale and Neil: Twins in Daytona
by Tom Higgins

Dale Earnhardt and Neil Bonnett unleashed virtually identical, final-lap slingshot passes Thursday to win wreck-marred twin 125-mile qualifying races leading to Sunday's Daytona 500.

Earnhardt, set up in a Ford Thunderbird draft with Buddy Baker, swept past leader A.J. Foyt's Monte Carlo in the third turn the final time around in the first race. The aerodynamic factor enabled Baker to follow, but Earnhardt cut his Lake Norman neighbor off coming to the checkered flag through the track's dogleg homestretch. He won by a car length.

"I was in exactly the place I wanted to be during the final laps," said Earnhardt. "I had no intention of trying to make a move till the last lap."

July 2, 1983
A tough-luck driver
by Tom Higgins

Daytona Beach, Florida—As the stock car racing season's second half begins, Bobby Allison and Sterling Marlin lead a couple of points races.

Allison holds a 189-point lead over Darrell Waltrip for NASCAR's Grand National championship. Marlin is 44 points ahead of Ronnie Hopkins, Jr., in the rookie of the year competition.

But it's much, much closer in another category; one in which drivers don't want the lead and, in fact, don't even want to be in the standings.

That's the imaginary "Tough Luck Driver Of The Year."

Dale Earnhardt's record shows three top-five finishes and three more top 10s. But those are the only races in which he has been running at the finish. Earnhardt, the 1980 Grand National champion from Lake Norman, dropped from contention in eight of the season's first 10 events. He is 11th in the points.

He has blamed the woes of his Bud Moore-led team on what he calls the failure of Ford officials to deliver promised high performance parts for the Thunderbirds.

July 17, 1983
WIN NO. 1: NASHVILLE
Back in Victory Lane

August 1, 1983
WIN NO. 2: TALLADEGA
Draft with me, Bobby

by Jody Meacham

Nashville, Tenn. — Dale Earnhardt had been a non-winner his last 39 times out on the NASCAR circuit but he broke that streak impressively Saturday night in the Busch 420.

The Kannapolis driver averaged 85.726 mph around the 596-mile Nashville International Speedway to outdistance two-time defending points champion Darrell Waltrip by one-half lap.

In the process of winning his first race since the 1982 Trans-South 500 at Darlington, Earnhardt snapped Waltrip's four-race victory streak at NIR.

"It's been a long time since we won a race," said Earnhardt, who started the race in the third position. "We did a little extra work to prepare the car for the short track, and it worked super.

"We didn't run hard at the first and we kept adjusting as the race went on. The car just kept getting better and better," Earnhardt said.

"We've been through some hard times lately but it looks like we've finally got things together."

Earnhardt's Ford took the lead for the third and final time when it beat Neil Bonnett's Chevrolet out of the pits during the race's fourth caution flag.

Talladega, Ala. — Dale Earnhardt picked up the victory in Sunday's Talladega 500, but for those of you scoring along at home, credit Bobby Allison with the assist.

Allison, not really out of modesty, declined having anything to do with the outcome.

But Darrell Waltrip, not really out of generosity, said Earnhardt ought to split the $49,950 winner's purse with Allison.

"He won the race for Dale," Waltrip said after coming up half a car length short at the finish line. "I never thought he (Allison) would get up there in the way like that."

But why wouldn't he? Allison, after all, is trying to maintain his lead in the NASCAR Grand National point standings over second-place Waltrip, and anything that hurts Waltrip's finish position does just that.

So on the last lap of the race with Waltrip, Earnhardt and Allison running 1-2-3 on the track-although Allison was 2 laps back-Allison became Earnhardt's drafting partner and both cars went around Waltrip on the backstretch.

"He (Allison) helped me a little by pushing me past Darrell," said Earnhardt, who won his second race in the last three events. "I don't think I could have gotten by before the corner without him, but I think I would have gotten past him on down in the corner."

That, of course, is Earnhardt's opinion and there's no way of knowing if he could have made the pass alone.

October 5, 1983
Earnhardt's '80 championship remembered as rare
by Jody Meacham

Three years ago Sunday, it was Dale Earnhardt who drove into Victory Lane following the fall race at Charlotte Motor Speedway, then called the National 500.

He had led more laps than anyone else in the race and he beat second-place Cale Yarborough by 1.5 seconds.

No one could know it at the time, but most suspected that Earnhardt was well on the way to his first NASCAR Grand National championship. That, in fact, is exactly what happened, but it took two more years before the full magnitude of his accomplishment could sink in.

What drivers with the experience, financial backing and support of long-established teams such as Richard Petty and Bobby Allison could not do, a second-year driver with a small-time sponsorship, a green crew and a team put together only two years before did.

And Earnhardt did it against the same team that beat Petty and Allison for the title five times in seven seasons—Junior Johnson's operation from the Blue Ridge foothills near North Wilkesboro.

"I don't think another team like that could win the championship today," Earnhardt said.

Perhaps Earnhardt's pessimism springs from the experience of poor seasons since, and from his own growing appreciation of how tough Johnson's team is to beat over the long course of a 30-race season. But the man who guided Earnhardt's championship effort in 1980 says it could be done if the same formula were followed.

"I would say especially from my experience of running a team, I'd like to put another team together and do it just to prove a point," said Roland Wlodyka, who was the team manager for California developer Rod Osterlund's racing outfit. "How many times has all the money and all the names been a flop? It ain't

the big names that make things happen in racing, it's other people doing it for them."

In 1980, at least, that was true.

Earnhardt was not a big name in stock car racing, although his father, Ralph, had been a noted sportsman division driver and he had been named Grand National rookie of the year only the season before.

Wlodyka's team, like himself, consisted largely of young Californians recently transplanted to North Carolina to fulfill his own promise to Osterlund to win the national championship in four years.

It only took three, and the team did it on the short tracks and down the season's fall stretch—on Junior Johnson's home turf, in other words—against all odds.

"This team hasn't been around long enough to recognize the pressure," Wlodyka said of the late-season period when Earnhardt won on consecutive Sunday's at Martinsville, Va., and Charlotte. "They don't realize what they're about to accomplish."

Maybe that was the secret.

"Rod Osterlund was sort of keeping me in the dark about how much money we were making," said Earnhardt, who wondered how long their effort could continue without sponsorship. "I guess we were spending all of it because he got out of racing the very next year.

"But at the time, he was always around telling me not to worry about anything, that it would all work out."

By the next year, Earnhardt was with his current team owner, Bud Moore.

"I think it was more exciting after we did it and sat down and sort of thought about it so we could grasp what we did."

Had they known what they were doing, they might not have done it.

October 18, 1983

Missed deadline means Moore-Earnhardt split

by Tom Higgins

Dale Earnhardt apparently is leaving the stock car racing operation of veteran team owner Bud Moore.

Earnhardt, the 1980 NASCAR Grand National champion, missed a decision-making deadline with Moore at 5 p.m. Monday.

"As far as I'm concerned, Dale is through with us," Moore said from his shop in Spartanburg. "We have no choice but to go to work on some other things (driver possibilities).

"A good while back, we both agreed that Dale would give me a decision by 5 o'clock on Oct. 17 on whether he was staying or leaving to join another team. But I haven't heard from him since last Thursday, when he called to say he'd be down on Friday to talk things over.

"I have to assume, then, that he's leaving."

Earnhardt, 32, couldn't be reached. Associates said he was in Fairfield County, S.C., on a deer hunt.

A source close to Wrangler Jeans, which has sponsored the Earnhardt-Moore team, said it probably will be announced Wednesday that Earnhardt is rejoining a team owned by Richard Childress. The source asked not to be named.

Earnhardt would replace Ricky Rudd in the cars fielded by Childress from a Winston-Salem shop.

Wrangler will honor a commitment to sponsor Moore's team during the 1984 season while also backing the Earnhardt-Childress duo, the source said. Moore said that was his understanding, also.

Earnhardt drove for Childress during the second half of the 1981 season. He joined Moore's outfit in '82, winning one race. He has two victories and 13 top-10 finishes this year, and ranks eighth in the point standings.

"I'm not worried about not getting a top man," said Moore. "We've got a good operation, and everyone in racing knows that.

"I can't quite understand Dale's thinking, though. I agree we got off to a shaky start. But good racing pieces (parts) just recently started being made available by Ford and we've done some strong running since July 4 (including victories in the Busch 420 at Nashville and the Talladega 500 in Alabama). And we ain't going to get no worse. Only better.

"I hate this time of year every season and all the changing and ride-jumping it brings. It gets aggravating and confusing.

"Why, it has been like 'ring-around-the-rosey' around here."

October 22, 1983
Hurting but still up front
by Tom Higgins

Rockingham, N.C.—Dale Earnhardt, limping and requiring assistance to get in and out of his car, nevertheless paced American 500 time trials Friday.

Although injured in a crash during practice Thursday, Earnhardt returned to earn the 16th starting position for Sunday's NASCAR Grand National stock car race with a fast lap of 143.876 mph at N.C. Motor Speedway.

"Not really bad for our old car considering the amount of time we've had to work with it," said Earnhardt, whose Bud Moore-led team had to revert to a backup Ford because the new Thunderbird was damaged so heavily in the wreck. Earnhardt lost control going into Turn 1 and slammed savagely into a new concrete retaining barrier.

"It's hard to believe how sore I am," said Earnhardt, who was lifted through the window of the car by crewmen. "I know now how hard we hit the wall Thursday. My left leg is giving me a fit."

Cartilage in Earnhardt's left knee was damaged and he had the knee drained Thursday night. It's the same knee he fractured last season at Pocono, Pa. and which is held together by bolts.

"But the worst thing is how sore I am about the shoulders and neck. On account of them, I expect we'll have to call on a relief driver Sunday." he said. "I don't think I'll be able to go the distance in the race. We're talking to Benny Parsons about possibly standing in for me."

October 28, 1983
Rudd changes mind on 1984 ride
by Tom Higgins

The plot thickened considerably Thursday in the ride-swapping drama involving top NASCAR Grand National drivers, and Ricky Rudd was stirring it with some help from Richard Petty.

The Observer learned that Rudd was in Spartanburg to sign with the Bud Moore team for 1984. That pairing—engineered by officials of Moore's sponsor, Wrangler Jeans—came about when Rudd, 27, was able to secure release from a verbal commitment to join another team.

Rudd, of Chesapeake, Va., had been headed to the RahMoc organization, and conceded before last Sunday's rainout of the American 500 at N.C. Motor Speedway "that everything about the deal is completed, but the signing of the contracts."

However, another arrangement that also would involve the RahMoc team with Petty mushroomed into a much larger scale program than originally anticipated. So Rudd opted for the opportunity to drive for the veteran Moore.

Essentially, the deal amounts to a swap of rides between Rudd and 1980 Grand National champion Dale Earnhardt.

The position with the Moore team was available because Earnhardt left to join an outfit owned and led by Richard Childress which also is to be sponsored by Wrangler in '84. Rudd has been the driver for Childress the past two seasons.

Rudd has won two races and four poles this year, Earnhardt two races and no poles.

The unconfirmed word on Petty last weekend is that for the first time he has plans to drive a car not fielded by Petty Enterprises, a family operation. Garage area insiders said at N.C. Motor Speedway that Petty is to compete in '84 in a car prepared by longtime crew chief Buddy Parrott with RahMoc supplying the engines.

Find all this confusing?

If so, it's understandable.

Chapter Seven:
1984: Back in a Chevy, and in Victory Lane

Races	Won	Top 5	Top 10	Poles	Earnings
30	2	12	22	0	$ 616,788

March 16, 1984

Jury out on Earnhardt-Rudd trade

by Tom Higgins

Hampton, Ga.—All the evidence won't be in—can't be in—until NASCAR's Grand National season ends next November at Riverside, Calif.

Only then will the jury, the nation's stock car fans, be able to deliberate and deliver a verdict.

The case:

Who came out best in the Dale Earnhardt-Ricky Rudd trade? The two drivers essentially swapped teams during the 1983-84 offseason, Earnhardt moving from the Ford outfit of Bud Moore to the Chevrolets fielded by Richard Childress. Rudd jumped from Childress to Moore.

"I think in the long run that the moves we made will prove equally good for both me and Ricky," Earnhardt said Thursday in the garage area at Atlanta International Raceway during preparations for Sunday's Coca-Cola 500. "And I'm not saying that to be diplomatic. I really believe it.

"In the meantime, I still feel and say what I have all along.... That if I'm going to win another Grand National championship this year, or anytime soon, I had better get

back in a Chevy to do it. Why? The Chevys are just better cars if you're going to chase the championship. You have to be consistent to win the (Grand National) title and consistency seems to be one of the strong advantages of the Chevrolets."

After 1984's first three races, Rudd and the Moore team of Spartanburg are third in the Grand National standings, 12 points behind leader Darrell Waltrip. Rudd's best showing is a triumph in the Miller 400 at Richmond, and he has won $81,890.

Earnhardt and his Winston-Salem-based crew are fifth, 38 points behind Waltrip. His best finish was second in the rich Daytona 500, a showing that has boosted his earnings to $99,835.

"Right now, I guess most folks would figure that Ricky is up on us, because he has won this year and we haven't," continued Earnhardt. "Even so, I'd still do it over again, definitely.

"I don't think there has been a time in my career when I've felt any better about a situation or been any more optimistic than I am now.

"I honestly think that me and Richard and the rest of the boys are ready to fire on 'em. We're running better and better each time out and we've got some tracks where I normally do pretty well coming up on the schedule."

"I know Bud was hurt and disappointed when I decided to move on," said Earnhardt. "I understand. We're friends now. In fact, I consider Bud as good a friend as I've got."

Even so, the two keep trying to beat each other, intent that the jury's verdict go their way next November.

April 15, 1984
Riding shotgun . . . with turkeys
by Tom Higgins

Darlington, S.C.—No matter what happens the rest of the way, it has been Dale Earnhardt's best season.

That estimation came Friday from NASCAR's 1980 Grand National champion himself.

How can Earnhardt make such a statement? Going into today's TranSouth 500 at Darlington Raceway, the season is only one-fifth of the way through. And while Earnhardt, from rural Doolie in Iredell County, is a solid fourth in the point standings. 49 behind leader Terry Labonte, he has won neither a race nor a pole in '84.

So where is Earnhardt coming from with this best season silliness?

Avid outdoorsman Earnhardt can say it because we're talking turkey, not stock car racing.

An accomplished deer hunter and angler, Earnhardt, 32, discovered wild turkey hunting this spring. Now he's hooked, an addiction that only other turkey hunters will understand.

April 2, Earnhardt called in and bagged his first wild turkey, a fine gobbler weighing 18 pounds and sporting a 10-inch beard and 1-inch spurs.

Turkey enthusiasts might say that a newcomer making such a kill is like a rookie

winning a superspeedway race, as Earnhardt did in 1979.

"I've won some big 500-mile races, I've won a Busch Clash on national TV, I've bagged a 12-point buck and I've caught a 25-pound striper on light tackle," Earnhardt said between practice runs at Darlington. "But the biggest thrill and sense of accomplishment right at one particular moment that I've ever known came when I got that turkey.

"As much as I like to hunt, I'd never thought much about turkeys, because we're always so busy racing in the springtime," said Earnhardt. "And mostly, in the spring is the only time you can turkey hunt in the Carolinas.

"But during the offseason, me and a bunch of buddies were sitting around in the basement of my next-door neighbor on Lake Norman, Lee Slater, talking hunting and fishing...Lee and the others got to messing around with different types of turkey calls and talking about how hard it is to fool an ol' gobbler.

"Well, you know me and a challenge. I borrowed one of Lee's slate box calls and started practicing all through the winter, getting instruction from him all along."

And immediately after the April 1 Valleydale 500 at Bristol, Tenn., he headed for

Chester County, S.C. and his chance to open the turkey season.

Chester was chosen because Earnhardt and a group of acquaintances have prime hunting property leased there.

"I walked way into the woods before daylight and it was pitch dark," said Earnhardt. "I doubt I could have found my way without a light, except that the spot I planned to hunt is on a ridge just 80 yards from my deer stand, and I've been to that so many times I know the way by heart.

"I went ahead and got situated, with a good-sized pine at my back and an old blown-down cedar sort of in front of me. I was in camouflage head to toe."

Earnhardt clucked a couple of times on the slate call, "and from my right there was a responding gobble. I could tell this turkey

was on the ground and coming toward me. My stomach was in my throat.

"I decided to gamble and make the slate box cluck one more time. But I had made a scratching sound and I knew that the turkey on the right was lost. It's incredible how smart and suspicious wild turkeys are.

"I was startin' to cuss myself when from the left I heard one from farther away, coming down the ridge."

Glad for a second chance, Earnhardt started clucking and the bird approached.

"I'll never forget the sight. Here he comes around the end of that blown-down cedar, his tail fanned out and his head thrown back to impress that sweet thing he thinks he has a date with. Right then, raising that shotgun, was as excited as I ever have been."

July 30, 1984
WIN NO. 1: TALLADEGA
Smiling in a photo finish
by Tom Higgins

Talladega, Ala.— Dale Earnhardt swept to the most satisfying victory of his career Sunday, taking a Talladega 500 thriller that could rank as motorsports' greatest race.

Earnhardt, fuming all week because he felt his driving style had been impugned, whipped into the lead in Turn 3 during a last-lap charge at Alabama Motor Speedway. He held on to first place when a pack of rivals went abreast in his wake and began dicing for position down the homestretch of the 2.66-mile track.

"This undoubtedly is the most exciting race I've ever been involved with."
—Dale Earnhardt

There were 10 drivers in the lead aerodynamic draft, and any of them conceivably could have won.

Terry Labonte, leading at the start of the final lap before a crowd of 94,000 and a national CBS-TV audience, appeared to salvage second place in a photo finish with Buddy Baker, Bobby Allison and Cale Yarborough.

However, two hours after the race, second was awarded to Baker with Labonte third.

Finishing fifth through 10th were

Darrell Waltrip, Harry Gant, Lake Speed, Tommy Ellis and Bill Elliott. A NASCAR record 15 drivers completed all 500 miles.

There were 68 lead changes among 16 drivers, both event records.

Baker led 41 laps, one more than Earnhardt. Yarborough, the pole winner at a record 202.474 mph, was in front 34 laps, Labonte 19 and Allison 16. Other leaders were Ron Bouchard, Trevor Boys, Elliott, Geoff Bodine, Dave Marcis, Gant, Ellis, Neil Bonnett, Ken Ragan, Clark Dwyer and Waltrip.

Earnhardt's 1.66-second margin of victory was the biggest advantage any driver held under the green flag.

"Just call me 'Stroker,'" Earnhardt, 33, said with an impish smile when he arrived in the press box for the winner's interview.

Early in the week some drivers were quoted as saying Earnhardt had become a "stroker" or gone conservative. That was cited as the reason for his leading the point standings toward the Grand National championship, which he won in 1980.

It had Earnhardt seething.

"Just because I hadn't won this year, they were taking shots at me," said Earnhardt. "I'd finished second four times, right on the bumper of the winners almost, and I was supposed to be stroking. Now that doesn't make sense."

The outcome padded Earnhardt's lead in the point standings to 65 over Labonte.

Earnhardt, who won $47,100 Sunday for the Richard Childress-Wrangler team of Winston-Salem, became the first driver to win back-to-back Talladega 500s. He averaged 155.485 mph in the 10th triumph of his career as seven yellows slowed the pace for 38 laps.

Two of the cautions were caused by scary Elliott Forbes-Robinson and Trevor Boys wrecks, but neither was seriously hurt.

"This undoubtedly is the most exciting race I've ever been involved with," said Earnhardt, the 12th different winner this season, tying a modern-era NASCAR record established last year. "There always seemed to be 10 or 12 of us up there fighting for the lead. Every little bit, you'd find yourself racing someone else for position."

Earnhardt, driving a Chevrolet, took an unusual outside route to make the decisive pass of Labonte's Chevy.

"Terry favored the inside route the last few laps," said Earnhardt. "So the last time around I just held mine straight and went outside because I figured it was too muddy to race in the infield."

Earnhardt grinned.

"My crew chief, Kirk Shelmerdine, was yelling over the radio as I came through turn four- 'Drive that thing! Drive it!'" said Earnhardt. "I started to answer him with something cute, but about that time I saw Buddy and Terry side-by-side in my mirror, and I pretty well knew it was mine. So I just waved at the crew and the fans down the homestretch toward the checkered flag."

"You waved and it was that close?" someone asked incredulously.

"Yeah, I was a-waving," came the reply. "I was tickled to death. Still am."

Earnhardt said Baker's following along as he (Earnhardt) began the move on Labonte was a critical factor. "Fortunately Buddy sensed what I was going to do and came out with me," he said. "It's not that he was trying to help me or Terry, he was trying to win the race himself. But it happened that his draft gave me a boost."

Earnhardt said Labonte slowed the pace the last few laps, "but I wasn't about to go around and give him the slingshot position." Because of the aerodynamics, second place generally is favored on the last lap at this speedway.

September 22, 1984
A 2nd-day qualifier
By Tom Higgins

Martinsville, Va.— Dale Earnhardt used the second round of Goody's 500 qualifying Friday as an expression of his determination to tighten the chase for the NASCAR Grand National championship.

Driving a Chevrolet fielded by the Richard Childress-Wrangler team of Winston-Salem, Earnhardt posted a fast lap of 88.747 mph to take the 11th starting spot for Sunday's stock car race at Martinsville Speedway.

The first 10 positions were determined Thursday, with the pole going to Chevy-driving Bodine at 89.523 mph.

"We're right there with Geoff and the others in the faster bunch now," said Earnhardt, whose speed was sixth-quickest overall. "I feel a whole lot better now about our chances Sunday and in turn about getting closer in the point standings."

Going into the 12:30 p.m. race at the boxwood-lined .525-mile track, Terry Labonte is the leader in competition for the lucrative title, worth an estimated $500,000 to $750,000. Labonte, who starts fourth at 88.797, has an 81-point advantage over second-place Harry Gant and he's 105 ahead of Earnhardt, who is third.

"With just six of the 30 races left, counting Sunday's, it's time to make a move and I intend to give that a shot," said Earnhardt, "I've got to go for it, and I'm not scared to...

"I've got to win some races and finish second or third in the ones I don't win. Considering the competition nowadays, that sounds tough, I know. But we can do it.

"My main concern here is wearing out the brakes. Getting overly aggressive on this tight little track sometimes causes you to use up your brakes. And I've got to be aggressive.

"You can't count Harry or me out. I'll tell you I certainly ain't giving up.

"Really, I think today is an example of our determination. I'm really glad to come back with such a good time.

"The problem was a plug that kept fouling. It really cut down our speed in the corners. That's where we made our big gain today."

Fred Wilson/The Charlotte Observer

November 12, 1984
WIN NO. 2: ATLANTA
Good win; terrible day
by Tom Higgins

Hampton, Ga.—Dale Earnhardt won the Atlanta Journal 500 Sunday, a NASCAR Grand National race in which driving newcomer Terry Schoonover crashed on Lap 130 and died from the resulting internal and head injuries.

Schoonover, 32, a novice making only his second Grand National start, wrecked on the backstretch. Schoonover, from Royal Palm Beach, Fla., was pulled unconscious from his Chevrolet, treated at the infield care center, then transferred to an Atlanta hospital. He was declared dead there.

"I'd just met him recently....I didn't know him well," said Earnhardt. Schoonover was the first stock car driver to be killed in a Grand National event since 1975 when Tiny Lund was killed in the Talladega 500, and the first to die at Atlanta International Raceway.

"I'm sorry it happened," Earnhardt continued. "Real sorry. It's something you don't want to think about happening, and I try not to."

Earnhardt flashed his Chevrolet across the finish line just .75 seconds ahead of Ford-driving home-state favorite Bill Elliott before a crowd of about 30,000.

Ricky Rudd, Benny Parsons and Bobby Allison followed, completing all 328 laps on the 1.522-mile track, but well out of contention.

Nowhere to be found among the finishers were Grand National points champion-ship contenders Terry Labonte and Harry Gant. Both were on the sidelines after enduring a day of roller-coaster emotions.

Labonte finished 30th, blowing an engine in his Chevy on Lap 205. Gant was 26th after pitting repeatedly, finally retiring on Lap 315.

The outcome left Labonte with a 42-point lead going into the season-finale Western 500 at Riverside (Calif.) Raceway next Sunday.

Earnhardt was near the front from the start of the 500-miler, delayed a week by rain. Yet he led just three times for 49 laps, including the final 36.

Earnhardt watched almost in disbelief as challenger after challenger succumbed to mechanical attrition.

Cale Yarborough, for example, fell steadily back after leading at the halfway point for a $10,000 bonus. A broken A-frame put him 11th.

Geoff Bodine, leading strongly, suddenly slowed coming off Turn 2 on Lap 293 and pulled over to let Earnhardt by. The engine had failed, but Bodine had led six times for 125 laps, far more than anyone else, a feat also worth $10,000.

Earnhardt said his car, backed by Wrangler and fielded by the Richard Childress team of Winston-Salem, also had difficulty in the final stages of the season's 29th race.

"With 19 laps to go, a piece of one of the header pipes flew off," said Earnhardt. "That caused a lot of smoke and the sparks just flew

> "It's something you don't want to think about happening, and I try not to."
> —Dale Earnhardt

as we went into Turn 3. I thought that was it.

"Well, turns out it wasn't all that bad. The piece had just bounced up and knocked a small hole in the oil pan.

"Bill (Elliott) was right behind me, and I guess he thought it was going to go, too, 'cause he backed off. He never made the margin up again...

"It seems like this one was meant for us. Earlier, my alternator went out. I turned off the pumps to preserve power. But when a hole was knocked in the pan, I had to turn 'em back on. Obviously, it didn't hurt us."

Said Elliott: "I had no chance to overtake Earnhardt there at the end. With about 25 or 30 laps to go his car started to throw oil. It got all over my windshield, and I couldn't judge distance....I kept waiting for his engine to blow, but it didn't.

"Also, let me tell you Geoff Bodine had one strong car. He'd have been hard to deal with if he'd been there at the finish."

"This was the race of my life on a superspeedway," said Bodine. "And this (blown engine) had to happen....But I have no complaints, really. We've won two races this year in our team's first season and have a lot to look forward to next year."

It was almost as if Earnhardt had cavesdropped on Bodine's comments. "What you saw from us today is what you're going to see a lot of in '85," he predicted.

It was Earnhardt's second victory this season, 10th of his career, and worth $40,610. He averaged 134.610 mph as seven yellow flags slowed the pace for 45 laps. Five of those were caused by spins or wrecks. Schoonover was the only person injured.

Races	Won	Top 5	Top 10	Poles	Earnings
28	4	10	16	1	$ 546,596

February 25, 1985
WIN NO. 1: RICHMOND
Earnhardt survives wreck-filled race
by Tom Higgins

Richmond, Va.—Dale Earnhardt came back from a potentially ruinous collision in the pits and won a wreck-strewn Miller 400 Sunday at Richmond Fairgrounds Raceway.

Earnhardt whipped into the lead with 15 laps to go on a restart after the 10th caution flag and outran Geoff Bodine and Darrell Waltrip in a Chevrolet showdown.

Tim Richmond led after the final yellow flag and appeared to be running strongly. But the rear end was going out on his car, and he gambled on staying out and nursing his Pontiac home. The bid failed when the right rear tire started losing air and he had to pit under green.

"It's hard to believe the way things fell in place for us," said Earnhardt. "Especially after the wreck with Terry Labonte (on lap 93). That knocked the toe-in out of line and we just had to keep adjusting and adjusting."

There were 10 yellow-flag periods in all, slowing the pace for 70 laps. This held Earnhardt's average speed to just 67.945 mph.

Earnhardt, 33, collected $33,265 for his first victory at Richmond and the 12th of his career.

Of the last restart, Earnhardt said: "I was looking to get a good run on (Richmond) and I did."

> "It's hard to believe the way things fell in place for us."
> —Dale Earnhardt

April 7, 1985

WIN NO. 2: BRISTOL
Power without power

by Tom Higgins

Dale Earnhardt relaxes in his car before practice for the Miller 500 at Charlotte Motor Speedway. (Fred Wilson/The Charlotte Observer)

Determined Dale Earnhardt manhandled his way to victory in the Valleydale 500 stock car race Saturday, toughing it out in a Chevrolet that had lost its power steering.

Persevering at Bristol Raceway despite arm fatigue that at one point put the limbs to sleep, Earnhardt used a late pit stop to gain the advantage he needed to outrun Ricky Rudd by 1.14 seconds in the wreck-filled NASCAR Grand National event.

With just 25 of the 500 laps to go, Rudd appeared en route to the winner's circle in his Ford. Earnhardt's car had become skittish because of a worn left rear tire, and the Lake Norman driver was falling back.

However, on Lap 477 Don Hume spun in Turn 2, bringing out the 15th caution flag, a record for the .533-mile track and just two short of the all-time Grand National mark.

Rudd roared out of the pits first and held the lead when the green showed on Lap 480.

Alone in the lead for the next 2 laps, the drivers battled side-by-side, sending sparks flying by rubbing metal five times. On Lap 483, Earnhardt edged ahead in the homestretch and went in front to stay.

"It overworked me a little bit today," Earnhardt, 33, said. "The power steering went out about Lap 100. I didn't think then that it would be possible to go all the way.

"Fortunately, the car was sticking to the track, handling pretty good, or there's no way I could have lasted in it."

All the while, Earnhardt, winning his second race this year, a third at Bristol and the 13th of his career, was working his forearm back and forth to revive it.

"Without the last yellow and the pit stop it gave us, Ricky would have won. I couldn't have caught him," said Earnhardt.

April 27, 1985
All's well between Earnhardt, Petty
by Tom Higgins

Martinsville, Va.—Despite appearances, there's no feud brewing between stock car racing's most dynamic young drivers.

Kyle Petty and Dale Earnhardt made that apparent at Martinsville Speedway, where Mike Alexander led the second round of time trials Friday for the Sovran Bank 500 with a lap of 89.485 mph. The NASCAR Grand National event is Sunday at 12:30 p.m.

Petty and Earnhardt shook hands and were grinning amicably after discussing an incident in last Sunday's Northwestern Bank 400 at North Wilkesboro Speedway that led to angry words and more.

It started when Petty's Ford and Earnhardt's Chevrolet tangled between Turns 3 and 4. Petty was running a strong third at the time, spun out, lost 2 laps and eventually finished 12th.

Immediately after the mishap, Petty pulled along Earnhardt on pit road, shouted something and made a gesture that was shown nationwide by ESPN. The network was airing the race live and had a camera in Petty's car.

Somewhat comically, Petty's car stalled adjacent to the Earnhardt pit. He had to be push-started by the crewmen of the driver he was berating.

"Dale spun me out and took away any chance I had of winning the race," Petty charged in postrace comments. "Somebody is going to have to do something about him."

Sensing things had cooled Thursday, he jokingly walked up to interrupt while Earnhardt was being interviewed for a TV news show. Their talk followed.

"By the way," Petty said afterward, "I'm going to be wearing mittens to drive here. They're specially designed so fingers don't show."

> "I'm going to be wearing mittens to drive here. They're specially designed so fingers don't show."
>
> **—Kyle Petty**

August 25, 1985
WIN NO. 3: BRISTOL
Caution and confusion
by Tom Higgins

Bristol, Tenn.— Dale Earnhardt wound up having to work for a Busch 500 victory that appeared his easily Saturday night in a wreck-strewn NASCAR Grand National race that ended in some confusion.

From Laps 366-434 in the 500-lap event at Bristol Raceway the Chevrolet- driving Earnhardt was leading in a lap by himself. But two wrecks by Kyle Petty enabled Tim Richmond, Neil Bonnett and Darrell Waltrip to make up the deficit and give a record, standing-room-only crowd of 33,000 and a national ESPN television audience some excitement.

When the green showed for the final time on Lap 460, Richmond was leading in his Pontiac with Earnhardt second.

On Lap 483 Earnhardt muscled past Richmond coming out of Turn 4 at the .533-mile track and led to the conclusion, finishing three car lengths ahead.

Chevy teammates Bonnett and Waltrip followed in the lead lap, and then came Ford-driving Bill Elliott in fifth place, a lap down. Completing the top 10 were Harry Gant, Ron Bouchard, Richard Petty, Ricky Rudd and Lake Speed.

NASCAR officials had some trouble sorting out what the lineup should be for the restart following the final caution-flag period on Laps 446-459, and Waltrip contended he was incorrectly placed in an unfavorable position, almost a full lap behind the leaders.

The triumph gave Earnhardt and his Richard Childress team a sweep of Bristol's two Grand National races this season. It was his third win this year, all on short tracks, and the 14th of the Lake Norman driver's career.

"When I got a lap ahead, I knew it wasn't going to be easy, not the way things were going tonight," said Earnhardt. "So I kept going hard. The car felt comfortable at a fast pace so I didn't slow down any.

"Tim gave me a good race at the end. He didn't give it to me. He ought to be a winner, too, as well as he drove tonight."

Earnhardt impatiently waits out a rain
shower in the back of his team's transporter
at Charlotte Motor Speedway. (Fred Wilson/
The Charlotte Observer)

WIN NO. 4: MARTINSVILLE
Surviving bumper cars
by Tom Higgins

Martinsville, Va.—Dale Earnhardt scored a "smashing" victory Sunday in a rough, wreck-strewn Goody's 500 in which one grinding accident helped runner-up Darrell Waltrip move to within 23 points of NASCAR Grand National standings leader Bill Elliott.

The suddenly luckless Elliott was the major victim of a multicar crash on the 343rd of 500 laps at Martinsville Speedway. He wound up 17th— 33 laps behind Earnhardt and Waltrip.

As a result, Elliott, who won his 10th race of the season just three weeks ago, lost much of his points lead for the third straight race. He dropped 63 points Sunday after leading by 206 Sept. 1.

Earnhardt collected $37,725 for his fourth stock car racing victory this season, all of which have come on the so-called short tracks.

"I earned every penny of it today," said a beaming Earnhardt, 34, after edging Waltrip in a duel of Chevrolet drivers. "It was tough here, like always, and we had a lot of pressure

> **"I earned every penny of it today."**
> **—Dale Earnhardt**

because of a big gamble right at the end."

That came with only eight laps to go on the .526-mile track when Bobby Hillin spun in Turn 3, bringing out the last of 12 yellow flags.

Earnhardt, Darrell Waltrip and Harry Gant were running 1-2-3 at the time.

Waltrip and Gant whipped into the pits for two fresh tires each, while Earnhardt stayed on the track.

"I was asking the boys in my pits (the Richard Childress team) by radio what they wanted to do," Earnhardt said. "They were asking back what I wanted to do. Finally, I said, 'Let's gamble,' and I didn't come in."

The field went back to full speed on lap 497, all except Gant, who'd taken on a flat tire.

While Gant pitted, Waltrip maneuvered alongside Earnhardt on the backstretch. With a race record crowd of 37,000 cheering, Earnhardt cut the third corner close, forcing Waltrip to back off slightly, and he was unable to get in passing position.

Another way Dale Earnhardt finds success and relaxation: deer hunting. These trophies weren't won at the race track. (Fred Wilson/The Charlotte Observer)

November 17, 1985
Over here, deer
by Tom Higgins

When an overwhelming majority of hunters enter the woods Monday to open the regular firearms deer season in North Carolina's central counties, they'll be reeking. Ditto for the northwestern and western area hunts beginning Nov. 25.

In addition to the normal body odors, they'll carry along the aroma of breakfast, bacon and eggs and coffee. Quite likely the air about them will be tinged with the scent of cigarettes, too, no matter whether they're smokers or not.

The fumes from tobacco used by their hunting buddies will have permeated their clothing.

Dale Earnhardt can't imagine anyone going deer hunting while sending out such a smelly message of warning to whitetail deer, whose greatest protective instinct probably is that sense provided through the nose.

"And then hundreds of hunters wonder why they never get a chance to bag a buck," says Earnhardt, shaking his head.

Of the state's well-known—or celebrity — deer hunters, Earnhardt quite likely is the most successful. The 1980 NASCAR Grand National champion, a four-time winner on the big league stock car racing circuit this year, has taken trophy-sized bucks each of the past several seasons, including an 11-pointer with a 21½-inch antler spread, a 12-pointer with a 20½-inch spread, and a 13-pointer. The 12-pointer weighed a whopping 230 pounds. Earnhardt has averaged four good-sized deer every season for the past 10 years. It's no accident.

Earnhardt, 34, is no luckier than the next hunter. He has no secret strategy for befuddling big bucks. The answer is that Earnhardt works at making his favorite recreation produce, never depending on chance to get a shot.

Here are some of his thoughts, which "will help hunters who might not otherwise get a deer" this year: "While I'm very big on thinking that odors play a part in deer hunting, I'm not into the store-bought buck lures or masking smells.

"Rather than using them, I use natural stuff. For example, a day or two before going hunting I put the clothes I plan to wear in a plastic trash bag. Then I throw a bunch of pine cones and leaves out of the woods in there with them and hang the bag outside in the air. My clothing absorbs the smell of the pine cones and leaves.

"When I get up on the morning of the hunt I avoid the kitchen where breakfast is being cooked. You can't stand around fixing breakfast then expect to go out and kill a deer. I take a shower, but don't use any deodorant, lotion or talc. I then fetch my clothes and put them on. When I get to my stand I feel like I smell as natural, as much like the woods, as is humanly possible.

"Occasionally I will use a store-bought scent, Tink's doe-in-heat lure, dousing it on a rag and tying that to my boot. I usually try this when I'm hiking a long way to a stand with the idea that a buck might cross the scent and trail along out of curiosity."

"Scouting is tremendously important to putting fresh venison—which I love, by the way—in the freezer. I spend about every free day during the preseason at it. I pick a lot of places with good potential for tree stands, then start narrowing the selection down to the sites that look the very best.

"The main sign to me is a pawing, where a buck is marking a place for does to come and meet him. I think pawings are far more productive places to hunt than tree rubs.

"The tree stands I use take a lot of work to build and then to get high up into a tree, but I think it's paid off... No, I know it has." Earnhardt laughed.

"These stands are pretty heavy, of course, so hoisting them up is a job. If the sites I've selected are near logging roads or the like, it's easier, 'cause my Blazer has a winch on the front of it and we can lift them right up. If not? Well, I sweet-talk three or four buddies into helping me with block and tackle and we do a lot of huffing and puffing.

"You've got to go to where the big bucks are to get one. It's very seldom they'll come to you. And if that's in an area that's aggravating to reach, well, tough."

"You've got to go to where the big bucks are to get one. It's very seldom they'll come to you. And if that's in an area that's aggravating to reach, well, tough."
— Dale Earnhardt

Chapter Nine:
1986: Almost did . . .
and almost didn'ts

Races	Won	Top 5	Top 10	Poles	Earnings
29	5	16	23	1	$1,783,880

February 17, 1986
Funny? It's a gas.
by Ron Green

Daytona Beach, Fla.—If it hadn't been dripping with irony, it would have been funny.

Aw, to heck with irony. It *was* funny.

Even Dale Earnhardt laughed about it, and he had just had his heart carved out by a gas gauge.

The Daytona 500 had ended Sunday, and the cars were circling the track one more time after the checkered flag had waved over Geoff Bodine. And there was Bill Elliott's Ford, battered in a midrace multi-car wreck and slapped around again in a supermarket parking lot fender bender on pit road. And it was pushing Dale Earnhardt's stalled Chevrolet back to the pits, the lame helping the lame. Along the way, they stopped and picked up Ron Bouchard's dead mount as well.

"Bill was the cleanup man, I reckon," said Earnhardt. Even he thought it was funny and he had just seen a dreamy chance at winning the the sport's richest race disappear with 3 laps to go when he ran out of gas.

Elliott and Earnhardt had been the names on the marquee over the past several days, between them winning everything there was to win in the elaborate preliminaries.

Elliott had led qualifying and won a 125-mile race. Earnhardt had won the Busch Clash, which matches pole winners from the previous year; the other 125-mile race and a 300-mile sportsman race.

Sunday's 500-miler was supposed to be their show with Bodine's Chevy lurking in the wings.

Elliott, who had a charmed, 11-win, $2 million season in 1985, finished two laps down in 13th place. His agony was prolonged. Earnhardt's came like a sucker punch.

With three laps to go, Bodine was running in front and Earnhardt was an inch or two behind, exactly where he wanted to be. He would wait until the last lap, then use the peculiar aerodynamics of these high-speed tracks to slingshot around. It was all but inevitable. Being second on the last lap here is better than being first. Bodine slowed, hoping Earnhardt would go around, but he knew better. "I think if I had gone down pit road, he would've followed me," said Bodine.

But halfway through the 197th turn around the 2-mile course, Earnhardt looked at his gas gauge and said, "Aw, no," or something like that. The needle normally stays around 6 or 7. When it drops to 5, you're running on fumes. His read 3. He had no choice but to dive onto pit road as Bodine sped away.

Earnhardt's engine died in the pits, and a crewman shot ether into it to get it restarted. When Earnhardt hurried back out to try for the highest finish he could manage, the ether detonated, broke the engine and left him sitting on the backstretch, nothing more than a spectator while cars flew by. By the time the thing ended, he had been dropped all the way back to 14th.

But as he climbed out of his car in the garage, he smiled and said, "Well, bleep."

"If I hadn't run out of gas, it would've been a helluva finish, wouldn't it?" said Earnhardt. "Who knows what would've happened.

"But when you see the gas gauge go down what can you do? You come in and get some gas."

Earnhardt seemed remarkably placid after his 15th-round knockout when he was in position to become the only man to win four races at Daytona during a single Speed Week session. He didn't throw any tool boxes or kick his car or eat a wrench.

"I can take losing just like I can take winning," he said. "Ain't nothing to complain about. It's been a helluva week for me.

"But now the party's over."

April 14, 1986

WIN NO. 1: DARLINGTON
Patience pays

By Tom Higgins

"When the last yellow came out, I thought, 'Oh no, here we go again.' I told Richard on the radio, 'Here it comes, spooking us another time.' But then I told him, 'Don't worry about it.' I knew this car was just too strong to lose unless something really crazy happened." —Earnhardt

Darlington, S.C. — Through the season's first five races there had been enough problems and tactical errors to make many stock car racing drivers try to bite a tire tool in two.

Twice, for example, Dale Earnhardt had run out of gas, costing him victory chances because of miscalculation in the pits.

Another time his Chevrolet's engine failed just 2 miles from the finish.

And then, there was the wreck with Darrell Waltrip at the conclusion of February's Miller 400 at Richmond as they battled for the victory with 3 laps to go.

It was a nettlesome start to the season, all the more nagging because of this development: Despite leading 677 of a possible 1,920 laps, Earnhardt had failed to triumph. During it all, though, Earnhardt demonstrated restraint rare for such a high-charged competitor.

"Things will come around," said the Lake Norman driver. "We've got too good a team for them not to fall into place."

Sunday he finally prevailed, running away with the TranSouth 500.

"We've been the car to beat every race this year," said a pleased Earnhardt after showing the field the rear bumper of his blue and yellow Monte Carlo for 335 of 367 laps. "So there wasn't any use to get all tore up over the bad luck.

"Sure, it was frustrating to be running up front and not winning. But part of racing is that to be a good winner, you've got to be a good loser. . .

"I knew it'd turn around."

April 21, 1986

WIN NO. 2: NORTH WILKESBORO
A win, but not by much

By Tom Higgins

"I was trying to get close enough at the end to give him a 'Dale Earnhardt' (bump) in the rear bumper and maybe get around, but I couldn't reach him." —Ricky Rudd

North Wilkesboro, N.C.—Dale Earnhardt held off Ricky Rudd by 2 car lengths and won the First Union 400 stock car racing thriller Sunday at North Wilkesboro Speedway.

It was the second straight victory on NASCAR's Winston Cup circuit for the Chevrolet-driving Earnhardt, snapping a streak of 11 winners in as many races dating to September.

Earnhardt, who won the TranSouth 500 at Darlington Raceway on April 13, whipped out of the pits first during Sunday's final caution period and held the lead the final 46 laps, scoring his first triumph at North Wilkesboro in 16 starts.

Rudd, driving a Ford, kept a North Wilkesboro Speedway-record crowd estimated at 29,500 on its feet by riding Earnhardt's bumper and making several daring attempts to pass.

Earnhardt and the other challengers maintained a hard pace throughout, as rain threatened to bring the race to a premature conclusion.

"It looked like it was going to pour all afternoon," said Earnhardt. "I was standing on the throttle hoping to be in front if the race was stopped, and the others were, too. I think it was about as good a racing as there has been here in a while. I know I wasn't bored."

May 24, 1986

Other drivers notice when Earnhardt's around

by Ron Green

Charlotte, N.C.—Dale Earnhardt's nickname around the NASCAR Winston Cup circuit is "Ironhead," an obvious play on his last name.

To some, it's an affectionate sobriquet. Others feel the appellation should be Hardhead.

Nobody among the upper echelon of stock car racing drives harder, battles more fiercely or takes more chances than Dale Earnhardt. He hurls his car around a track in a style that is often chilling to competitors and fans alike. He drives like a New York cabbie with his throttle stuck.

How are we to regard the 35-year-old son of a former national sportsman champion who has notched his 16th and 17th Winston Cup victories in this, his eighth full year on the circuit, and is contending for the national points and money-winning titles?

Fellow driver Neil Bonnett said, "He's the most aggressive driver out here, but I've raced him since long before we got into Winston Cup racing, and I've always liked it. A lot of drivers don't.

"I catalog drivers and react to them accordingly. When I see Richard Petty coming up on me, I think 'smooth.' When I see Earnhardt's car in my mirror, it registers 'aggression.'

"It's just Dale's type of driving. The name of the game is racing, and that's what it means to me. Digging, shoving. People are saying he's overly aggressive, but I don't want to see high-speed parading where you go around single file and then try to win at the end. That's not racing. I don't want them telling me I can't bump somebody going down the stretch, that I've got to stay 5 feet behind them or 6 inches to the side of them. If they do that, we might as well park these things because the quality of the show is going to hell.

> "People are saying he's overly aggressive, but I don't want to see high-speed parading where you go around single file and then try to win at the end. That's not racing."
> —Neil Bonnett

"He beat on me at Richmond one time, and I tried for 2 laps to wreck him but I couldn't catch him. And he knows that."

On the other hand, Darrell Waltrip, who is battling Earnhardt for the points lead going into Sunday's Coca-Cola 600 at Charlotte Motor Speedway and who has more than once been a victim of Earnhardt's driving ferocity, said, "Aggressive? I guess you could call it that.

"I like to race with him—as long as it stays within the realm of racing. I look at it as what's necessary and what isn't. Some people do some unnecessary things and cause problems. Some do what's necessary and don't cause problems."

In last year's 600, which Waltrip won, there was a $10,000 bonus for the halfway leader. Earnhardt had the lead coming off the fourth turn. Waltrip moved under him and suddenly found himself riding on the infield grass.

"That was my money," said Earnhardt. "I'd done counted it coming off Turn 4. I just kinda pinched him off."

Earlier this year, Earnhardt was fined $5,000, placed on probation for a year and ordered to post a $10,000 bond after he wrecked Waltrip and two following cars at Richmond when Waltrip tried to pass him with 3 laps to go. NASCAR officials charged Earnhardt with reckless driving. The penalties were later lifted except for a $3,000 fine.

"Richmond is behind us," said Earnhardt, who lives in Mooresville. "It hasn't changed anything in my style or my feeling. I just hate that I made a mistake. It cost both of us a race car. I did all I could to win. I made a judgment, and it was a mistake.

At a black-tie awards dinner in New York last winter, driver Ricky Rudd jokingly told the audience, "If you're wondering why we're all dressed up like this but our shoes aren't shined, it's because we were standing around backstage and Earnhardt walked all over us."

After finishing second to Earnhardt in a race, Rudd said, "I was trying to get close enough to give him a 'Dale Earnhardt' in the rear bumper and maybe get around."

Earnhardt ponders the question of his slashing style and says, "I have a race team that puts 100 percent into what it does, and I feel like I ought to do the same. I want to give more than 100 percent every race, and if that's aggressive, then I reckon I am.

"To be good out here, to be here awhile, you've got to go out and try to win, show what you can do, what the team's capable of doing. That makes the sponsors, the fans, everybody happy.

"It's not a sport for the faint of heart."

Dale Earnhardt wore many hats in 1986, including that of TranSouth 500 champion at Darlington. (Diedra Laird/The Charlotte Observer)

May 26, 1986

WIN NO. 3: CHARLOTTE
600 lands in Earnhardt's lap

by Tom Higgins

"As the race wound down, I knew Bill had to make another pit stop . . . So I was content to just run behind him, not pressure the tires, save my stuff and wait for him to go in."

— Dale Earnhardt

Charlotte, N.C. — Dale Earnhardt abandoned his usual attacking style in favor of patience Sunday and allowed developments to bring him victory in the Coca-Cola 600 stock car race.

Earnhardt, driving a Chevrolet, was ahead only two times for just 25 of the 400 laps at Charlotte Motor Speedway, including the last 16. But he won because:

- Bill Elliott had to pit while leading on Lap 384 for fuel to finish the NASCAR Winston Cup Series race. His Ford failed to get gas mileage equal to the Chevrolets of Earnhardt, Tim Richmond, Harry Gant and Darrell Waltrip, and the Ford of Cale Yarborough, all of which swept by him during a 4.15-second stop.
- The 1.5-mile track's asphalt surface changed gradually throughout the 4-hour, 16-minute, 26-second race, and near the end its condition matched almost perfectly the high gearing chosen by Earnhardt, team owner Richard Childress and crew chief Kirk Shelmerdine.

Earnhardt, winning the 600 for the first time, finished 1.59 seconds ahead of Richmond, who nipped Yarborough by about a hood-length for second in a dash off the fourth turn. Farther back in the lead lap came Gant, Waltrip and Elliott.

Dale Earnhardt and Dale Jarrett battled for position. (Kent D. Johnson/The Charlotte Observer)

September 2, 1986
Let's (almost) make a deal
by Tom Higgins

Darlington, S.C.—If driver Cale Yarborough hadn't bought the Race Hill Farm team of Jack Beebe, then Dale Earnhardt was going to purchase it.

Earnhardt, the leader in NASCAR's Winston Cup Series point standings, confirmed the plan to *The Observer* after winning Monday's Gatorade 200, a Busch Series sportsman event.

"I definitely was going to do it," said Earnhardt. "I already had the financing taken care of. All I had to do was take Jack the check.

"In fact, I thought we had a deal. But about 15 minutes after I told him I'd take the team, he phoned me back and said that Cale had bought it."

What were Earnhardt's plans for the Beebe cars and equipment, since he recently signed a three-year contract to continue with the Richard Childress team of Winston-Salem?

"I would have found some use for it," replied Earnhardt, grinning. "Eventually I would have moved it to a new shop I'm building on my farm near Mooresville. I would have put someone in the car for several races next season."

Someone like Al Unser, Jr., the Indy-car star?

"You've got a great source," said Earnhardt, grinning.

October 4, 1986
Verbal sparks fly
by Tom Higgins

> "(I'd put) some psychological stuff in the papers, but it wouldn't do any good 'cause Dale and his boys can't read."
> — Darrell Waltrip

As expected, the verbal sparks have flown between archrivals Dale Earnhardt and Darrell Waltrip at Charlotte Motor Speedway.

While preparations continued for Sunday's Oakwood Homes 500, the two top contenders for the Winston Cup Series championship engaged in one of their spiciest exchanges ever.

The battle of barbs became inevitable last Sunday when Waltrip, noted for his gamesmanship, cracked during the Holly Farms 400 victor's interview that he'd put "some psychological stuff in the papers, but it wouldn't do any good 'cause Dale and his boys can't read."

"I can read," responded a grinning Earnhardt, who leads Waltrip by 122 points in the standings toward the title. "Just like in a kid's early reader. See Darrell run his mouth. See Darrell fall.'"

October 6, 1986

WIN NO. 4: CHARLOTTE
Back from 2 laps down

by Tom Higgins

> "Thank the Lord we caught those cautions just right, or we might not have made up the lost laps."
> —Dale Earnhardt

Charlotte, N.C.— Flashing the form of a champion, Dale Earnhardt charged back from a 2-lap deficit Sunday for an Oakwood Homes 500 victory that may have delivered him the NASCAR Winston Cup Series stock car racing title.

The victory left Earnhardt with a commanding 159-point edge over Darrell Waltrip in the chase for the championship with only three races remaining.

Tim Richmond, who appeared headed to victory lane until his obviously superior car's engine failed on the 266th of 334 laps, dropped practically out of contention in the points race, 232 points behind.

Waltrip finished ninth and lost 37 points to Earnhardt; Richmond wound up 27th and dropped 88.

Early in the race it appeared that Earnhardt and his Richard Childress-owned, Kirk Shelmerdine-led team from Winston-Salem faced almost certain continuation of a nonwinning streak of 15 races, dating to May's Coca-Cola 600. After dueling closely with Richmond for the lead, Earnhardt suddenly flashed into the pits on Lap 37 for left side tires. The left rear had equalized, or gone out of balance. The stop cost Earnhardt a lap.

On Lap 47, Earnhardt again pitted, this time because of a cut right rear tire, the possible result of cans and bottles being thrown on the track in Turn 1. He lost another lap.

"To say I was concerned then isn't the word," Earnhardt said. "Worried is the word.

"But Richard (Childress) kept talking on the radio, leading the cheers and keeping me pumped up."

Earnhardt got one lap back when a wild, multi-car crash on the backstretch enabled him to beat Benny Parsons, then the leader, back to the flagstand on Lap 85 as the caution light came on. On the restart after that yellow flag, Earnhardt passed leader Geoff Bodine to work back onto the lead lap.

A frontstretch wreck involving Bobby Hillin and Bill Elliott on Lap 120 helped Earnhardt erase his deficit totally, and he was in or near the lead the rest of the way.

October 6, 1986

A racing rivalry that runs flat-out

by Ron Green

Charlotte, N.C.—They are neighbors on Lake Norman and brothers in spirit when they are behind the wheels of their race cars.

And for a while Sunday in the Oakwood Homes 500 at Charlotte Motor Speedway, Dale Earnhardt and Tim Richmond let their kinship and their feisty natures soar like children at play.

It was a dangerous game of "chicken," played at high speed. But these two, probably the most daring drivers on the NASCAR Winston Cup circuit and clearly the hottest going this year, enjoyed it.

For about 3 laps around the midway point of the race—when they were dividing the lead for 134 of 135 laps—they drove side-by-side around the mile-and-a-half speedway broiling under a July-like sun, first one pushing his nose ahead, then the other, traveling 150 miles an hour or faster.

Although it was no time to be taking wild chances, neither would yield.

They were having too much fun.

It was the kind of stuff people pay to see. Earnhardt and Richmond regularly give the customers more of that than anyone nowadays.

The shootout finally ended when Earnhardt went too high coming out of the second turn and scraped his car along the wall for about 30 or 40 yards, allowing Richmond to move out well ahead of him.

As it turned out, it was wasted effort—in a way—for Richmond. His engine broke on the 266th lap, and he had to park his car, eventually finishing 27th. Earnhardt, who at one point early in the steamy afternoon was 2

laps down, won the race.

For Richmond, the encounter wasn't a total waste.

"I liked it," he said. "That's what it's all about. We were racing."

Earnhardt liked it, too.

"I was having so much fun, I just got caught up in the competition and the fun we were having and forgot we still had a lot of racing to do," he said. "When I hit the wall, it sort've made me calm down."

There was a time a couple of years ago when their relationship was strained. Earnhardt pushed Richmond around a couple of times on the track, and Richmond barked that he wasn't going to put up with it anymore.

But that has passed. They're pals.

And since he's gotten married, Earnhardt doesn't even come around Richmond's house at two or three o'clock in the morning and blow the horn or fire his shotgun to wake Richmond anymore.

"Earnhardt and I have more desire to beat one another than probably anybody out there," said Richmond, "but we trust each other's ability. When you race that close that long, you're not worried about each other's ability.

"Our relationship is like two boxers. When they start a fight, they're ready to whip one another bad, but the longer the fight goes on, the more respect they gain. Lots of times you see boxers put their arms around each other after a fight, because they know what each other had to go through to get to the end and not play dirty."

> "Our relationship is like two boxers. When they start a fight, they're ready to whip one another bad, but the longer the fight goes on, the more respect they gain."
> —Tim Richmond

November 3, 1986

WIN NO. 5: ATLANTA
Earnhardt wins points title

by Tom Higgins

Hampton, Ga.— Whoever said you can't have it all forgot to tell Dale Earnhardt.

Charging characteristically, Earnhardt swept to a record-smashing Atlanta Journal 500 victory Sunday and in the process clinched NASCAR's rich Winston Cup Series stock car racing championship with one race remaining.

The triumph, combined with Darrell Waltrip's 39th place finish after leaving the Atlanta International Raceway event with a failed engine on the 85th of 328 laps, left Earnhardt, 35, who also won the championship in 1980, with a 278-point lead going into the season finale Western 500 at Riverside (Calif.) Raceway on Nov. 16. The most points Waltrip could gain even if Earnhardt finished last in that race is 148.

It marks the first time since Cale Yarborough clinched with two races remaining in 1978 that the chase for the championship hasn't ex-

tended to the final race.

"I'm not going to compare the two titles, but this one means an awful lot because of the dedication of the boys on my crew and Richard Childress," said a surprisingly subdued Earnhardt, whose '80 crown came with a long-defunct team. "Richard was our key to winning the championship. His effort as team owner put us where we are. All the glory is his."

Dale Earnhardt raises his arms in celebration. (Jeff Siner/The Charlotte Observer)

November 15, 1986
Sweet memories
by *Tom Higgins*

Riverside, Calif.—A few weeks after Ralph Earnhardt died unexpectedly of a heart attack at his Kannapolis home in 1973, his son, Dale, decided to sell their prized bird dogs.

"It got to where I couldn't look at them. It was too painful," Dale once recalled. "They'd make me think of all the good times we'd had hunting together, and it was too much for me. I was only 20 then, and I couldn't handle it.

"So with permission from my mom, Martha, I let them go."

Dale Earnhardt says he still feels the pain of losing the father he had idolized. However, the years and maturity have changed his attitude toward thinking about the driver who was one of stock car racing's pioneers in the 1950s and '60s.

Nowadays, Dale evokes his dad's memory often and touchingly, crediting him with shaping his own career as a second-generation driver.

"Daddy was honest, quiet and independent," Earnhardt said. "I think it was his independence that maybe was the reason he didn't go much further in racing.

"Lord knows, he had the know-how to have gone on. I stood on his tow truck as a boy, and I think I must have seen every lap he ever drove. I guess you could say I adopted his style of driving, and I've tried to capitalize on what he told me, all the advice he gave me. I wish I'd paid more attention.

"It has been a long time, but he's still an everyday thought. Whenever I have a problem, inside the race car or out, I still think, 'How would he have handled this situation. What would he have done?' He's still a big part of me."

"They're two peas in a pod," said Spartanburg's Bud Moore, for whom Dale drove during the 1982-83 seasons. "The same fire is there in both father and son."

In addition to memorializing his father, Earnhardt credited his wife, Teresa, for his career advancing as far as it has.

Four years ago in Mooresville, Dale and Teresa Houston were married.

She had a racing heritage, too. Teresa's father is Hal Houston, a former driver at Hickory Speedway. She's the niece of NASCAR Busch Series sportsman veteran Tommy Houston.

"Today's our fourth anniversary," said Earnhardt. "I can't say what she has meant to me. She's such a positive influence—very supportive and helpful in the planning."

Friends of the Earnhardts generally credit Teresa with Dale's increasing openness and smoother image.

> "I've tried to capitalize on what he told me, all the advice he gave me. I wish I'd paid more attention."
> —Dale Earnhardt, on his father's influence on his career

Charting the Domination

Race	Finish	Money	The Season Rank (+/- Lead)
Daytona 500	14	$61,655	14 (-59)
Miller 400	3	19,310	4 (-31)
Groodwrench 500	8	19,510	3 (-42)
Motorcraft 500	2	51,300	3 (-27)
Valleydale 500	6	10,650	3 (-58)
TranSouth 500	1	52,250	2 (-48)
First Union 400	1	38,550	2 (-33)
Sovran Bank 500	21	9,915	2 (-5)
Winston 500	2	53,900	1 (+109)
Budweiser 500	3	24,900	1 (+124)
Coca-Cola 600	1	98,150	1 (+144)
Budweiser 400.	5	14,125	1 (+119)
Miller 500	2	29,750	1 (+251)
Miller 400	6	17,650	1 (+251)
Firecracker 400	27	14,895	1 (+178)
Summer 500	7	14,655	1 (+159)
Talladega 500	26	15,355	1 (+161)
Budweiser Glen	3	25,250	1 (+151)
Champion 400	5	18,750	1 (+141)
Busch 500	4	12,800	1 (+121)
Southern 500.	9	15,735	1 (+109)
Wrangler 400	2	24,525	1 (+118)
Delaware 500	21	10,750	1 (+138)
Goody's 500	12	11,770	1 (+136)
Holly Farms 400	9	9,500	1 (+122)
Oakwood 500	1	82,050	1 (+159)
Nationwise 500	6	15,750	1 (+144)
Journal 500	1	67,950	1 (+278)

Rank refers to Earnhardt's standing in the points race and +/- Lead refers to how many points he trailed the leader or by how many points he led.

Chapter Ten

1987: Driver of the Year . . . for 11 reasons

Races	Won	Top 5	Top 10	Poles	Earnings
29	11	21	24	1	$2,099,243

March 2, 1987

WIN No. 1: ROCKINGHAM
Big time in the Sandhills
by Tom Higgins

"I messed up so bad in qualifying, I felt I had to show how good our car was."

—Dale Earnhardt

Rockingham, N.C.—Dale Earnhardt dominated the field Sunday and sped to an impressive victory in the Goodwrench 500 stock car race.

Earnhardt, NASCAR's defending Winston Cup Series champion, crossed the finish line in his Chevrolet 10.58 seconds, or about a half-lap, ahead of runner-up Ricky Rudd's Ford for his first big-time triumph in 17 starts at N.C. Motor Speedway.

Charging characteristically, Earnhardt moved from his 14th starting position to take the lead just 30 laps into the event on the 1.017-mile Sandhills track.

Earnhardt, a fiery competitor, said he came into the race with more determination than ever.

"I owed it to Kirk Shelmerdine, my crew chief, and the rest of the boys," Earnhardt said after his 21st career victory. "I messed up so bad in qualifying, I felt I had to show how good our car was to make it up to them. So there was double incentive there."

March 9, 1987

WIN NO. 2: RICHMOND
Bent, not broken
by Tom Higgins

Richmond, Va.—Dale Earnhardt, although wheeling a bent and beaten Chevrolet, showed his rear bumper to the field Sunday and won the Miller 400 at Richmond Fairgrounds Raceway.

Earnhardt, NASCAR's current Winston Cup Series champion, flashed across the finish line .57 seconds ahead of runner-up Geoff Bodine, also in a Chevy.

It wasn't nearly as close as the time indicates. Earnhardt's car was clearly dominant.

It was the second straight victory in three races this season for Earnhardt, and it propelled him into a 530-510 lead over Bill Elliott in pursuit of the rich driving title.

Earnhardt's chances seemed tremendously diminished Saturday when the throttle hung on his car, causing a violent crash into the first turn wall during practice. However, his team took the car to a local racing shop and made repairs, including straightening of the frame.

"Obviously, I can't say enough about my crew," said Earnhardt. "What a job! The car essentially was totaled out. Not only did they have to put a new engine and front suspension in, they had to put the car on a frame machine, a difficult deal.

"I didn't know what the car was going to do, but they assured me it was going to be all right. They were right, and I can't say enough for them. They put the car back together, and I put my trust in their promising it was OK and went out there and ran it hard.

"Oh, there was some good racing out there," said Earnhardt, who honestly loves it when the competition is close. "Me and ol' Bill (Elliot) had a pretty good time out there (running side by side and at close quarters from laps 211-231). We enjoyed it and I know the fans did. That's what it is all about, for everyone to have a good time all day."

March 30, 1987

WIN NO. 3: DARLINGTON
Elliott gambles, Earnhardt collects
by Tom Higgins

Darlington, S.C.—Dale Earnhardt raked in all the chips from a Bill Elliott gamble Sunday and won the TranSouth 500 stock car race at Darlington International Raceway.

Earnhardt swept into the lead in Turn 3 at the 1.366-mile track on the last of the 367 laps as Elliott's Ford ran out of gas down the backstretch before a crowd estimated at 60,000.

"I saw him get slowed down going up the backstraight," Earnhardt said.

"That made me drive mine all the harder. I saw Bill coasting and I said that's the end of it.

"But truthfully, I can't believe he ran out of gas."

Earnhardt overtook Elliott between the third and fourth turns and sped to the checkered flag 1.23 seconds ahead.

Said Elliott, who finished second:

"We did the only thing we could do. It just ran out of gas. Gambling to go all the way was the only way we could have beaten Earnhardt."

It was Earnhardt's 23rd career victory and second straight TranSouth 500 triumph.

April 6, 1987

WIN NO. 4: NORTH WILKESBORO
Six starts, four wins, one tough car
by Tom Higgins

North Wilkesboro, N.C.—Dale Earnhardt is doing his best to deny NASCAR its claim of being the most competitive form of motorsports in the world.

Charging in a Chevrolet like a man possessed, Earnhardt continued domination of Winston Cup Series stock car racing Sunday by rolling to victory in the First Union 400, his fourth triuumph in six starts this season.

In the process, Earnhardt led 319 of the 400 laps at North Wilkesboro Speedway. This pushed his season total to 1,210 laps led of a possible 2,187, or 55.3 percent. His $44,675 share of Sunday's purse padded the 1987 winnings of Kannapolis native Earnhardt, 35, to $298,155, or $49,692.56 per start.

For the record, Earnhardt flashed to the finish at the five-eighths-mile track 1.72 seconds ahead of Ford-driving Kyle Petty.

Only caution flags for a variety of incidents kept Earnhardt's potent Chevrolet, engineered by the Richard Childress team of Winston-Salem, from lapping the field not only once, but possibly twice.

On Lap 225, for example, Earnhardt was within 4.1 seconds of lapping all his rivals, but Geoff Bodine blew an engine, bringing out the yellow flag.

No one passed Earnhardt under green. The only time he relinquished the lead was while pitting.

"I had a good time today, 'cause Richard Childress, Kirk Shelmerdine (the crew chief) and the rest of the boys had my Cadillac running well." Earnhardt cracked. "Seriously, I know we've got an awful good team, but it amazes me that our cars and the crew can be so consistent.

"If I keep my head screwed on, we're going to have a great year. It'd be great to win 12 to 15, and we're shooting for that."

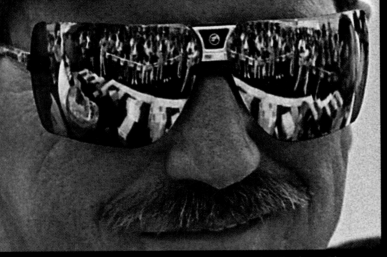

Patrick Schneider/The Charlotte Observer

April 13, 1987

WIN NO. 5: BRISTOL
Good show, bad soundtrack
by Tom Higgins

"The deal with Sterling was a little close. I thought I had him cleared. ... I had got under Sterling several times and he either chopped me off or hit the brakes."
—Dale Earnhardt

Bristol, Tenn.— Dale Earnhardt sped from a lap down Sunday to win the Valleydale 500 and continue his stock car racing tear, but rolled into another controversy in the process.

Winning for the fifth time in seven NASCAR Winston Cup Series starts this season, the Chevrolet-driving Earnhardt finished .79 seconds, about five car lengths, in front of runner-up Richard Petty's Pontiac.

Taking positions 3-6, all in the lead lap, in the event delayed 1 hour by rain and marred by 13 yellow flags for a track record 127 laps, were Ricky Rudd, Bill Elliott, Alan Kulwicki, Harry Gant and Kyle Petty.

Eight of the yellows were for crashes or spins. One of the worst wrecks resulted in harsh words for Earnhardt from Sterling Marlin and his team owner, Wayne King. Marlin wrecked while battling Earnhardt for the lead on the 254th of the 500 laps at the .533-mile track.

"First of all, there was a lapped car in the hole where he (Earnhardt) was trying to get by me," said Marlin, who had applauded Earnhardt sarcastically while walking back to the pits from his car. "If he had been up beside me it might have been different, but he hit me and spun me.

"I'm the leader of the race and it's my track. He has to pass me, not spin me out. The hard thing about this whole deal is that I was running damn good and I had a real chance of winning this race. That hurts even more than him spinning me out.

"Don't worry, his day is coming and he'll get it, too."

"If that's what it takes to be national champion, then they (Earnhardt and his Richard Childress team) can have it," said King, referring to the fact that the winner padded his lead toward a second straight national championship.

"That's exactly what I want to say. I'd like to use a little stronger language. There's at least three cars today I know that he's run all over."

April 27, 1987

WIN NO. 6:MARTINSVILLE
They call him the Streak

by Tom Higgins

Martinsville, Va.— Dale Earnhardt got an unintentional assist from Kyle Petty in the Sovran Bank 500 and continued his sensational stock car racing victory streak Sunday at the expense of arch-rival Geoff Bodine.

The victory in the NASCAR Winston Cup Series event before an overflow, record crowd of 40,000 at Martinsville Speedway was Earnhardt's fourth straight, sixth in eight starts this season and eighth in the last 12 races dating to last October.

Earnhardt's victory embellished what already ranked as the fastest start in NASCAR history. Previous best before Earnhardt's start was Richard Petty's four victories in the first seven races of 1975. No one ever had won more than five of the first 10 before.

Sunday's victory gave Earnhardt a sweep of the four short track events in the season's opening half. No one had done that since Cale Yarborough in 1977.

However, as the chase at the .526-mile track wound down, it appeared that Bodine, who has been plagued by mishaps while racing this season, had finally snapped his slump and that at last someone had Earnhardt's number.

As Bodine sped into the 484th lap he had a comfortable five-second lead over Earnhardt, driving a Chevrolet.

Then, to the disbelief of spectators, it happened.

Just as Bodine worked his Chevrolet abreast of Petty on the outside, Petty's Ford, which had been lapped, lost traction and swerved right. Although only clipped slightly, Bodine's car spun atop the inside curbing and onto a grassy strip.

Tires spinning, Bodine quickly got back on the track. By then, though, both Earnhardt and Rusty Wallace, driving a Pontiac, had swept by.

NASCAR officials deemed no caution flag was necessary, and Earnhardt simply rode to the checkered flag from there. He finished 2.28 seconds ahead of runner-up Wallace, who had Bodine right on his bumper.

"If you don't have a little luck, you can't win races," said Earnhardt, 35, who appeared a bit in disbelief at the good fortune of his Richard Childress team. "And this one was all luck. Geoff definitely had us beat.

"I had knocked the toe-in out of line on that inside curbing while racing with Rusty, and I couldn't do anything with Geoff. I was racing as hard as I could to try to catch him, but I wasn't gaining."

Earnhardt's hot start

Dale Earnhardt has won six of the first eight races in the 1987 NASCAR season, the best start since NASCAR started keeping records.

Date	Race	Winner	Finish
Feb. 15	Daytona 500	Bill Elliott	5th
March 1	Goodwrench 500	Dale Earnhardt	1st
March 8	Miller High Life 400	Dale Earnhardt	1st
March 15	Motorcraft 500	Ricky Rudd	16th
March 29	TranSouth 500	Dale Earnhardt	1st
April 5	First Union 400	Dale Earnhardt	1st
April 12	Valleydale 500	Dale Earnhardt	1st
April 26	Sovran Bank 500	Dale Earnhardt	1st

May 18, 1987
Pass the dirt and some moonshine, boys
by Ron Green

> "It was worth being in third (where he finished) just to watch the show. It was like bumper cars that last 10 laps. ... It's not his fault. They're letting him get away with it."
>
> —Tim Richmond

Charlotte, N.C.—For three years now, NASCAR has been trying to find a suitable home for The Winston, a race featuring its brightest stars.

May we recommend holding it next year at a rural dirt track? Way, way out in the country, where people still carry sidearms and make moonshine. On a Saturday night.

Dress the drivers in flowered print shirts, blue jeans, white socks, street shoes and some of those funny-looking old helmets.

Dale Earnhardt and Bill Elliott might just as well have been a couple of ol' redneck boys at Charolette Motor Speedway on Sunday, juiced up with a bellyfull of bourbon, whopping each other up against the fence and raisin' hell.

But this was grim business they were about Sunday. When drivers start turning left or right into each other with malice aforethought at speeds of more than 150 mph, it is deadly grim. There's enough risk in stock car racing without having someone trying to take you out with a 3,500-pound weapon moving at high speed.

We chuckle at some of the little incidents that crop up fairly regularly in auto racing. Rubbing fenders, as they call it, blocking somebody, bumping someone from the rear to tell him to get out of the way, that sort of thing.

But Sunday's performance was terrifying. And, at whatever expense, including suspension, it ought to be the last we see of that kind of tactic.

Earnhardt tells it one way, Elliott another. Other drivers have their own versions.

Early in the last segment of this three-chapter race with a $150,000 difference between first money and second, Elliott hit Geoff Bodine, spinning him between the first and second turns.

Elliott says Earnhardt hit his right rear panel, causing him to lose control and run into Bodine. Tim Richmond, following close behind, verified that version. Earnhardt contended he didn't touch either.

On the next lap, Elliott forced Earnhardt off the track into the infield grass on the front straight. Two laps

---

April 27, 1987
Anyone else know how to drive?
By Tom Sorensen

NASCAR to Tim Richmond: Save us, please.

All those fans who pay all that money to watch all those drivers make all those left turns might begin to stay home if Dale Earnhardt continues to win. NASCAR has had eight races this season, and Earnhardt has won six of them.

Richmond, who has not raced all season while recovering from pneumonia, said he plans to return to the sport May 17 at The Winston. That alone makes the race, which will be held at Charlotte Motor Speedway, the most fascinating of the year. Richmond might not beat Dale Earnhardt. But he might. There aren't many others you can say that about.

later, Elliott had a tire go down, almost wrecking him. He said it was the result of Earnhardt's hitting him, forcing his fender in and cutting the tire.

"When a man pulls over and lets you beside him, then tries to run you into the wall, is that racin'?" Elliott said.

But he slammed into Earnhardt on the backstretch after Earnhardt had won the first prize and was taking a victory lap.

"That bothered me," Earnhardt said. "We'll have to see what NASCAR has to say about that. It was a little bit unsportsmanlike, I thought."

Unsportsmanlike! Those two had been playing a deadly game of bumper car and Earnhardt's talking about sportsmanship? Gimme a break.

Two drivers who had choice seats for much of this war were Bodine and Richmond.

Bodine, who has been a vocal critic of Earnhardt's style in the past, said, "You race hard and you do everything you can, you even rub and bang with people, but you don't try to kill them.

"If he thinks that's racing, he's sick. I don't care if it was for $200,000 or $2 million, and I'd tell him this to his face, my life is worth more than $200,000."

Richmond said, "It was worth being in third (where he finished) just to watch the show. It was like bumper cars that last 10 laps.

"I watched that fiasco. I guess no matter how many boos there are (Earnhardt heard plenty before and after the race), you've gotta keep doing your deal. I think if I got all those boos, I'd have to rethink.

"It's not his fault. They're letting him get away with it."

All in all, an ugly and shameful day for Winston Cup racing.

Besides that, except for the last 10 laps, the race was lousy.

Dale Earnhardt and wife Teresa keep company with two of the faster machines around— Earnhardt's race car and an Air Guard jet fighter. (Davie Hinshaw/ The Charlotte Observer)

June 13, 1987

WIN NO. 7: MICHIGAN
New contract, new sponsor

by Tom Higgins

Brooklyn, Mich.—Dale Earnhardt, his Chevrolet suddenly sputtering with a mysterious fuel problem, held off Davey Allison's fast-closing Ford to win a dramatic Miller 400 stock car race Sunday at Michigan International Speedway.

Celebrating the signing of a $2.2 million contract extension with his Richard Childress team and sponsor, Goodwrench, Earnhardt flashed across the finish line a scant four car lengths in front.

> **"Yes, he (Davey Allison) was catching me, and yes, he'd have got by me in a lap or two. But the end of the race came before that could happen."**
>
> **—Dale Earnhardt**

The Observer learned that the deal, agreed to Saturday night but still unannounced officially, pairs Earnhardt and Childress for two more seasons and includes an option year. The pact confirms Goodwrench's replacement of Wrangler as primary backer of the NASCAR Winston Cup Series championship team from Winston-Salem during that period.

Allison almost spoiled the party for Earnhardt and hundreds of executives of Chevrolet and Goodwrench, a General Motors subsidiary, attending the event from nearby Detroit.

Closing in during a 12-lap dash to the checkered flag following a fifth caution period, Allison drew his Thunderbird alongside Earnhardt's Monte Carlo in the fourth turn on the final lap at the 2-mile track. However, he couldn't complete the pass and eased off to finish .296 seconds behind.

"With about five laps to go, something went wrong with the fuel system," said Earnhardt. "The engine was sputtering and actually cutting off at the end of the straightaways, like the gas wasn't getting picked up. Meanwhile, Davey got tough there at the end."

Pressed in a post-race interview about that tense situation, Earnhardt said, "Yes, he was catching me, and yes, he'd have got by me in a lap or two. But the end of the race came before that could happen."

July 20, 1987

WIN NO. 8: POCONO
Bump, brake, flag

by Tom Higgins

Long Pond, Pa.— Dale Earnhardt regained the lead from upset-bound Alan Kulwicki halfway through the final lap Sunday and won a stirring, "rocky" Summer 500 stock car show at Pocono International Raceway.

Kulwicki swept his Ford in front of the favored Earnhardt's Chevrolet on the 200th lap of the NASCAR Winston Cup Series event, making the pass between Turns 1 and 2 at the triangular track.

However, the momentum and a bit of apparently inadvertent bumping between the cars carried Kulwicki high in the second corner. This bobble enabled Earnhardt to slip back under Kulwicki and continue to his eighth checkered flag in 16 races this season.

Earnhardt finished two car-lengths in front to foil Kulwicki's bid for a first-ever Winston Cup victory.

"Alan was awful tough at the end," said Earnhardt, who boosted his lead toward a second straight driving championship to a commanding 401 points for the Richard Childress team of Winston-Salem. "He's a good racer.

"It was awful close racing the last three laps. Fender to fender. After Alan got by between Turns 1 and 2, I got on my brakes going into the second corner so I'd have a better chance to duck low under him. We bumped bumpers, and I guess that helped make him go higher than he wanted to go. It wasn't intentional. It was scuffing cars in close racing."

When Kulwicki, the circuit's Rookie of the Year in 1986, first returned to the garage area he appeared upset about the last lap contact, although the runner-up finish was the best of his NASCAR career. However, a few minutes later he joined Earnhardt on a stage in the track's infield media center and refused to criticize his rival.

"I'm not going to complain," said Kulwicki, who owns his team based in Concord. "It was just NASCAR racing, and I guess I'm going to have to learn to race harder.

"It's the best race I ever ran, so there's a lot to be pleased with.... But at the same time I admit that to come this close and not win is very disappointing."

Kulwicki shook his head and added softly, "I thought I had it won when I got by him."

August 23, 1987
WIN NO. 9: BRISTOL
Dale 5, short tracks 0
by Tom Higgins

Bristol, Tenn.—Dale Earnhardt pushed his season record to 5-0 on NASCAR Winston Cup Series short tracks Saturday night by dominating the Busch 500 at Bristol Raceway.

Earnhardt led 414 of the 500 laps at the .533-mile track and finished a comfortable 5.59 seconds ahead of the Pontiac of runner-up Rusty Wallace.

Earnhardt, winning for the ninth time in 20 regular-season races this year, led the final 152 laps on the track that gave him his first big-time victory in 1979 and has produced three other checkered flags for him since.

The triumph put Earnhardt, 36, in position to challenge for NASCAR's modern era record of seven victories on short tracks—speedways of less than a mile in length—set by seven-time winners Cale Yarborough in 1976 and Darrell Waltrip in 1982.

Three short track races remain among the nine '87 events still on the schedule—at Richmond on Sept. 13, Martinsville, Va., on Sept. 27 and North Wilkesboro on Oct. 4.

"The driver was giving out a little bit at the end," conceded Earnhardt. "I've been a little sick all week. The crew made it better for me. They challenged me to keep up with them. It was tough to do."

September 7, 1987
WIN NO. 10: DARLINGTON
Rain, rain . . . who cares?
by Tom Higgins

Darlington, S.C.—Dale Earnhardt further enhanced his sensational stock car racing season Sunday by winning a thrilling Southern 500 that was shortened by rain to 275.932 miles, the event's least distance ever.

In capturing the NASCAR Winston Cup Series classic at Darlington Raceway for the first time, Earnhardt drove to his 10th victory of 1987 in a roll toward a second straight championship in the Chevrolet fielded by the Richard Childress team of Winston-Salem.

With dark clouds moving in and lightning flashing about the 1.366-mile track, Earnhardt took the lead in a furious duel with sentimental favorite Richard Petty on Lap 191, sweeping by the Pontiac driver in the treacherous third turn.

The storm arrived on Lap 198 with Earnhardt about 10

> "I felt it was our day all the way, but at this place, you never know."
> —Dale Earnhardt

Earnhardt holds the trophy during a steady downpour after winning the rain-shortened Southern 500 at Darlington. (Diedra Laird/The Charlotte Observer)

car lengths ahead, and it scattered a crowed estimated at 75,000 and brought out the yellow flag.

On Lap 202 the red flag was shown and the field ordered to a stop on the front stretch at 3:40 p.m.

The rain set in and there was no chance for a restart, although NASCAR officials waited until 5:11 p.m. before declaring the event official.

The outcome increased Earnhardt's lead toward a second straight Winston Cup championship to a runaway 583 points over Bill Elliott and gave him a sweep of Darlington's Winston Cup events this year. He also won the TranSouth 500 in March.

With a car that was clearly superior, Earnhardt wasn't about to be denied.

"I felt it was our day all the way." He said. "But at this place, you never know. It's a challenge to drive, and so much can happen. Strange things.

"The wall just reaches out and rushes at you sometimes here. I've hit it a bunch of times. I did in the TranSouth 500 this spring but was lucky enough to win anyway.

"Who knows what could have happened if we'd gone 500 miles? I think we probably still would have won. Does it diminish the victory by the race being shortened? No way. It's still the Southern 500 and I'll take it."

September 14, 1987
WIN NO. 11: RICHMOND
Green flag, red flag, checkered flag
by Tom Higgins

Richmond, Va.—Dale Earnhardt escaped one of the biggest pileups in Richmond Fairgrounds Raceway history, narrowly evaded two other accidents and overcame a NASCAR penalty Sunday to edge Darrell Waltrip in the final Wrangler 400.

The triumph in the Winston Cup Series stock car race improved Earnhardt's overall record this season to 11-for-22 and left him 6-0 on the circuit's short tracks, speedways of less than a mile in length.

The triumph was Earnhardt's third straight and the 31st of his career, leaving him just one behind Hall of Famer Fireball Roberts.

"I don't keep up with records, so I don't have any certain goals in that respect," said a delighted Earnhardt. "I just try to win every one we go to."

Earnhardt, 36, now has driven his Chevrolets fielded by the Richard Childress team of Winston-Salem to a stunning 608-point lead toward a second straight Winston Cup championship and third of his career. With only seven races left it's considered virtually impossible for anyone to catch him for the title, although not mathematically so.

The stirring run between archrivals Earnhardt and Waltrip to the checkered flag was set up on Lap 295 when oil on the track swept Alan Kulwicki, Phil Parsons and Sterling Marlin into a grinding first-turn crash. No drivers were hurt, but damage to the railing was so severe that the red flag was shown and the field stopped for 18 minutes while repairs were made.

Green flag action resumed on Lap 312, and some of the season's best racing ensued. From Lap 320-399 Earnhardt and Waltrip were never more than a foot or so apart. The two frequently ran side-by-side as Waltrip's Chevy worked best in Turns 1-2 and Earnhardt's in turns 3-4.

However, Earnhardt was credited with leading every one of those closely contested laps. He led the final 156 and 219 overall.

"I didn't develop no big game plan as to what I was going to do at the end if necessary," said Earnhardt. "I just ran my route, which was a little higher than Darrell's.

"I stayed relaxed and cool and ran my car and let him worry about getting around me. We bumped a little, but nothing serious. When you race that close you're bound to scuff some. It was good racin'.

"If Darrell had ever got around me, I don't think I could have got back by. That's why we were running each other so hard.

"I knew it. He knew it."

> "I didn't develop no big game plan as to what I was going to do at the end if necessary. I just ran my route."
> —Dale Earnhardt

January 25, 1988
Trophy time
by Tom Higgins

Charlotte, N.C.— Dale Earnhardt was honored Sunday in Charlotte as the National Motorsports Press Association's driver of the year for 1987.

Rival NASCAR Winston Cup Series driver Richard Petty presented the trophy during the NMPA, which is holding its annual convention at the Adam's Mark hotel in Charlotte.

In presenting the trophy to Earnhardt, Petty might have realized an even bigger honor. It certainly is one that will be enduring.

The trophy, new this year, is named for Petty and bears an etching of his likeness in the center of a steering wheel. As far as can be determined, no other major sports figure who is still active has an award of such significance named for him.

"I always thought things like this came after the fact (retirement)," said Petty, 50, a 200-time winner and seven-time Winston Cup champion. "Maybe people have been watching me run lately and figure it is after the fact."

Earnhardt, 36, who won 11 races and his third Winston Cup title in '87, appeared touched to have won the first Petty award.

"I've always admired Richard, and one of my biggest thrills was getting to race on the same track with him the first time," said Earnhardt.

Petty, asked what he would do if he should win his own trophy, replied with a grin, "I'm going to make Dale come back and present it to me."

Earnhardt meets with the press after a race. (Christopher A. Record/The Charlotte Observer)

Chapter Eleven:
1988: Three-by-Three

Races	Won	Top 5	Top 10	Poles	Earnings
29	3	13	19	0	$ 1,214,089

February 8, 1988
The Busch Clash: Earnhardt 1, Allisons 0
by Tom Higgins

Daytona Beach, Fla.—Dale Earnhardt thwarted the father-son tag team of Bobby and Davey Allison and won a Busch Clash stock car racing thriller Sunday at Daytona International Speedway.

"When I saw Bobby pull into third place behind Davey with a couple of laps to go, it worried me," Earnhardt said after taking his Richard Childress team's Chevrolet to Victory Lane.

"Davey was already competitive, and when his daddy came up, I was afraid they were going to pull their "Alabama Shuffle" on an ol' Carolina boy. Davey tried everything, but I was able to hold him off."

Earnhardt effectively blocked the younger Allison's Ford and Bobby Allison's Buick going into Turn 3 on the last lap around the 2.5-mile track, then repeated the maneuver through the homestretch. The margin of victory in the 50-mile dash for 1987's NASCAR Winston Cup Series pole winners was a car length.

That difference meant earnings of $75,000, including $25,000 in lap-leader bonuses, for Earnhardt's record third Busch Clash triumph. He also won in 1980 and 1986.

Earnhardt whipped into the lead off the fourth turn on Lap 7 and was never headed, although Davey Allison certainly tried, moving up from the ninth starting position.

"The Chevys certainly look tough with the new 1-inch carburetor rule," said Allison. "But our Ford hung in there. I congratulate Dale, but I also want to let him know that we're coming after him.

"It was fun racing out there with Dad. I knew he'd be tough at the end.

"I just ran out of room with Dale, that's all. Our cars touched, but there was a lot of that going on. I'd bet every car in the race has got some dings and dents on it."

Bobby Allison said, "We were in hot pursuit, but Dale was holding too many aces. When he pulls away like he once did on the straightaway, it's a pretty hopeless situation. But it was a good race. The new (carburetor) rule gave us a little closer racing."

Earnhardt indicated approval of the carburetor rule, which has dropped speeds at Daytona about 15 mph.

"I thought it produced good racing," said Earnhardt, a three-time Winston Cup champion. "It has put drafting strategy back into racing here at Daytona, and I'm sure the fans will like that. It's going to take two cars hooked up to pass one."

Maybe that'll work later. It didn't Sunday for the Allisons.

Dale Earnhardt peers down pit row as he gets ready to climb into his car prior to the start of the race. Wife Teresa stands by, watching her husband's race preparations. (Jeff Siner/The Charlotte Observer)

March 21, 1988
WIN NO. 1: ATLANTA
Told you so . . .
by Tom Higgins

"That 'Bama bunch has won enough. It's time for us Tar Heels to take back over."

—Dale Earnhardt

Hampton, Ga.—Dale Earnhardt, seldom a reserved sort, didn't mince words Saturday in looking to the Motorcraft 500 stock car race.

"They better get ready," Earnhardt said of his NASCAR Winston Cup Series rivals. "I'm going to unload on all of 'em tomorrow."

Well, they can't say they weren't warned.

Earnhardt, driving a Chevrolet fielded by the Richard Childress team of Winston-Salem, was equal to his boast Sunday at Atlanta International Raceway, taking the 500-miler in almost embarrassingly easy fashion.

Earnhardt, 36, led 269 of the 328 laps at the 1.522-mile bowl-shaped track, including the final 63.

The winner of two straight Winston Cup national driving championships, Earnhardt flashed to the finish line 1.05 seconds ahead of Pontiac-driving Rusty Wallace, the only other competitor in the lead lap.

Earnhardt was so dominant no other driver was able to lead more than three laps.

It was the first triumph of the regular season for Earnhardt, who had seen Bobby Allison and Neil Bonnett, both from Ala-bama, win the year's first three events. Allison took the Daytona 500. Bonett, Earnhardt's best friend among the drivers, won both the Pontiac 400 at Richmond and the Goodwrench 500 at N.C. Motor Speedway near Rockingham.

"That 'Bama bunch has won enough," Earnhardt, who took the Busch Clash special event for 1987 pole winners in February at Daytona, said with a grin Saturday. "It's time for us Tar Heels to take back over."

Driving a black and silver Monte Carlo, he wrestled the lead from pole winner Geoff Bodine on the second lap. He subsequently led stretches of 21, 43, 12, 28, 56, 42 and 63 laps. At one point, caught back in the pack as a result of a pit stop during a yellow flag caution period, Earnhardt had the crowd estimated at 70,000 standing and stomping as he charged back to the front.

"Yeah, I could see 'em getting excited and waving me on," said Earnhard. "It tickled me. It made it a lot more fun."

It was the 32nd career victory for Earnhardt. He now has four triumphs at the Atlanta track.

Earnhardt won 11 times last year en route to a $2.4 million season. However, he hadn't triumphed in almost six months, last winning on Sept. 13 in the Wrangler 400 at Richmond.

Whispers had started:

"What's wrong with Earnhardt?"

"I was asking myself the same thing," Earnhardt said, nodding his head. "But I knew nothing was wrong. Just that we had run into some very good competition. I knew things would come around. This is too good a team to go without winning for long."

March 26, 1988

Question and answer man
"You make your own luck"

Excerpts of an interview with Earnhardt by *Observer* staff writer Tom Higgins:

Q. A few drivers, including Bill Elliott, have said that in racing side-by-side with you they have seen you grinning at them. If so, is it because you're having so much fun or is it a form of intimidation?

A. Yeah, I know people say that. But no one has ever made me grin at them on a race track. I'm so busy driving my own race car I haven't got time to be looking at anybody else.... Well, now, a time or two me and Rusty Wallace have been racing and laughed and shook our fists at each other.

Q. Your most bitter rivalry is with Geoff Bodine. Lately you've been seen chatting and laughing with him. Has the animosity eased a bit?

A. Not on my part. I don't like him and never will. But I'll stay on good terms with him as long as we just race without any of the other stuff (bumping and verbal barbs).

Q. Only Richard Petty and Cale Yarborough have won three straight Winston Cup championships. How much would tying their record this year mean to you?

A. It means everything, because that's the only way I can win four in a row and break their record. ... My greatest goal is to equal or surpass Richard's overall record of seven championships. I hope I stay healthy enough to get that shot.

Q. You're building a shop complex on the 300-plus acre farm you own in the Coddle Creek section of Iredell County. Any plans for your own Winston Cup team in the future?

A. I have no plans of ever doing that. It's true I'm building a facility out there, but it'll house my Busch Series Grand National (sportsman) team. Why would I ever want to leave (Richard) Childress and that ugly bunch of crewmen he has got after the success we've had?

Q. After the recent Atlanta victory, which ended a 10-race non-winning streak for your team, you conceded that you'd been asking yourself, "What's wrong with Dale Earnhardt?" Were you really worried?

A. Uneasy is a better word. I was saying, well, maybe my luck has changed. I've always felt you make your own luck, and I wasn't making any.

Q. You had one big victory before the racing season even began. Can you explain it?

A. Oh, man yeah. I was lucky enough to get invited to the Buckmaster Classic, an event at Southern Sportsman Lodge west of Montgomery, Ala. A big group of athletes and show buisness people who like the outdoors were invited—guys like Bo Jackson, Rick Sutcliffe, Jody Davis, Johnny Lee—along with some of the country's top hunters such as Noel Feather and Ben Lee. ... I also outran Bo Jackson, who may be the fastest man in baseball, in a special race—I just don't tell people I did it riding an all-terrain vehicle, not on foot.

April 25, 1988

WIN NO. 2: MARTINSVILLE
Change tires, change outcome

by Tom Higgins

Martinsville, Va.—Dale Earnhardt got a pivotal tire adjustment well into the race, and won a Pannill Sweatshirts 500 Sunday that appeared to belong to Harry Gant and then Sterling Marlin.

Earnhardt's Chevrolet passed the checkered flag 1.99 seconds ahead of Marlin's Oldsmobile before a track-record crowd of about 42,000 at .526-mile Martinsville Speedway.

For the first three-fifths of the race, Earnhardt hardly appeared a contender.

The crew kept working with tire sizes to improve handling in the corners. Finally, a pit stop during a caution period from laps 312-318 produced the combination Earnhardt wanted.

He took the lead on lap 319 and stayed in front the rest of the way.

"At the start of the race the car was a little too tight," Earnhardt said. "We kept working with the tire stagger (the match among different size tires) to make it freer in the corners. Once we got it right, that enabled me to get back on the gas quicker off the turns, and we put the pressure on from there."

The victory—Earnhardt's fourth at Martinsville, the 33rd of his career and his second this season—padded his point lead toward a third straight Winston Cup championship to 77 over Marlin, who moved from fourth place to second in the standings.

Earnhardt won six of eight on NASCAR's short tracks last year, but this was his first win on one in 1988. His other win this year came in Atlanta's Motorcraft 500

"We could have won three more already, except for two flat tires and a broken motor mount," said Earnhardt, who averaged 74.740 mph as seven cautions slowed the race for 46 laps.

"Last week at North Wilkesboro Speedway (when a leaking tire cost Earnhardt almost certain victory) was definitely on my mind the last 20 laps today. But I was determined to run hard regardless."

> "We kept working with the tire stagger to make it freer in the corners. Once we got it right ... we put the pressure on from there."
> —Dale Earnhardt

Dale Earnhardt sits in his car while his crew
makes changes during a practice session.
(Davie Hinshaw/The Charlotte Observer)

And now a word from... The boogie man?
by Tom Higgins

Charlotte, N.C.—Among the characters of people at Charlotte Motor Speedway on race weekends is a beefy, unshaven man named Billy Wood.

He claims to have dark powers over the fortunes of stock car drivers.

Wood, 55, comes from Norfolk, Va., for Charlotte's spring and fall races. He stands in front of the infield media center, from where he can see some of the backstretch and the third turn. From time to time, he will fix his eye on a car he wants to hex, raise his arms parallel to the ground and cross his forefingers.

Wood is not to be taken seriously, of course.

Still, some drivers wince at the sight of him, some stop to shake his hand and talk a while and some fuss about his presence. Darrell Waltrip, perhaps out of the kindness of his heart, gives the man caps and shirts and money. Wood says it's in return for the good fortune he can heap on Waltrip.

But this has not been a great season for Waltrip, and Saturday, in the Winn-Dixie 300 for Busch Grand National cars, his racer broke early.

Asked about this, Wood, holding two hot dogs and a Coke, seemed to search for an explanation, then said, "He figures I did my best."

With his hero out, Wood focused his attention on Geoff Bodine and Dale Earnhardt. He was pulling for Bodine and putting his hex, which he claims to have learned more than 40 years ago, on Earnhardt.

Everyone else in the place focused on those two as well. There's not a rawer rivalry in stock car racing than theirs. On the same speedway last year, they tangled in The Winston and again a week later in the Winn-Dixie 300, drawing fines and admonition from NASCAR.

Saturday, they gave the 300 its heart and soul, racing each other at close quarters—close enough to see each other's grimace—for about 100 miles.

On Lap 105, Earnhardt moved up on Bodine's bumper. Suddenly, at the top of the backstretch, Bodine was sliding. He spun three times, winding up in the grass. Earnhardt raced on.

Billy Wood was furious, raging. "You see what kind of driver Earnhardt is," he shouted. "See what he did to my man?"

After Bodine spun in front of Earnhardt, he was a lap down. He later chased Earnhardt down, after NASCAR officials advised his crew to radio him and advise him against any retribution, if that's what he had in mind.

He passed Earnhardt to get back into the lead lap, and then they raced, hard, hotly, lap after lap. Door to door or bumper to bumper. Earnhardt finally backed off a length or two. He was leading. Bodine was almost a full lap behind. There was nothing to be gained by racing Bodine so hard. Except, of course, to race him.

On lap 198—two away from the finish—Earnhardt's car suddenly spat out a cloud of white smoke. His engine had blown. He was out of it.

Billy Wood heard.

He smiled.

Earnhardt autographs the shirts of fan Henry Clay of Concord at Charlotte Motor Speedway during "Fan Appreciation Day" activities. (The Charlotte Observer)

August 28, 1988

WIN NO. 3: BRISTOL
Bump and roll
by Tom Higgins

Bristol, Tenn.— Dale Earnhardt ran the last 10 laps with Bill Elliott on his bumper, and held on to win the Busch 500 at Bristol Raceway Saturday night.

Elliott finished second as he and Earnhardt lapped third-place finisher Geoff Bodine on the final lap.

"My car was pushing (understeering in the turns) at the end, but we had just enough to hold off Bill," Earnhardt said of his Richard Childress team. "I was able to get off the corners a little stronger, and that was my ace in the hole."

Said Elliott, "Of course, I'd like to have won, but it was an excellent night for us. We just wanted to keep up and play Dale's game."

The outcome enabled Elliott to sweep into the Winston Cup point lead, taking the top spot from Rusty Wallace, who had to turn his Pontiac over to relief driver Larry Pearson on the 211th of the 500 laps on the .533-mile track.

> "I feel fine. But I'm probably going to use a neck brace during the race."
> —Rusty Wallace

Wallace had been shaken up in a savage crash during practice Friday and his neck tired. Pearson brought the Wallace backup car in ninth.

Elliott gained 37 points to lead by 16 over Wallace, who fell to second place. Earnhardt picked up 31 points and now trails in third place by 126.

An overflow record crowd of 53,100 watched Earnhardt win for the fifth time in the last eight 500-lap races at Bristol.

"It was a rough night with all the accidents," said Earnhardt, who won $48,500. "Seems like I was dodging the whole night. I seemed to be right in the middle of everything that happened, but I didn't get involved in any of it.

"I think the fans got their money's worth.

"I can't remember a race where everyone had a lot of trouble. I guess it was the full moon."

Clash follows crash
by Tom Higgins

North Wilkesboro, N.C.—Ricky Rudd and Dale Earnhardt clashed with their cars on the track and then angrily with words in the garage area Sunday during and after the Holly Farms 400 at North Wilkesboro Speedway.

Rudd accused Earnhardt of a "dirty move," of "taking cheap shots," and seemingly threatened to get even. Earnhardt said "Rudd hit me intentionally and wrecked my car."

The incident that triggered the most ill will on the NASCAR Winston Cup Series tour this season started on Lap 361 of the 400-lap event as Rudd and Earnhardt dueled for the lead.

Rudd, in a Buick, appeared to make contact with Earnhardt's Chevrolet in pulling ahead in Turn 3. Earnhardt tagged Rudd back in Turn 1 as Lap 362 began, causing him to spin and bringing out the yellow flag.

For the restart, NASCAR officials ordered both Rudd and Earnhardt to line up behind the other drivers on the lead lap—Geoff Bodine, eventual winner Rusty Wallace, Bill Elliott and Phil Parsons. The penalty essentially ended the victory hopes of both drivers, although their cars appeared the race's strongest.

Earnhardt finished sixth, Rudd seventh.

"He (Earnhardt) went into the corner, looking into his mirror and overdrove and I got around him clean," said Rudd. "My car was working good down low, and that's where I was running. He turned to the bottom of the track like he didn't even know I was there. He wrecked himself.

"Then, he comes back and spins me in Turn 2, knocking my front end out of line. Clearly, that was a dirty move. NASCAR put us both at the rear and cost us a chance to win. We got beat by a cheap shot. ...

"If he wants to play this game, then he can forget the championship. We have nothing to lose. Next year, too, if he wants it.

"I'm not going to be like Geoff Bodine. I'm not going to take this crap."

Earnhardt, who fell 193 points behind points-standings leader Elliott in a bid to take his third straight championship, denied intentionally ramming Rudd.

"He turned me sideways in Turn 3," said Earnhardt. "Then I got into him. I didn't mean to. Even if I had, I didn't hit him any harder than he hit me. I backed off so he could straighten up, but he went on around (spun).

"Did they penalize Ricky when he spun me out the last time (with four laps to go in Turn 3, briefly bringing out the yellow flag)? No.

"He's the one that got rough. I wasn't worried about the points race. I was trying to win this race."

Races	Won	Top 5	Top 10	Poles	Earnings
29	5	14	19	0	$ 1,435,730

April 17, 1989

WIN NO. 1: NORTH WILKESBORO
Tire wars: Radials vs. Hoosiers
by Tom Higgins

North Wilkesboro, N.C.—Dale Earnhardt and Goodyear Tire Co. shared victory Sunday in a First Union 400 thriller at North Wilkesboro Speedway that may have revolutionized NASCAR's Winston Cup Series with the advent of racing radial tires.

Earnhardt held off Alan Kulwicki in a Chevrolet-Ford duel to take the checkered flag by 2.20 seconds before a record crowd of 36,000 at the five-eighths-mile track.

The convincing victory—Earnhardt led 296 laps—snapped a 15-race nonwinning streak for the three-time national champion. And it enabled Earnhardt and his Richard Childress team to regain the point standings lead from Geoff Bodine, 1,054-1,051.

Earnhardt, 37, was so tickled to finally win again that he announced a "Dale Wins Sale, one time only, every car on the lot at cost" today at his Chevrolet Dealership in Newton.

Earnhardt's 35th career Winston Cup victory moved him into 13th place on NASCAR's all-time list, breaking him out of a tie with the late Fireball Roberts.

As the race neared the 275-lap mark Earnhardt and Rusty Wallace bumped several times as the latter tried to unlap himself.

NASCAR radioed a warning for the two to "calm down a little."

"Hell if I know why they (NASCAR officials) did that," said Earnhardt. "They always get excited if I bump somebody. Me and Rusty weren't giving each other a hard time. We were having a fun time."

Following the final caution period on Laps 355-357, Earnhardt surged to a lead of about half a straightway. "My car, in a change for us, ran really good on new tires," said Earnhardt.

> **"They always get excited if I bump somebody."**
>
> **—Dale Earnhardt**

June 5, 1989

WIN NO. 2: DOVER
"Ain't no Ford track"

by Tom Higgins

> "All I'd heard all week was Ford track, Ford track. Well, a race track is a race track and a race car is a race car. There ain't no Ford track, or Chrysler track in the world, and today proves it."
> —Dale Earnhardt

Dover, Del.— On Saturday, Dale Earnhardt argued strongly that Dover Downs should not be classified a "Ford track."

On Saturday in the Budweiser 500, he proved it.

Driving one of Chevrolet's highly regarded new Luminas, Earnhardt led an overwhelming 454 of the 500 laps, including the final 63, in the NASCAR Winston Cup Series stock car race at the speedway nicknamed "The Monster Mile."

Earnhardt flashed to the checkered flag a half-second ahead of runner-up Mark Martin's Thunderbird, ending a streak of five straight wins for Ford at Dover Downs, where the make also has a string of five poles.

"All I'd heard all week was Ford track, Ford track," said Earnhardt after his second victory this season and the 36th of his career, but the first at Dover. "Well, a race track is a race track and a race car is a race car. There ain't no Ford track, Chevrolet track or Chrysler track in the world, and today proves it.

"Ford cars won here because of good drivers and circumstances."

The circumstance Sunday was that the meanest "Monster" at the Monster Mile was under the hood of Earnhardt's menacing-looking No. 3 Chevy.

Finishing third through sixth were Ken Schrader, Chevrolet; Terry Labonte, Ford; Rusty Wallace, Pontiac; and Ricky Rudd, Buick. Wallace made the only pass among the leaders in the final eight laps to take a position from Rudd.

Schrader was the only driver besides Earnhardt to crack double digits in fronting the field, leading 24 laps. Included was Lap 250, when Schrader bumped his way by Earnhardt to collect a $10,000 bonus as halfway leader.

Their battle for that bonus produced perhaps the best action of the season's 11th race.

"It got a little rough there when I was running Kenny," said Earnhardt. "I didn't want to get knocked out of the groove and hit the wall, so I let him go, much as I'd liked to have won that halfway money."

Earnhardt, who had to settle for $59,350 after averaging 121.712 mph, added: "I'll file the memory of that one away."

July 18, 1989
Hall of Fame honors Daddy
by Tom Higgins

Charlotte, N.C.— Ralph Earnhardt and Jerry Cook, two auto racing champions from different eras and different sections of the country, have been elected to the National Motorsports Press Association Hall Of Fame.

Induction ceremonies—posthumous for Earnhardt—are scheduled Sept. 2 at Florence (S.C) Country Club on the eve of the 40th Southern 500 at nearby Darlington Raceway.

Earnhardt was a Kannapolis native and father of three-time Winston Cup champion Dale Earnhardt. He won NASCAR's national sportsman division championship in 1956 driving cars he built and engineered himself. His success that season is perhaps unrivaled in the sport as it produced track championships at 11 different speedways and 32 feature victories.

He was runner-up for the national title in 1955 and '57. His most impressive victory came in 1965 when he won a 250-mile late-model sportsman race at Charlotte Motor Speedway.

Those who saw Earnhardt drive on the South's numerous dirt tracks during a 23-year career—but especially in the late 1950s and early '60s—rate him the best on that type lay-out.

Few records were kept in those days, and it's uncertain exactly how many races Earnhardt won, but the number definitely is in the hundreds.

> "Everyone in the family loved to watch daddy race. I know this means a lot to my mother and my brothers and sisters, and I can't begin to say how much it means to me."
> —Dale Earnhardt

Earnhardt was known for a tough, relentless driving style, a trait he obviously passed on to Dale, presently leading the Winston Cup point standings toward a fourth championship.

"Everyone in the family loved to watch daddy race," Dale Earnhardt said upon learning of his father's election to the hall.

"I know this means a lot to my mother and my brothers and sisters, and I can't begin to say how much it means to me."

August 20, 1989

Ba-a-a-d in black

by Tom Higgins

Brooklyn, Mich.—Who ranks as the most menacing driver in NASCAR Winston Cup Series stock car racing, and maybe tops in that category for all of motorsports?

Who else?

It's Dale Earnhardt.

And not just because he drives that ba-a-ad-looking black car.

Ask other NASCAR competitors who they least like to see in their rear view mirror, the answer is Earnhardt.

Ask who they dread trying to get around most, the answer is Earnhardt.

Ask who'll go harder to the ragged edge of control in a gambling situation, the answer is Earnhardt.

Going into today's Champion Spark Plug 400 at Michigan International Speedway, Earnhardt stands especially imposing in terms of the Winston Cup championship and its $1 million prize.

Earnhardt and his Richard Childress-owned team based near Winston-Salem, hold a 126-point lead after 18 of the season's 29 races.

The mood in the garage area Saturday at the Michigan track was that if the challengers—Mark Martin, Darrell Waltrip, Rusty Wallace and Bill Elliott—don't gain significantly today, their hopes will be sharply diminished.

Earnhardt, 38, was grinning before the time trials, a certain sign that he's savoring the pressure that's on his rivals. Then, he turned it up a notch.

"They're in trouble," said Earnhardt, seeking to become only the second driver to win as many as four championships and take sole possession of second place on the all-time list behind Richard Petty's seven titles.

"They've been in trouble all season, but they're in big trouble now. We're in good shape in the points race."

> Ask other NASCAR competitors who they least like to see in their rear view mirror, the answer is EARNHARDT.

September 4, 1989
WIN NO. 3: DARLINGTON
Dad in Hall of Fame, son in Victory Lane
by Tom Higgins

Darlington, S.C.—Dale Earnhardt strengthened his bid for NASCAR's Winston Cup Series championship Sunday by winning a "sentimental journey" Southern 500 in which Darrell Waltrip's shot at the Winston Million bonus went astray.

Earnhardt, driving a Chevrollet, rolled to the checkered flag 1.45 seconds ahead of runner-up Mark Martin's Ford in averaging a Darlington Raceway record 135.462 mph for the 40th running of the sport's oldest superspeedway race.

Earnhardt called his 37th career victory "maybe the most satisfying of all" as it followed by about 20 hours the induction of his late father, Ralph, into the National Motorsports Press Association Stock Car Racing Hall Of Fame.

The outcome boosted Earnhardt's lead toward a fourth title to 73 points over Rusty Wallace, a gain of 20, with eight races remaining.

"I'm tickled to pad it, but we didn't gain as much as we'd lost to Rusty the last two weeks," said Earnhardt after his second Southern 500 triumph and fifth in a 500-miler at Darlington. "He's going to be tough to beat."

Overall, it was perhaps the tamest Southern 500 ever at the storied speedway dating to 1950, with only four caution flags covering 27 laps.

However, the race—and the walls in the turns—were marked by cars frequently scraping the concrete.

> **"I don't know exactly why I'm so successful here. . . . I know you've got to give this race track your highest respect and not drop your guard for a second."**
>
> **—Dale Earnhardt**

Earnhardt also had wall trouble in his Lumina. He scraped the concrete in Turns 1-2 on Lap 166 while leading and had to pit under green for four tires.

Earnhardt barely stayed on the lead lap, but went from three seconds ahead to 25 behind Harry Gant, whose car appeared exceptionally strong.

But on Lap 178 Gant scuffed the wall for the first of six times in Turns 1-2, and Earnhardt steadily drove back into contention. The third caution period starting on Lap 227 for Larry Pearson's spin in Turn 2 enabled Earnhardt to catch up. He was in the lead or near it the rest of the way.

"Our car was just mediocre, but it was consistent," said Earnhardt, who earned $71,150 in becoming a winner for a third time this season. "We finally dodged the bullets that have been getting us—like the wreck while leading at Bristol (in the Busch 500 on Aug. 26). That was my fault, but the crew stood behind me, and this is the payoff.

"After the last stop (on Lap 301) they told me from the pits we had enough gas to go all the way, and that was the last words said on the radio.

"I don't know exactly why I'm so successful here. . . . I know you've got to give this race track your highest respect and not drop your guard for a second. I guess some of the guys are intimidated by it, and that makes it easier to beat them."

Fans approach NASCAR great Dale Earnhardt as he relaxes near his trailer. (Jeff Siner/The Charlotte Observer)

September 18, 1989

WIN NO. 1: DARLINGTON
The lead grows

by Tom Higgins

"It was a good battle. Mark (Martin) run me real hard. I was worried about him."

—Dale Earnhardt

Dover, Del.—Dale Earnhardt outdueled Mark Martin in a classic Chevrolet-Ford confrontation Sunday and won the Peak 500 stock car race at Dover Downs, adding his lead toward the NASCAR Winston Cup Series championship to 102 points over Rusty Wallace.

Earnhardt, in a Chevy, took the checkered flag two car lengths ahead of runner-up Martin's Thunderbird after they'd battled at close quarters the last 34 laps around the mile track, touching sheet metal twice.

Marring the triumph somewhat for Earnhardt was an injury to Neil Bonnett, his best friend among the drivers. Bonnett suffered a broken sternum when his Ford slammed into the Turn 4 wall on the 455th of the 500 laps. Bonnett is expected to be hospitalized at Kent General in Dover for at least two days.

The accident involving Bonnett forced the race to be red-flagged for about 10 minutes while he was cut from his car. The stoppage bunched the field and set up a sprint to the finish among Earnhardt, Martin and Ken Schrader, the only drivers remaining on the lead lap. Schrader's Chevy couldn't keep up and he placed third, about 4 seconds behind.

"It was a lot of fun racing Mark, but I'd have preferred a little bit more of an edge," Earnhardt, unaware of Bonnett's fracture, said with a grin after his fourth victory this season, including a sweep of Dover's two 500-milers.

"It was a good battle. Mark run me real hard. I was worried about him.

"I got to judging him after we'd run close there awhile and I saw he couldn't do much with me on the bottom of the track. So I tried to run up high where I could keep my tires cool and make him run down low, heating his tires up. That worked to my advantage."

Although a first Winston Cup victory eluded him by only one-tenth of a second, Martin was upbeat following his fourth runner-up showing this season, and the fifth of his career.

"It was a great race," said an excited Martin. "I don't mind running second when it's a race like this. Dale gave me all the room I needed, but my car just wasn't quite strong enough. He was a true sport."

On Lap 195, Earnhardt passed the Pontiac of Wallace to put his main rival for the $1 million Winston Cup title a lap down. Wallace eventually wound up three laps behind in seventh place and lost 39 points, a possibly costly chunk of Winston Cup money with only six races remaining.

"Rusty might as well get ready to go to New York (for the post-season NASCAR awards program) and get second place money," needled Earnhardt, who has finished first, second, first in his last three races.

This is real. Really it is.
by Tom Higgins

Martinsville, Va.— It was a plot so hokey that even Hollywood probably would have been reluctant to produce it.

The scene: Martinsville Speedway, where time trials are scheduled for the Goody's 500, an important NASCAR Winston Cup Series stock car race.

The dire situation: Dale Earnhardt, the sport's most dynamic driver who is leading the point standings toward a fourth championship, is delayed in reaching the track because of a violent storm, Hurricane Hugo.

The solution: A down-on-his-luck local driver, good ol' boy Jimmy Hensley, is asked by Earnhardt's team to qualify its hot Chevrolet in the star's absence. He agrees, and dramatically outruns Darrell Waltrip, the leading money winner in all of motorsports, for the pole.

Hokey?

Sure is.

Nevertheless, it happened just that way Friday at the .526-mile track where the 500 is scheduled Sunday.

Hensley, 43, who lives at nearby Ridgeway, Va., qualified Earnhardt's Richard Childress-fielded Lumina at 91.913 mph to put the potent Chevy on the pole. He wrested the No. 1 spot from Waltrip, who'd logged a lap of 91.833 in a Chevy.

Hensley's lap time was 20.602 seconds, Waltrip's 20.620. That's a difference of 18-thousandths of a second.

Earnhardt arrived at the track just four cars before his machine was to go under the clock. He had time to get in it, but NASCAR rules require that a driver qualifying a car practice in it first. Earnhardt hadn't practiced.

"I've been sick to my stomach knowing this was going on up here," said Earnhardt. "I got away as soon as I could. Everything is torn up around my house (in Iredell County), I bet there's $40,000 damage at the farm. I had to play it safe and get fences back up so animals didn't get out in the roads and hurt somebody. . . . I tried to call up here, but the phones were out."

Waltrip was almost in disbelief after the pole was taken from him. "Oh, well. I had it for almost 21 seconds," Waltrip said. "This shows just how strong Earnhardt's car really is."

November 20, 1989

WIN NO. 5: ATLANTA
Dale wins race, Rusty wins title, Grant Adcox dies

by Tom Higgins

Hampton, Ga.— **Rusty Wallace hung on Sunday to win the NASCAR Winston Cup Series championship by 12 points over Journal 500 victor Dale Earnhardt in a season finale at Atlanta Raceway that took the life of driver Grant Adcox.**

By the time Wallace sprayed champagne in Victory Lane and arrived in the press box for the new champion's interview, he had been informed of the Adcox fatality and opened with a somber statement:

"I want to offer my deepest sympathy to Herb Adcox (the driver's father) and his family. It was one of the hardest licks I've ever seen and I was worried it might be bad . . . "

Tennessean Adcox, 39, slammed almost head-on into the Turn 1 wall on Lap 202. He was taken to the infield infirmary, then to Georgia Baptist Hospital in Atlanta, where he was pronounced dead at 4:15 p.m. of massive head and chest injuries.

Wallace raced through several problems to finish 15th, three laps down to Earnhardt, who led an overwhelming 294 of 328 laps and got the checkered flag 25.71 seconds ahead of runner-up Geoff Bodine.

However, Wallace started the 29th event of 1989 leading Mark Martin by 78 points and Earnhardt by 79, and needed only to finish 18th or better on the 1.522-mile track to take the title, worth $1.5 million in postseason bonuses.

In claiming the national championship for the first time, Wallace and his Charlotte-based Blue Max team finished with 4,176 points to 4,164 for Earnhardt and 4,053 for Martin.

That 12-point margin is the second closest since the scoring system was introduced in 1975, edged only by Richard Petty's 11-point triumph over Darrell Waltrip in 1979.

On Lap 187 Wallace briefly dueled abreast with Earnhrdt, trying to regain a lap, but Earnhardt exerted his car's power and pulled away.

"I said to myself, 'This can't be happening,'" Wallace said. "I thought the championship was slipping away. It was scary. It was hair-raising. Along with the other problems, we'd jetted the carburetor too rich and I'd missed bad on the chassis setup.

"This isn't the way we wanted to win, but it was all we could do. We hung in there."

"We did what we said we were going to do," said Earnhardt, who averaged 140.229 mph and earned $81,700 plus a $25,000 boat for his fifth Atlanta Raceway victory.

"I drove with all my heart. I didn't give the car a rest, and it was prepared so well it stood the pace. If the green had stayed out, we'd have lapped the field.

"I wish we'd been close enough in the points starting today that Rusty would have had to race me for it."

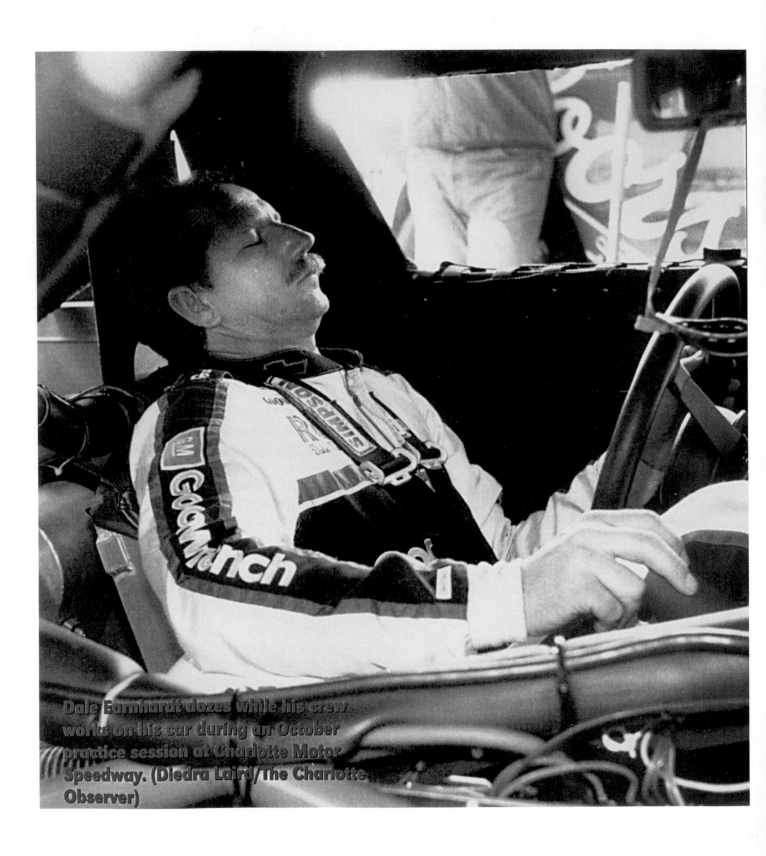

Dale Earnhardt dozes while his crew works on his car during an October practice session at Charlotte Motor Speedway. (Diedra Laird/The Charlotte Observer)

Chapter Thirteen:
1990: From chicken bone to champion

Races	Won	Top 5	Top 10	Poles	Earnings
29	9	18	23	4	$ 3,083,056

February 19, 1990
Drumstick ruins drum roll
by Ron Green

Daytona Beach, Fla.—What Rusty Wallace and Darrell Waltrip and Terry Labonte and others couldn't accomplish with their snapping, growling 3,500-pound racers in the Daytona 500 Sunday, a chicken bone may have.

Beg pardon? A chicken bone?

That was the sniffy suggestion tossed out by Dale Earnhardt after he cut a tire less than a mile from the finish when it appeared he would win a race he had dominated like Secretariat.

That allowed Derrike Cope, who had lurked near the front all day, to go by him for the victory and three others to pass him as well.

> "You can't see everything on the race track."
> —Dale Earnhardt

The only grandstands at Daytona International Speedway other than those on the front straight is a small section of bleachers at the end of the backstretch. The cheap seats.

It was there that Earnhardt ran over something that cut his tire.

"We had a tire go right in front of the chicken-bone grandstands on the backstretch," said ol' Ironhead, making no bones about it. "I hit some debris, something. I heard it hit the bottom of the car and then it hit the tire and then the tire went.

"If I had known that debris was back there, well, there ain't nothing you can do. You can't see everything on the race track."

Especially a chicken bone.

February 20, 1990

Daytona: Reflections

by Tom Higgins

> "I never thought I had it in the bag."
> —Dale Earnhardt

Daytona Beach, Fla. — Relaxed and confident, Dale Earnhardt sat in the garage area at Daytona International Speedway Wednesday chatting with members of the media.

Earnhardt, a three-time NASCAR Winston Cup Series champion from Kannapolis, once abhorred having to meet the press.

Even when he did, he was careful to guard his private feelings.

The last couple years have revealed a more friendly Earnhardt, and during this time an openness has emerged.

Still, it was a bit surprising last week to hear Earnhardt, 38, admit how deeply it had hurt to lose the 1989 Winston Cup championship after holding a big points lead with four races to go.

"It has taken me three months since the season ended in November to get over it," said Earnhardt. "Back earlier in the winter I'd get in my Blazer and drive out to the farm and think about coming so close.

"I guess I'm not all the way over it yet. ..."

Imagine, then, how Earnhardt must feel after the Daytona 500.

Earnhardt had it won for the first time in his career. Dominating at Daytona as few have, he put his class-of-the-field Chevrolet in front for 155 of the 200 laps, once leading by more than half a lap.

Then, with a mile to go, the right rear tire was cut by a piece of metal on the track, forcing Earnhardt to slow and enabling Derrike Cope to pass him and take the checkered flag.

How long will it take Earnhardt to get over this?

For Earnhardt, it's too painful to ponder.

He has been denied before at Daytona, most notably in 1986 when he led with two laps to go but ran out of gas and Geoff Bodine won.

This was more cruel.

Earnhardt sat in his car for about a minute, composing himself. No one intruded.

"I never thought I had it in the bag," Earnhardt said later. "I was counting them corners all day."

Earnhardt and his team likely will go on from the Daytona disaster to dominate the rest of the season, starting Sunday in the Pontiac 400 at Richmond.

But when will Dale Earnhardt really get over those two corners that never came Sunday?

March 19, 1990

WIN NO. 1: ATLANTA
Good race, bad belly

by Tom Higgins

> "My stomach really started cramping. I was only about 50 percent of what I should have been, but I decided to stick it out."
>
> —Dale Earnhardt

Hampton, Ga.— Dale Earnhardt humbled his NASCAR Winston Cup Series rivals Sunday through much of the Motorcraft 500 at Atlanta International Raceway, but at the end it took one of his stirring charges to barely beat Morgan Shepherd, Ernie Irvan, Ken Schrader and Mark Martin.

Earnhardt, despite becoming so ill he almost asked for a relief driver, led 214 of the first 275 laps in the 328-lap event. He also built advantages of up to 16 seconds.

It appeared the team would easily take its first checkered flag of 1990.

But a slow pit stop by Earnhardt because of a faulty air wrench turned the lead over to Ford driver Geoff Bodine for Laps 276 through 320. Then, Shepherd became the leader when he kept his Thunderbird on the track while the other contenders pitted during two caution periods in the last 10 laps.

A blown engine on current Winston Cup champion Rusty Wallace's Pontiac on Lap 319 and a spin by Bobby Hillin's Buick on Lap 325 after a tap by Bodine, forced the yellow flags.

When the green showed for the final time on Lap 327 the order was Shepherd, Earnhardt, Martin, Irvan, Schrader.

"When the last restart came, I wondered if I could get around Morgan. I was worried about him," Earnhardt said.

"Then, that hole opened up for me down low. I went lower on the bottom of the track than I usually do, but there was still room for me to get by and that left me with a clear shot for the rest of the last two laps."

The 40th victory of Earnhardt's career tied him for 11th on the Winston Cup all-time list with Charlottean Tim Flock, a hall of famer.

Earnhardt was so ill near the race's midpoint that he "was on the verge of asking for a relief driver."

"I don't know why I got sick," said Earnhardt. "But my stomach really started cramping. I was only about 50 percent of what I should have been, but I decided to stick it out a little further. Then that air wrench deal (on Lap 276) put us behind (requiring a 19.9 second stop compared to 13.2 for Bodine) and I forgot about being sick. I had to concentrate then."

**Dale Earnhardt talks with crew chief Kirk Shelmerdine in the garage.
(Mark B. Sluder/The Charlotte Observer)**

April 29, 1990

WIN NO. 2: DARLINGTON
Made in the shade

by Tom Higgins

Darlington, S.C.— Earnhardt used a late-race assist from Darlington Raceway's scarred old Turn 1-2 wall Sunday to roll to victory in the TranSouth 500 that earlier appeared destined for either Geoff Bodine or Morgan Shepherd.

As the sun set behind the infamous corner in the closing laps at the 1.366-mile track, it shaded the banking and further hampered visibility for drivers already struggling to see through sandblasted, greasy windshields.

On the 306th lap of the NASCAR Winston Cup Series race, Shepherd, who was leading in a Ford, went into Turn 1 too high and scraped the concrete barrier for about 100 feet. Earnhardt steered his Chevrolet low, as Shepherd's momentum slowed, and swept into a lead he was to hold for 60 of the remaining 61 laps.

Earnhardt then charged to good jumps on restarts from two caution periods in the last 18 laps, and outran Ford drivers Mark Martin, Davey Allison, Bodine and Shepherd, in that order, to the checkered flag. Allison sped back from a lap down to finish third in the 367-lap race.

Earnhardt's $61,985 share of the purse gave him career winnings of $10,060,638 and enabled him to join Darrell Waltrip as the only drivers to achieve the $10-million plateau.

Said Earnhardt: "You've almost got to feel your way through and make sure that ol' wall doesn't jump out and get you. It was so tough to see today I gave myself an extra inch or two in that corner.

"I had a lot of concern all week, mainly over using the radials here for the first time," said Earnhardt. "I was cautious when I got out of bed this morning and tried to be all day ... This is Darlington."

> "You always have trouble seeing late in races here. You've almost got to feel your way through and make sure that ol' wall doesn't jump out and get you."
>
> —Dale Earnhardt

"That's a pretty phenomenal amount of money." —Dale Earnhardt

May 7, 1990

WIN NO. 3: TALLADEGA
NEXT stop is the bank

by Tom Higgins

Talladega, Ala.—This time, there was no cut tire in the final mile for Dale Earnhardt, and he held off Greg Sacks to win a Winston 500 thriller Sunday at Talladega Superspeedway, becoming the all-time leading money winner in motorsports.

Earnhardt, who lost the season-opening Daytona 500 on the last lap after a dominating run, experienced no such disappointment in Sunday's Winston Cup Series race.

Earnhardt led 113 of the 188 laps on the 2.66-mile Talladega track in front of approximately 140,000 fans.

"I was really racin' ol' Greg those last few laps," said Earnhardt, who won by two car lengths. "I was throttling up in the corners, because we were both guessing and playing, trying to figure what the other one was going to do.

"The last lap I stayed in the gas a little more, and I believe it surprised him."

The 42nd victory of Earnhardt's career was worth $98,975, pushing his Winston Cup winnings to $10,213,178. That purse was enough to move Earnhardt, 38, into No. 1 all-time, passing Darrell Waltrip, who finished 10th Sunday for $24,725 and a total of $10,201,565.

"That's a pretty phenomenal amount of money," Earnhardt said. "I don't know what went with all of it."

May 26, 1990

The man, the fans

by Ron Green

"Dale would have made a good cowboy, a gunfighter."
—Racing historian Bob Latford

Charlotte, N.C.—There was a time when they weren't sure he wasn't a devil, that ol' Dale Earnhardt, the way he drove that race car and knocked their favorites around.

Gradually, though, they've come around, the people in the stands. More and more wear his color, black. It was inevitable.

And when Earnhardt is introduced before the Coca-Cola 600 Sunday at Charlotte Motor Speedway, the applause that will wash down on him will probably be equaled only by that for Richard Petty, the King.

It just may be that in Earnhardt, the fans have found a man to fill the void being left by the aging Petty. Another consummate race driver.

Earnhardt is that. He was born in Kannapolis in the heart of racing country, the son of a race driver, Ralph, who was a national sportsman champion. He learned on dirt, where the roots of the sport put down.

He looks like a stock car racer, That, of

course, may only be a perception but there is something about the eyes.

He talks like a stock car racer, sometimes dropping in the obligatory "throwed" or "blowed."

"His grammar's not polished," said one racing official, "but when he speaks, people listen because he knows what he's talking about."

Ask racing historian Bob Latford who among the old drivers Earnhardt resembles and you know what he's going to say. "Junior Johnson," says Latford. "Hard-charging, running for the front and don't worry about the sheet metal.

"Dale would have made a good cowboy, a gunfighter."

Under tow in a battered race car, Dale Earnhardt heads for the garage after blowing a tire and hitting the wall in the Coca-Cola 600 at Charlotte Motor Speedway. (Dick Van Halseman/The Charlotte Observer)

June 25, 1990

WIN NO. 4: MICHIGAN
Excuse me, Ernie, this one's mine

by Tom Higgins

Brooklyn, Mich.— Dale Earnhardt out-dueled Ernie Irvan at Michigan International Speedway in a Miller 400 thriller Sunday that appeared to belong to Bill Elliott.

After Elliott's dominant Ford dropped out of the NASCAR Winston Cup stock car race with a blown engine, Earnhardt and Irvan were left to tussle for the triumph. Misfortune struck Elliott as he was pulling away on the 186th of 200 laps.

Earnhardt, driving a Chevrolet, led Laps 186-187 before Irvan put his Oldsmobile in front for seven laps. Earnhardt then took the lead for good on Lap 195.

Earnhardt, snapping a four-race run of bad luck, rolled to his fourth checkered flag this season, a car length ahead of Irvan. For Irvan, it was the best finish of his career.

He was closely followed by Ford drivers Geoff Bodine and Mark Martin, third and fourth respectively. Harry Gant took fifth in an Olds.

"I'll be jumped up if it doesn't feel good to win again," said Earnhardt, who led the Winston Cup standings by 90 points before the slump, which began in Charlotte's Coca-Cola 600 and produced finishes of 30th, 31st, 34th and 13th. The outcome of the 400—the 14th of the season's 29 races—left him in fifth place, 118 points behind current series leader Martin, with Morgan Shepard, Geoff Bodine and Rusty Wallace in between.

"How could I have won?" Irvan, 31, said in response to a question. "I could have taken Dale out, but that's not racing.

"It was good, clean racing. Dale didn't race me dirty. He got behind me, figured out my weak points and knew where to pass me. He never pushed me. We had a close run, but Dale had a good car."

June 8, 1990

WIN NO. 5: DAYTONA (SORT OF)
One wreck, two wreck, I wreck, you wreck

by Tom Higgins

"In the mirror I saw a couple of 'em side-ways and I knew it was going to be a mess—it is anytime there's a big tangle that close to the front early in a race. Guys should know you can't jump around in a big pack like that."

—Dale Earnhardt

Daytona Beach, Fla.— Dale Earnhardt dashed to the front immediately Saturday in the Pepsi 400 at Daytona International Speedway, a move that enabled him to miss a second-lap melee and then dominate the race.

Earnhardt flashed to the checkered flag for a first NASCAR Winston Cup Series victory at the track, so cruelly elusive to him previously, with his Chevrolet a comfortable 1.6 seconds ahead of Alan Kulwicki's Ford to complete a run in which he led 127 of 160 laps on the 2.5-mile raceway.

Earnhardt lists 10 victories at Daytona, but none in a regular-season Winston Cup race, although he has threatened repeatedly. The worst disappointment came in Daytona 500 in February when a cut tire victimized him while he was leading in the last mile.

"The last three laps I thought about that and ran right in the middle of the track where there was the least chance for debris," Earnhardt said with a grin. "I took no chances."

July 30, 1990
WIN NO. 6: TALLADEGA
DieHard III—Dale owns Alabama
by Tom Higgins

Talladega, Ala.—Dale Earnhardt added to his long list of auto racing accomplishments Sunday by becoming the first three-time winner of the DieHard 500 at Talladega Superspeedway, an event that has produced 19 different winners in 22 runnings.

In successfully stretching a dwindling supply of fuel in his Chevrolet to finish two car lengths ahead of runner-up Bill Elliott's Ford, Earnhardt charged to within a point of leader Mark Martin in the chase for the $1 million NASCAR Winston Cup Series championship.

Martin, who had to pit his Ford for gas while running third with nine laps to go on the 2.66-mile track, finished ninth and lost 47 points to Earnhardt, a three-time national driving champion.

"I ran out of gas going to victory lane," said Earnhardt, who has made that trip a season-leading six times, including three of the last four races. "Richard Childress, my team owner, told me on the radio he felt we could make it all the way, but that it could be close, so I throttled up a little bit to save fuel.

"Then, Richard hedged and said we might not, could make it, and I dropped back and drafted Bill a bit to save as much gas as I could." Elliott, who had ample fuel to go the distance in the 188-lap event, led Laps 151-168, the longest stretch of anyone other than Earnhardt.

"With 20 laps left I decided to go on back ahead," said Earnhardt. "I just feel more comfortable out front, and the last five laps I ran pretty hard because I saw Bill's car was getting loose (slipping) in the corners."

"My knees were knocking, we knew it was going to be so close," said the normally cool Childress. "We figure we can go 46 laps here on a tank of gas, and we were looking at going 47."

Earnhardt last pitted on Lap 141, Elliott on 145, both under the green flag.

"When Earnhardt made his last move and got around me, I pretty much knew that was it," Elliott said. "I kept trying, but boy, was he strong."

> **"We figure we can go 46 laps here on a tank of gas, and we were looking at going 47."**
> **—Richard Childress**

(Gary O'Brien/The Charlotte Observer)

September 3, 1990

WIN NO. 7: DARLINGTON
Tough track? What tough track?
by Tom Higgins

The payoff enabled Earnhardt, 39, to become the first driver in all of motorsports to officially top $11 million in winnings. He has $11,190,358.

Darlington, S.C.— Because of Dale Earnhardt, officials at Darlington International Raceway face finding a new nickname for the place.

"The Track Too Tough To Tame" doesn't apply anymore.

At least not for Earnhardt. Not after Sunday's Southern 500.

He enhanced his domination of the 1.366-mile speedway that has daunted so many competitiors through its 40-year history, outracing the NASCAR Winston Cup Series field for yet another Darlington victory.

In finishing 4.08 seconds ahead of runner-up Ernie Irvan's Chevy, Earnhardt embellished his record at Darlington Raceway to read:

- Six 500-mile victories in his past 10 starts, including three of the past four Southern 500s.
- Three straight 500-mile wins.

- A second sweep of the speedway's two annual Winston Cup events, matching his feat of taking the 1987 Southern and TranSouth 500s and making him the first driver to achieve that twice.
- Seven 500-mile triumphs overall, second to David Pearson's 10 at the track also known as "The Lady In Black" because of its treacherous nature.

Although it appeared a relative cruise of a ride for Earnhardt as he pulled away from Irvan and the others finishing on the lead lap—Alan Kulwicki, Bill Elliott, Harry Gant, Mark Martin, Ricky Rudd and Geoff Bodine—the victor revealed it actually wasn't comfortable at all.

"With about 30 laps to go a terrible vibration developed in the rear of my car," said Earnhardt, who averaged 123.141 mph as 10 caution periods slowed the pace for 52 laps. "It felt like a tire had equalized. The steering wheel was really shaking, and it made my hands and fingers numb.

"... Ernie couldn't come on up to me because he'd used his tires up trying to catch me earlier, before my vibration started. Ordinarily I would have pitted with a car shaking that bad, but me and the crew agreed to stay out since the stopwatches showed Ernie wasn't making up ground."

September 3, 1990

The couple wore black

by Ron Green

Darlington, S.C.—On the Sunday before Labor Day each year, they should hang a sign outside Darlington International Raceway that reads, "Men At Work."

The Southern 500 stock car race is fun only for the thousands who come to this old peanut patch to roast their semi-bare bodies, eat chicken and quaff a celebratory libation or two. The race is hard labor, and only tough guys need apply.

The toughest of the racers, Dale Earnhardt, won his third Southern 500 in four years Sunday, surviving more than four hours of wild racing that left the retaining walls of this old track black and blue. And red and yellow and assorted other colors, where spinning, sliding cars kissed the concrete.

When he had parked his black racer and crawled out to accept $205,350 in assorted prizes and bonuses, Earnhardt, red-faced, tired and numb in his fingers, said, "I had to work hard today. Any time you race at Darlington, it's tough. Add the heat and it's tougher.

"There are so many things here. You have to be careful. You can't ever forget where you're racing when you're racing here. When I got out of that car, I felt like I had run 100 laps on foot."

He was gulping a headache tablet as he spoke.

Once Sunday, Earnhardt forgot where he was racing. On the 133rd lap, falling behind because the tires he had just taken on weren't adhering well, he "overdrove" and slid into the second-turn wall.

Earnhardt, the best at saving a car out of control, brought it back under rein and sped on.

"The old girl slapped me when I got a little fresh," he said.

Because nobody has more nerve or skill than Earnhardt and because those are the qualities Darlington demands of its Southern 500 winners, this is a perfect marriage. They even have his-and-her nicknames. By appropriate coincidence they call Earnhardt the "Man In Black" because of his racing colors and Darlington the "Lady In Black," for her mood on race days.

The list of men who have won the Southern 500 over the past 41 years reads like a hall of fame. Ordinary guys don't win this one. Earnhardt said Ernie Irvan, who is ordinary in that he has won only one Winston Cup race, could have won Sunday had things fallen a little differently. But that's the point. For whatever reason, there's never an upset in this one.

On a day when 10 caution flags flew and cars were going sideways everywhere, Earnhardt had only a couple of close encounters.

"When you look at this race track, it doesn't look so tough," Earnhardt said. "But then you get into a race car and get into traffic and you know it's tough."

> "There are so many things here. You have to be careful. You can't ever forget where you're racing when you're racing here. When I got out of that car, I felt like I had run 100 laps on foot."
>
> —Dale Earnhardt

September 10, 1990

WIN NO. 8: RICHMOND
Running on empty

by Tom Higgins

Richmond, Va.— Dale Earnhardt won a gamble on gasoline Sunday and literally coasted to victory in the Miller 400 at Richmond Raceway, edged Mark Martin, his leading rival for the NASCAR Winston Cup championship.

"The car ran out just as I went under the checkered flag," Earnhardt said after pushing his season-leading win total to eight and cutting 10 points off Martin's advantage to trail by 16 in the chase for the $1 million title. "I had to coast to get back around to Victory Lane."

Earnhardt's Chevrolet crossed the line .43 seconds ahead of Martin's Ford.

As Earnhardt crawled atop his car in Victory Lane, he was shaking his head and saying, "We ran out of gas. ... We ran out of gas and still won. I can't believe it."

The yellow flag showed on Lap 396 after Ernie Irvan spun in his Chevy while attempting to get on pit road for refueling, erasing Earnhardt's big edge of eight seconds at that point.

Earnhardt's crew put out the pit board signaling him to come in, and had the gas can on the wall ready to put a splash in the tank. But he stayed on the track and nursed the car to the flag on fumes.

"We knew we could make it. ... That was a just-in-case situation," Earnhardt said of the pit board's display. "We had talked on the radio and they were telling me, 'Stay out! Stay out!'

"We're lucky to win this race. I admit it. The car was handling too tight from the start and geared a little too high for the conditions the weather put the track in. Then, we cut it pretty tight on gas."

October 3, 1990

Brakes?
Never heard of 'em

by Tom Higgins

"I'll run as long as my ol' head will stay on my neck and I can turn a steering wheel."
—Dale Earnhardt

Charlotte, N.C.—With an all-time motorsports record $11 million earned and with businesses established that should set him for life, it wouldn't surprise some stock car racing fans if Dale Earnhardt started looking to slow down.

They should look again.

The way Earnhardt figures it, he is just reaching his prime racing years.

And this season's NASCAR Winston Cup Series figures confirm that contention.

Earnhardt leads practically every superlative statistic.

This is why Earnhardt, in assessing career plans, talks of accelerating, not braking.

"I've never given a thought to quitting or cutting back on any aspect of my racing," Earnhardt, 39, said. "Just the contrary.

"If I stay healthy, I plan to drive as long as I can. I'll run as long as my ol' head will stay on my neck and I can turn a steering wheel.

"I think the neck is the first part of the body that a driver has to go, because of all the pressure put on it through the years by the pull of the centrifugal force at high speed.

"My neck is still really strong and I think it has a lot of years left in it. I guarantee my body will wear out before my will and desire to win do."

November 5, 1990

WIN NO. 9: PHOENIX
Close, and counting

by Tom Higgins

"We're making it interesting, aren't we?"
—Dale Earnhardt

Phoenix, Ariz.—Dale Earnhardt drove to a dominating victory Sunday in the Checker 500K at Phoenix International Raceway, and charged into a six-point lead over Mark Martin for the $1 million-plus NASCAR Winston Cup Series championship with one race remaining.

Earnhardt, driving a Chevrolet, made up 51 points as Martin finished 10th in a Ford. The outcome enabled Earnhardt to reclaim first place going into the 29-event-season's finale, the Journal 500 on Nov. 18 at Atlanta International Raceway, where he has won three of the past four.

The windup ranks as the second-closest in NASCAR history, surpassed only in 1979 when Darrell Waltrip led Richard Petty by 2 points starting the last race. Petty won the title by 11.

"We're making it interesting, aren't we?" Earnhardt said.

"This is just the thing we had to do. The race couldn't have gone any better for us."

November 19, 1990

Another title, please

by Tom Higgins

"Richard Petty is way away from anything I could be. He's 'the King,' and it makes me proud to do something only he has done."

—Dale Earnhardt

Hampton, Ga.—It was a modest, gracious Dale Earnhardt and a classy Mark Martin who concluded their chase for the NASCAR Winston Cup series title Sunday in the Journal 500 at Atlanta Motor Speedway.

Earnhardt won, padding a lead of six points going into the last race of the season, to 26 with a third-place finish. Martin was sixth.

The title is the fourth for Earnhardt, breaking him out of a tie for second all-time with Lee Petty, David Pearson, Cale Yarborough and Darrell Waltrip. The leader is Richard Petty with seven, a mark now seemingly in striking distance for Earnhardt.

"Three more is a long way off, way out there," said Earnhardt, who will collect more than $1 million in postseason bonuses. "I feel at age 39 I've got 10 more competitive years of driving left, so I might get that many.

"But even if I do, Richard Petty is way away from anything I could be. He's 'the King,' and it makes me proud to do something only he has done."

Earnhardt gives the Winston Cup trophy a victory hug after he finished third in the Atlanta Journal 500, but first in the points race. (Mark B. Sluder/The Charlotte Observer)

December 9, 1990
From dirt tracks to the Grand Ballroom
by Tom Higgins

It's likely Ralph Earnhardt, inducted into the National Motorsports Press Association Hall of Fame in 1989, was there. Invisible, certainly, but there at Dale's shoulder just as Dale had stood at his on the front seat en route to a race more than 30 years ago.

New York—Dale Earnhardt's earliest memory of stock car racing traces through time to the late 1950s.

Then, as a 5- or 6-year-old, he stood on the seat of a passenger car or pickup truck at the side of his legendary father, the late Ralph Earnhardt of Kannapolis, as Dad towed souped-up coupes to dirt short tracks around the Carolinas for weekend shows, most of which he won.

Dale Earnhardt's latest memory of stock car racing is of standing on the stage Friday night in the elegant Grand Ballroom of the Waldorf-Astoria, warm applause washing over him as he was honored for winning the NASCAR Winston Cup Series championship a fourth time.

The 1990 title gives Earnhardt four, second only to Richard Petty's seven, and the $1.3 million in bonuses accompanying it push his career winnings to $12,827,634, tops for all forms of motorsports.

What a journey three decades-plus have produced for the tow-headed lad with the mischievous twinkle in his eye from those days he spent idolizing his dad.

"I think I watched every foot of every lap he ever run after I started going to races with him and Mom," Earnhardt, 39, said Saturday at the Waldrof, where he and his family spent the week as series sponsors R.J. Reynolds Tobacco Company's guest in the $4,000-per-night Presidential Suite.

"And I was almost always at his elbow there in the garage in the backyard of our house on Sedan Street in Kannapolis, trying to see what he did that made his cars so strong."

Dale decided to become a race driver, too, in the early 1970s, wheeling his own "little ol'" 1956 Ford six-cylinder" at Charlotte's Metrolina Fairgrounds Speedway.

Devastated when his father died of a heart attack in the mid-1970s, Dale almost quit. But the sensation of speed generated by unmuffled engines had become too much a part of him. He stuck with it to become, in the opinion of NASCAR pioneer team owner Bud Moore, for whom Earnhardt once drove, "just simply the best overall that's ever been."

Not many can be found to dispute the grizzled Moore's contention, especially after Earnhardt's nine-victory 1990 season that produced world record single-year winnings of $3,089,056.

> "Friday night was the warmest in New York for me for a lot of other reasons, one of them being that it was the first time my mama, Martha, got to come to the Waldorf and be at the awards program in person. Her being here means a lot to me. I just wish daddy could have been, too, 'cause he never has left my heart."
>
> —Dale Earnhardt

Never mind that his 48 career triumphs tie him for only ninth place all-time, well below the 200 wins of Petty.

"Richard is the King, and always will be," said Richard Childress, a former driver himself who gave up the wheel in 1981 when he was able to hire Earnhardt to drive his Chevrolets. "But I have to agree with Bud. Dale is achieving all these things at a time when there are 20 to 25 competitive teams capable of winning rather than just five or six."

Earnhardt is modest in his thoughts on that matter, and on the fame and wealth and international adulation of motorsports fans that he commands.

"Being the champion a fourth time is a little overwhelming," he said. "It took some time to sink in that I'd broken out of a tie at three titles with drivers as great as Lee Petty (Richard's father), Darrell Waltrip, Cale Yarborough and David Pearson. And that it left me three behind the King with, I hope, a lot of racing years left.

"Richard, in my opinion, is in a class by himself, both on and off the track. To have people mention my name in the same breath with that man is about as big an honor as I could ever hope for.

Dale Earnhardt and Mark Martin competed for the 1990 Winston Cup. (Mark B. Sluder/The Charlotte Observer)

"Richard Childress and the crew guys likely aren't going to get as much credit for this season and what we've done together in the past seven years.

"I'm not just saying this, now, but this championship means more than the others, even that first one in '80, although it came in just my second year in the Winston Cup. I was younger then, and a heck of a lot wilder, and I didn't appreciate everything that winning meant. I do now.

"A big reason it stands out is that we had to race so hard to get it. Mark Martin and that team of his that Jack Roush owns gave us more than we wanted to have to handle.

"Friday night was the warmest in New York for me for a lot of other reasons, one of them being that it was the first time my mama, Martha, got to come to the Waldorf and be at the awards program in person. Her being here means a lot to me. I just wish daddy could have been, too, 'cause he never has left my heart."

It's likely Ralph Earnhardt, inducted into the National Motorsports Press Association Hall of Fame in 1989, was there. Invisible, certainly, but there at Dale's shoulder just as Dale had stood at his on the front seat en route to a race more than 30 years ago.

Chapter Fourteen:
1991: The drive for five

Races	Won	Top 5	Top 10	Poles	Earnings
29	4	14	21	0	$ 2,396,685

January 18, 1991
They're racin' and chasin'
by Tom Higgins

"I'm glad they're talking about us that way. If that's intimidation and it gives us a little edge, we'll take it."—Dale Earnhardt

Welcome, N.C.—Team owner Rick Hendrick predicted that for one of his two drivers—Ricky Rudd or Ken Schrader—to become Winston Cup champion in '91, they'd have to outrun Dale Earnhardt.

"If we can beat the No.3 car consistently, we can win the championship," Hendrick said. "I think the best chance of doing that is for our two teams to put their heads together, and that's our plan."

Hendrick's comments gathered added meaning at a luncheon in Lexington when a representative of a restaurant chain announced that a new racing-related promotional program would include addition of a large steak called "The Intimidator" to its menu.

"The Intimidator" is becoming one of Earnhardt's most widely used nicknames because of his charging, aggressive driving style.

"I'm not sure about some of this intimidation stuff," Earnhardt said with a grin. "Maybe that was the case a few years ago when I was wilder.

"I think as I've matured more finesse has figured in to go along with the aggression. Just look at how hard me and Mark Martin raced last year, and we didn't have any problems on the track."

Earnhardt beat Martin by 26 points for the 1990 Winston Cup title.

"It makes me feel good to hear that other teams think they have to beat us to win the championship," he said. "I'm glad they're talking about us that way. If that's intimidation and it gives us a little edge, we'll take it."

February 11, 1991
Dash for the Clash
by Tom Higgins

Daytona Beach, Fla.— Dale Earnhardt made what even he termed an "unbelievable" charge Sunday, dashing quickly from 14th—and last—in the Busch Clash's second segment to win the special event stock car race for the fourth time in six tries.

Driving his Chevrolet to the track's inside edge at Daytona International Speedway, Earnhardt surprised even himself by passing 13 rivals in just 1-plus laps around the 2.5-mile trioval layout.

"Man, that car really came around the track," Earnhardt said of the second-segment sprint. "It was awesome, wasn't it? All week long we thought about strategy, thought about maybe not winning the first half. But we decided we're a 'go for it' team and settled on trying to get it all. It's amazing to me. I can't believe we did it in 2 laps. I told everyone earlier in the week that King Kong couldn't do that."

Earnhardt averaged 189.474 mph and earned $60,000 overall.

Said one NASCAR insider: "Dale just drove a stake through the heart of every team in the garage area."

February 19, 1991
Daytona 500: This can't be happening...
by Tom Higgins

> "The best car doesn't always win. We proved that last year."
> —Dale Earnhardt

Daytona Beach, Fla.—Ernie Irvan, his Chevrolet almost out of fuel and sputtering although running slow under caution conditions Sunday, won a Daytona 500 that turned from boring to bizarre as three accidents altered the outcome in the last 40 miles.

"I ran out of gas under the last yellow flag with still about a lap to go," Irvan said after the stunning finish in the NASCAR Winston Cup Series opener at Daytona International Speedway.

"I said, 'This can't be true. This can't happen to me.'"

It didn't, although runner-up Sterling Marlin, alongside Irvan in a Ford, thought it might.

"Ernie's car was sputtering so bad when we got to Turns 3 and 4 I thought it was going to stop," Marlin said. "I was saying, 'Quit! Quit! Quit!' But it didn't."

The race's twists and turns also undoubtedly left Dale Earnhardt, Darrell Waltrip, Davey Allison, Rusty Wallace and Kyle Petty uttering "this can't be happening."

"The best car doesn't always win. We proved that last year," said Earnhardt, who finished fifth.

After a yellow flag, Earnhardt led the restart on Lap 194, but on Lap 198, Earnhardt's car lost its aerodynamics and spun out of control off Turn 2, wrecking both the Ford of Allison and Kyle Petty's Pontiac.

This created another caution period and with just two laps left Irvan was home free—if he had enough gas.

He did.

Barely.

"Ricky raced me strong, but clean, and I can't say enough about that. Hopefully, this will sort of set a precedent after all the bumps and run-ins and harsh feelings we've had."—Dale Earnhardt

February 25, 1991

WIN NO. 1: RICHMOND
It's Dale, by a length
by Tom Higgins

Richmond, Va.—Dale Earnhardt held off Ricky Rudd in a furious finish Sunday and won the Pontiac 400 at Richmond Raceway to regain a familiar position, the NASCAR Winston Cup Series point standings lead toward a $1 million championship. What looked like a romp for 1990 title winner Earnhardt, who had forged a 4-second advantage, became a battle when an accident involving Hut Stricklin and Brett Bodine forced a yellow flag on the 394th of 400 laps.

Earnhardt charged about three car-lengths ahead at the restart on Lap 398. However, he bobbled a bit in Turn 4 on Lap 399, enabling Rudd to take the low groove that Earnhardt had commanded through the last three-fourths of the race.

Their Chevrolets stayed abreast almost the rest of the way around, until Earnhardt said his tires "got a better bite" through the final corner and he took the checkered flag ahead by a car length.

"Ricky raced me strong, but clean, and I can't say enough about that." Earnhardt said of the rival with whom he has had several confrontations.

"Hopefully, this will sort of set a precedent after all the bumps and run-ins and harsh feelings we've had.

"I'll remember this and give Ricky room the next time I get under him."

WIN NO. 2: MARTINSVILLE
Happy Birthday. But which one?
by Tom Higgins

Martinsville, Va.—Dale Earnhardt got an early birthday present Sunday by winning a Hanes 500 stock car race that appeared gift-wrapped for Davey Allison at Martinsville Speedway.

Earnhardt, who is either 39 or 40 today, depending on whose date of arrival is accepted, got the break he needed to claim his 50th NASCAR Winston Cup Series triumph when Allison cut a right front tire while pulling away on the 457th of 500 laps at the .526-mile track. As Allison tried to get to pit road, a slight tangle with fellow Ford driver Alan Kulwicki resulted, forcing a caution flag.

This enabled Earnhardt, a half-lap behind at the time in fifth place and fading, to stop for new tires and a chassis adjustment his Chevrolet desperately needed.

On the lap 463 restart, Kyle Petty led in his Pontiac with Earnhardt second. The two raced abreast until reaching Turn 4, where Earnhardt edged in front to stay to become the first repeat winner in eight races this season. It was his fifth career Martinsville win.

"It'll be my 39th birthday, I don't care what my momma says," Earnhardt said with a grin after averaging 75.139 mph to earn $63,600 before a track record crowd estimated at 44,000. Martha Earnhardt of Kannapolis contends her son will be 40 today.

The win tied Earnhardt for seventh in all-time Winston Cup victories with hall of famers Junior Johnson and Ned Jarrett, who retired with 50 each.

"It feels good to be there with drivers like that," Earnhardt said. "They raced my dad (the late Ralph Earnhardt) and I watched 'em and admired them. I always imagined someday equaling what they had done."

July 29, 1991
WIN NO. 3: TALLADEGA
Out-running the Fords
by Tom Higgins

Talladega, Ala.—Dale Earnhardt prevailed in a furious DieHard 500 finish Sunday and became the all-time victory leader at Talladega Superspeedway with five NASCAR Winston Cup Series triumphs on the circuit's fastest track.

Earnhardt held off a line of Fords over the last three laps on the 2.66-mile track. He won by a car length over Bill Elliott.

Sterling Marlin conceded a strategy was concocted on pit road among the Ford teams to try to use the aerodynamic draft to beat Earnhardt as the 188-lap event ended.

"We were supposed to work together, but the battle plan got lost somewhere," Marlin said.

"It was a tough race, tough to stay in front of those Fords," Earnhardt said. "I saw what Bill was going to do the last lap. He laid off a little bit down the backstretch to try and get a run at me off Turn 4. I knew Bill had the experience to maybe make it work."

September 30, 1991
WIN NO. 4: NORTH WILKESBORO
Bad brake for Gant, lucky break for Dale
by Tom Higgins

North Wilkesboro, N.C.—Harry Gant's seemingly unstoppable string of victories in September's major NASCAR races came to a halt Sunday in the Tyson Holly Farms 400 at North Wilkesboro Speedway.

A 10-cent brake part failed, allowing Dale Earnhardt to pass Gant with nine laps left for the victory. The failure cost a fifth straight Winston Cup Triumph and approximately $200,000 that would have gone to Gant for winning from the pole.

"With 10 laps to go I had no brakes. Nothing," Gant said. "Before long, Dale caught me and I had to let him go or wreck him. I don't do people like that."

Earnhardt pulled away by 1.5 seconds for his fourth victory this season in a Chevrolet, but first since the DieHard 500 at Talladega (Ala.) Superspeedway in late July.

The Talladega victory pushed Earnhardt's points lead toward a fifth Winston Cup championship to 160 points. In the seven races since, his margin had dwindled as low as 36 over Ricky Rudd.

Sunday's outcome pushed the advantage to a commanding 112 ahead of Rudd—who was 12th in a Chevy—with four races left.

"The point situation is looking a lot better for us," Earnhardt said after his team gained several positions for him with quick pit stops.

"It's not over yet, though. The pressure is off us a little bit and more on Ricky and his team. He's got to make a move pretty soon.

"I think it has gone into a two-man race now. Hopefully after Charlotte it'll be one man—me."

November 15, 1991

The best ever?

by Tom Higgins

Hampton, Ga.—All that Dale Earnhardt has to do Sunday to win the NASCAR Winston Cup Series championship is lift a finger.

With that, Earnhardt will flip the ignition switch of Richard Childress racing's Chevrolet to start the Hardee's 500 at Atlanta Motor Speedway.

When Earnhardt takes the green flag for the last of the season's 29 races, the title and approximately $1.3 million in bonuses are his, no matter what happens afterward.

It is to be a fifth championship for Earnhardt, 40, second only to Richard Petty's seven.

Earnhardt's success in big-time stock car racing's modern era, which began in 1972, has stirred considerable speculation among those who follow the sport closely:

Is he the best driver ever?

The main argument of those who feel Earnhardt is the most talented is this:

Although Earnhardt has "only" 52 victories, four this year, to the record 200 lifetime of Petty, Earnhardt's wins and titles have come during a more competitive period.

It's pointed out that when Petty, 54, was winning so big in the 1960s the schedule included up to 60 races. The fields weren't always filled in those days at some short tracks, and often only two or three other cars anywhere near the equal of Petty's were present.

> "I've never thought about being the best or greatest. Not even when I started out in what amounted to jalopies back in the mid-'70s. I just wanted to drive a race car like my daddy."
> —Dale Earnhardt

Starting in '72 the schedule has ranged from 28 to 31 races, and since Earnhardt took his first title in '80 at least a dozen first-class cars ran every event.

Earnhardt, who leads Davey Allison by 156 points and Ricky Rudd by 165, seems embarrassed by the suggestion he's the all-time best.

"There is only one Richard Petty, and he's the King," Earnhardt has said repeatedly. "I don't think there's a comparison ... I could never top him as far as being a better driver.

"I've never thought about being the best or greatest. Not even when I started out in what amounted to jalopies back in the mid-'70s. I just wanted to drive a race car like my daddy."

Dale's father was Ralph Earnhardt, a two-time NASCAR national champion in the sportsman division, now known as the Grand National Series. The elder Earnhardt, rated by some as the greatest dirt track driver ever, died in 1973 of a heart attack.

Earnhardt concedes he hopes to equal or even surpass Petty's record for championships.

"If I can keep going strong as Harry Gant is, then the chance should be there," Earnhardt said. "Harry is 11 years older than me and he's won five races this year. ... If I can stay in as good a shape as Harry has, and

I plan to, I should have 10 more pretty good seasons of racing left."

Earnhardt already holds the motorsports record for prize winnings. His Winston Cup total is $13,909,874. Darrell Waltrip is second with $11,024,517.

Where do the experts rate Earnhardt in terms of all-time ability?

Very highly, but short of having him dethrone Petty.

Said Ned Jarrett, a two-time Winston Cup champion and now a broadcaster:

"From early in Dale's career I've said if there ever was a natural-born race driver, he is it. He just seems to have an uncanny ability to do incredible things with an automobile. He can save them when they're so far out of shape it's amazing."

Dale Earnhardt climbs out of his car after a qualifying run. (Diedra Laird/The Charlotte Observer)

Chapter Fifteen:
1992: One win, one new crew chief

Races	Won	Top 5	Top 10	Poles	Earnings
29	1	6	15	1	$ 915,463

February 16, 1992
0-for-Daytona, again?
by Tom Higgins

"We've been in strong shape the past several years down here but haven't won. Maybe we can do it this time with the fourth or fifth best car."
—Dale Earnhardt

Daytona Beach, Fla.—The day belongs to Richard Petty, starting his 32nd and last Daytona 500 in the final year of a storied career.

However, it appears the NASCAR Winston Cup Series season-opening classic at Daytona International Speedway possibly will wind up as the property of Dale Earnhardt—at long last. Five straight years in February, Earnhardt's strong runs in stock car racing's biggest show have ended agonizingly, producing three fifth-place finishes and a third. Until Thursday, he generally was given little chance of even being very competitive this time against a fleet force of Fords.

Then, using his Lumina's superior handling, the five-time Winston Cup champion edged the Thunderbird rated strongest of all on race set-up, that of Mark Martin, to win a 125-mile qualifying race.

With the drop of that checkered flag, Earnhardt became the favorite among most experts to win the 200-lap race. And he is at least co-favored by practically all the others who variously give co-billing to Martin and fellow Ford drivers Bill Elliott, Sterling Marlin, Davey Allison and Morgan Shepherd.

"We're handling really good, looking really good," said Earnhardt, who will start third behind time-trial leaders Marlin and Elliott when the green flag shows for the $2.3 million race. "A couple of cars have us outpowered, and Mark's is handling well to boot.

"We've been in strong shape the past several years down here but haven't won. Maybe we can do it this time with the fourth or fifth best car."

Three times Earnhardt's Daytona 500 hopes have been dashed when he was forced to make late pit stops for fuel. Last year he spun—and took Allison out of contention with him—when the aerodynamic slipstream whipped his Chevy around as the duo raced abreast in pursuit of eventual winner Ernie Irvan late in the race.

The toughest loss, the one that won't go away, came in 1990 when Earnhardt over-whelmed the opposition, only to cut a tire a mile from the finish and watch victory go to Derrike Cope.

"I come down here every year, excited about having a shot to win this race," said Earnhardt. "This is my 14th try. It took Darrell Waltrip 17 and Buddy Baker 18 to win the Daytona 500. I don't want to play on that so much, 'cause I don't want it to take me 17. I'd like for it to be 14. We're going to work hard on winning it. This is the race you want to win. There's not another one to match it."

February 17, 1992

Yes, 0-for-Daytona. Again.

by Tom Higgins

"The Daytona 500 can be cruel."—Michael Waltrip

Mark B. Sluder/The Charlotte Observer

Daytona Beach Fla.—Davey Allison made a heady move to avoid a wrecking trio of leaders just feet ahead of him Sunday and domi-nated the Daytona 500 afterward to win the NASCAR Winston Cup Series' biggest stock car race for the first time.

As Ford team-mates Sterling Marlin and Bill Elliott bumped along with Chevrolet driver Ernie Irvan and then spun out of control on the backstretch at Daytona International Speedway, Allison whipped his Thunderbird to the outside and cleared the trouble that swept up 11 other cars, including several top contenders.

Incredibly, the chain-reaction crash on the 92nd of 200 laps resulted in only one slight

injury, Ken Schrader's sprained ankle.

But it elimi-nated the cars of Dale Jarrett, Chad Little, Schrader and pole-winner Marlin, while erasing the chances of Dale Earnhardt, Mark Martin, Darrell Waltrip, Elliott, Hut Stricklin and Richard Petty, who was mak-ing his last start in the race.

Earnhardt fin-ished ninth.

Michael Waltrip burned a piston as he ran second eight laps from the finish. "We were in a position to at least try to make a run for the win," Waltrip said. "The Daytona 500 can be cruel. I think we could have made it inter-esting."

May 12, 1992

Driven a Ford, lately?

by Tom Higgins

"I just wanted to drive a Ford, see what the competition had."

—Dale Earnhardt

Charlotte, N.C.—Has Dale Earnhardt driven a Ford lately?

You bet.

He did it Monday at Charlotte Motor Speedway.

Earnhardt, a five-time NASCAR Winston Cup champion and perhaps the best-known Chevrolet driver in the country, surprisingly took to the wheel of one of the Fords fielded for driver Mark Martin by the Jack Roush Racing team. He ran 8 laps on the 1.5-mile track, with a best of 163.934 mph.

"I knew it had to be Earnhardt in the car when it came through the garage area and swerved at me," said driver Buddy Baker. "He's the only one mischievous enough to do that."

It happened in mid-afternoon during a busy test session at the speedway.

"I just wanted to drive a Ford, see what the competition had," said a smiling Earnhardt, who along with other Chevy drivers has seen Thunderbird teams win 13 straight races dating to last October.

However, there was speculation among other team members that there's more to it than that. Some feel Earnhardt has been approached by Roush about becoming part of that team in 1994.

"All I know is that Dale came by and asked if he could drive our car," said Steve Hmiel, team manager/crew chief for Martin. "I said, 'Sure, if you think you'll fit the seat.' Dale said he'd lower the seat, since he's so much taller than Mark. He did, and out he went."

How did Earnhardt rate the Ford to Hmiel when he came back in?

"Dale said, 'Nice handling car. ... But not much motor.'"

May 25, 1992

WIN NO. 1: CHARLOTTE
Pit, and make it quick

by Tom Higgins

Charlotte, N.C.—
Dale Earnhardt, bedeviled by mostly bad luck at Charlotte Motor Speedway since 1986, battled back with the help of a brilliant green flag pit stop Sunday and held off Ernie Irvan to win a Coca-Cola 600 thriller.

> "I fudged all I could on the speed limit (55 mph) on pit road without getting penalized. I judged 55 to be 4,000 rpms and I might have got up to about 4,050 leaving."

No. 13 figured prominently as Earnhardt edged fellow Chevrolet driver Irvan by 39-hundredths of a second, or about three car lengths, before a track-record crowd estimated at 160,000.

The outcome:
- Ended Earnhardt's NASCAR Winston Cup Series non-winning streak dating to last September at 13.
- Snapped Ford's victory string dating to the same month at 13.
- Marked the second time in 65 races dating to 1960 at the 1.5-mile track that a Winston Cup event has been won from starting position No. 13, which is where Earnhardt lined up the Richard Childress team's Lumina.

Pivotal to all this was a sizzling 19.40-second pit stop by Earnhardt's crew, led by Kirk Shelmerdine, on the 346th of 400 laps.

It enabled Earnhardt to return to the track slightly ahead of Irvan and the dominant Pontiac of Kyle Petty, both of whom stopped 2 laps earlier for service that required 21.19 and 19.72 seconds, respectively. Earnhardt wasn't headed afterward, leading the final 54 laps—the only time he was in front in the race.

"It was a great pit stop. That was the key," said current Winston Cup champion Earnhardt after his 53rd career victory and fourth at his Charlotte home track, two in the 600. "Me being in front made Ernie and Kyle run a little harder and use their tires up.

"I got in quick, whoa'd down within the limits, got gone quick and flat- footed around through Turns 1 and 2 on the return lane. I fudged all I could on the speed limit (55 mph) on pit road without getting penalized. I judged 55 to be 4,000 rpms and I might have got up to about 4,050 leaving.

"For years Charlotte was a great place to me and then bad things began happening. It's good to get back in Victory Lane."

May 25, 1992

Home, sweet home

by Ron Green

Charlotte, N.C.—As Dale Earnhardt wheeled his panting car into the Coca-Cola 600 victory circle Sunday afternoon, a couple of shirtless, sunburned fans with celebratory libations in hand hoisted a sign at the foot of the Charlotte Motor Speedway grandstand.

It read, "If God was a stock car driver, his name would be Earnhardt."

Well, maybe, but could He drive like Earnhardt, wheeling through three wrecks without a scratch, making a pit stop that was so fast it looked like magic and then muscling his Chevrolet home half a second in front of Ernie Irvan's?

That's how Earnhardt finally broke Ford's long winning streak and ended a personal string of disappointments dating to last September.

The Man In Black, as he's advertised, had a golden glow as he told how it felt to win.

"It felt great," he said. "I said before the race, 'It's time for something big to happen.' I picked Richard Petty to win. That would have been big. He didn't, but I did and that's big, too."

Earnhardt has been the dominant driver on NASCAR's Winston Cup circuit for years, and has five points championships to prove it, but he hadn't won a Winston Cup race in Charlotte since 1986.

He had to drive down pit road once to avoid a wreck. Another wreck forced him into the infield grass. And he had to scoot around another without leaving the track.

"I was lucky to get by," he said.

His last pit stop on Lap 346 (of 400) was a dazzler. He came into the pits third behind Kyle Petty and Irvan and came out leading. Petty had questions.

> "I picked Richard Petty to win. That would have been big. He didn't, but I did and that's big, too."
> **—Dale Earnhardt**

"There's no way a man can be two seconds behind you on a race track and everybody comes down pit road at the same time and he comes out a second ahead," said Petty. "I don't care what anybody says."

What Petty was intimating was that Earnhardt had exceeded NASCAR's 55-mph speed limit on pit road. So, Dale, were you under the limit?

"I must've been, they didn't black flag me," said Earnhardt, with what looked suspiciously like a little grin behind his mustache. "I got on pit road great, whoa'd down quick and got out quick.

"I don't like to run second to anything. I've not been in Victory Lane in a while and Ford's been winning. I hate to see anybody win, I don't care what they're driving."

May 25, 1992

Here's to you, the Earnhardt crew

by Liz Clarke

Charlotte, N.C.—With 2 laps left in Sunday's Coca-Cola 600, crew chief Kirk Shelmerdine snuck a peek at the black stopwatch cradled in his left hand.

At that point—well past a final, crucial pit stop—there was nothing Shelmerdine could do to help Dale Earnhardt through the race.

"It was something to do, more than anything," Shelmerdine said of the last-minute check on Earnhardt's pace—essentially a pointless exercise.

Earnhardt's crew had made the difference in the race. With 54 laps left, Earnhardt pitted for new tires and a tank of gas behind race leaders Kyle Petty and Ernie Irvan.

Just 19.4 seconds later, he zoomed back into traffic with the lead.

Earnhardt's team hadn't won a race since North Wilkesboro last September.

He'd come close May 16 in The Winston, only to spin out in the final lap.

Sunday, as Earnhardt fended off Irvan in the last 25 laps of the 600, his crew members milled about the pit area solemn and expressionless.

Shelmerdine kept to himself, leaning against a pole.

His headset shut out the commotion around him and kept him wired to Earnhardt by radio.

The rest of the crew did busy work.

Some rolled tires away; others tidied up. A few sat with their backs to the race.

But on lap 399 of the 400-lap race, the crew climbed on the wall. Still expressionless, they stood on tiptoe, cranings their necks for a better view.

And the moment Earnhardt roared across the finish line, 39-hundredths of a second and about 3 car lengths ahead of Irvan, they went berserk.

Two dozen men in grungy black racing suits leaped, spilled onto pit road and thrust their fists to sky, hooting and hollering, high-fiving and hugging like crazy.

Then they ran out to meet Earnhardt's car, which screeched to a brief stop, then roared off for victory circle.

In minutes, Earnhardt was surrounded by sponsors, track officials, TV cameras and photographers.

He waved, grinned and mugged for photos wearing a series of caps with corporate logos.

But the real celebration was going on behind the backdrop.

That's where Earnhardt's crew had gathered and was holding the most raucous party anyone ever had while guzzling nothing but Gatorade and Coke.

"We've been a little bit behind," said gas man Chocolate Myers, "and we're so damn used to winning. We're pumped up. We've been so damn close. It's almost like winning the first race."

> The real celebration was going on behind the backdrop. That's where Earnhardt's crew had gathered and was holding the most raucous party anyone ever had while guzzling nothing but Gatorade and Coke.

Sign on the dotted line
by Tom Higgins

> "This deal shows that we not only think we're capable of coming back from a tough season, but that we will."
> —Richard Childress

Charlotte, N.C.—Five-time NASCAR Winston Cup Series champion Dale Earnhardt and team owner Richard Childress scotched rumors of a breakup Tuesday by signing a three-year contract extension with Goodwrench, sponsor of their Chevrolets.

Earnhardt already was committed to Childress Racing of Welcome for 1993, so the deal will keep the duo together through 1996.

Speculation about a split, which Earnhardt and Childress have denied since the fall of '91, resurfaced when crew chief Kirk Shelmerdine re-signed last week, effective after the season finale Hooters 500 Sunday at Atlanta Motor Speedway.

Shelmerdine explained that he was "spent" after the team's least productive season since Earnhardt joined Childress in 1984. Earnhardt has only one victory this year—in May's Coca-Cola 600 at Charlotte Motor Speedway—and he's 11th in the point standings after being favored in preseason to win for a third straight year.

"Everyone involved in racing more than a couple years—including the Goodwrench people—know things run in cycles," said Childress. "The kind of numbers we've put up the last few years are hard to maintain. This deal shows that we not only think we're capable of coming back from a tough season, but that we will."

Earnhardt has scored 45 of his 53 victories and taken four of his titles in Childress-fielded cars. He couldn't be reached Tuesday, but had insisted for days the contract extension was imminent.

Welcome aboard, Mr. Petree
by Liz Clarke

As expected, **Andy Petree, the outgoing crew chief for Harry Gant's Skoal Bandit racing team, was officially named Monday as the next crew chief for Dale Earnhardt and the GM Goodwrench-Richard Childress racing team.**

Petree, 34, will start his new job around Dec. 15. He'll take over for Kirk Shelmerdine, who resigned unexpectedly, saying he needed a break from the sport.

Petree has 10 Winston Cup victories. Nine of those came with Gant's team.

Childress said he was pleased with the selection of Petree, though no one would be able to take Shelmerdine's place.

"We've been watching Andy work for some time and we like what we see," Childress said.

Races	Won	Top 5	Top 10	Poles	Earnings
30	6	17	21	2	$3,353,789

February 14, 1993
In a Daytona groove?
by Liz Clarke

"It's like waiting on Santa Claus."
— Dale Earnhardt

Daytona Beach, Fla.—The way Dale Earnhardt is driving, only bad luck or uncommonly bold driving by everyone else will keep him from winning today's Daytona 500.

Earnhardt manhandled the field in the Goody's 300 at Daytona International Speedway Saturday, slicing through packs and fending off challengers to storm to his fourth straight win in the season-opening Grand National race.

The blowout gives Earnhardt a perfect record since showing up in Daytona last week: three races, three black Chevrolets, three wins.

Not one has even been close.

The five-time Winston Cup champion led 10 of 20 laps in last Sunday's Busch Clash, 34 of 50 laps in Thursday's 125-mile qualifying race to set today's lineup, and 87 of the 120 laps Saturday.

For those without calculators, that means Earnhardt has led 69 percent of his 190 race laps on the 2.5-mile speedway.

"It's like waiting on Santa Claus," Earnhardt said, on anticipating the 1993 Daytona 500.

If ever there's a year Earnhardt ought to break his 14-year jinx in the Daytona 500—the only major title that eludes him—this seems to be it.

"I'm sort of scared to death my luck's gonna run out, you know," Earnhardt said after a final practice.

February 15, 1993

So much for Santa Claus

by Liz Clarke

Daytona Beach, Fla.—With his mother praying in the infield and his father about to jump out of the CBS anchor booth, Dale Jarrett blew past a seemingly cursed Dale Earnhardt Sunday to win the Daytona 500 in the final 2 laps.

Earnhardt, gunning for his first win in 15 tries, led more than half the race in a powerful Chevy that had drivers scared all week.

But with 3 laps left, Earnhardt got wobbly and Jarrett took advantage.

He drove around rookie Jeff Gordon, who had been hugging Earnhardt's bumper for a good 20 laps, to pull even with Earnhardt with about a lap and a half left.

His power fading, all Earnhardt could do was bump him. Jarrett hung on, and with a push from Geoff Bodine's Ford, he found just enough to blow past for the win.

Earnhardt finished second.

He had won all three races leading up to Sunday's race, and was considered a favorite to win his first Daytona 500.

It seemed ordained early on. Earnhardt ran close to the front all day, and waltzed unscathed around the seven wrecks that took out strong cars like Kyle Petty's, Rusty Wallace's, Jimmy Hensley's, Ernie Irvan's and Al Unser Jr.'s.

Earnhardt took the lead for the last time on Lap 179. With the rest of the pack in single file behind him, it seemed a battle for second.

When Jarrett bolted, his father, Ned, a former driver who was analyzing the race for CBS, cheered him on from the anchor booth.

Dale Jarrett couldn't hear, of course, but obeyed instinctively.

While Jarrett was being interviewed in the winner's circle, Gordon and Earnhardt pulled into the garage, one behind the other.

> "We've lost this race about every way you can lose it. We've been out-gased, out-tired, out-run, out-everythinged."
>
> **—Dale Earnhardt**

Gordon popped out at once, and couldn't wait to talk about his fifth-place finish. "One heckuva day! One heckuva day! I couldn't ask for a better day!" Gordon said, beaming.

Earnhardt just sat in his driver's seat, staring straight ahead. He wiped his face, sipped some Gatorade and stared some more.

A few minutes passed before he climbed out.

"We've lost this race about every way you can lose it," Earnhardt said. "We've been out-gased, out-tired, out-run, out-everythinged.

"It's tough to run the way we did all week, and have the success we've had all week and not win the big one. I'm getting tired of winning everything up until the 500 and then not win it."

March 29, 1993

WIN NO. 1: DARLINGTON
Black cloud; silver lining

by Tom Higgins

Darlington, S.C.—Dale Earnhardt, NASCAR Winston Cup racing's "Man In Black," got help from a black cloud Sunday and rolled to a dominating victory in the TranSouth 500 at Darlington Raceway.

The cloud cover that appeared midway through the 367-lap race changed conditions on the 1.366-mile track.

Turns out it was tinged with a silver lining for Earnhardt, whose Chevrolet had a chassis setup that obviously corresponded perfectly.

Earnhardt led 149 of the last 150 laps, including the final 46, after Mark Martin's Ford ruled the first half of the season's fifth event. Martin led 124 laps when the speedway was bathed in sunshine, taking over once Earnhardt had paced the first 49 laps from the pole.

"Our car worked better after the sun went in," said Earnhardt, who averaged a track record 139.947 mph, topping the 139.364 of Bill Elliott last spring. "When the sky got darker, it enabled me to change the line I was running in the turns. I went up high against the wall. My car got faster in that groove."

The result was an eighth major victory at Darlington for Earnhardt and the 54th of his career, tying the Iredell County driver for sixth place on the all-time Winston Cup list with NASCAR pioneer Lee Petty.

March 29, 1993

Hey, who's the new guy?

by Tom Higgins

Gordon was running an impressive second on the 100th of 367 laps in the TranSouth 500, contending with eventual winner Dale Earnhardt ... when a collision from behind sent his Chevrolet sliding.

Darlington, S.C.—Although Jeff Gordon is only 21 and a newcomer to NASCAR Winston Cup racing, he had heard some of the stories about Darlington Raceway's devious ways.

How the old speedway's walls sometimes seemed "to jump out and bite" drivers. ... How the track seemed "to have an invisible hand" that swept competitors into accidents. ... How "every inch of its walls are scarred with a story."

With shocking suddenness Gordon became a part of the track's lore Sunday in his first Winston Cup start at Darlington.

Gordon was running an impressive second on the 100th of 367 laps in the TranSouth 500, contending with eventual winner Dale Earnhardt and runner-up Mark Martin, when a collision from behind sent his Chevrolet sliding in Turn 1, the car's back half badly battered.

Michael Waltrip, overtaking Gordon after getting fresh tires on his lapped Pontiac, inadvertently had run into the rookie.

Gordon has been the epitome of diplomacy this season. But disappointment momentarily put a testy edge in his voice.

"He just drove into the back of me," Gordon said. "How smart do you have to be to know you run faster on new tires than someone else is on old tires? He was a lapped car and I was running second and out of nowhere I got hit from behind. ..."

May 31, 1993
WIN NO. 2:CHARLOTTE
Night moves
by Tom Higgins

Charlotte, N.C.—A post-race fireworks display couldn't compare with the ones ignited Sunday night by Dale Earnhardt, who twice overcame penalties imposed by NASCAR officials to win a wild Coca-Cola 600 at Charlotte Motor Speedway.

Earnhardt rallied from laps lost for speeding on pit road and rough driving to lead the final 39 of 400 laps on the 1.5-mile track and finish 4.1 seconds ahead of the runner-up, rookie Jeff Gordon. Dale Jarrett edged Ken Schrader by about a foot for third place and Ernie Irvan followed to give

Chevrolet a sweep of the top five positions before a speedway record crowd estimated at 162,000, attending the first day-into-night race in NASCAR history.

> **"They can start 'em whenever they like. I'll finish 'em."**
>
> **—Dale Earnhardt**

"They can start 'em whenever they like. I'll finish 'em," Earnhardt said.

Ford drivers Bill Elliott, Jimmy Spencer, Bobby Labonte, Morgan Shepherd and Geoff Bodine completed the top 10.

"I'm really excited about winning the first 600 to finish under the lights," said Earnhardt, NASCAR's Terminator, whose voice showed his emotion. "It's history, and it'll always be special."

Dale Earnhardt sprays the Victory Lane crowd, including his wife, Teresa, with champagne after his victory in the Winston at Charlotte Motor Speedway. A week later he completed the sweep of Charlotte by winning the Coca-Cola 600. (Gary O'Brien/The Charlotte Observer)

May 31, 1993

Oh, so he's a magician...

by Ron Green

Charlotte, N.C.—Had Houdini been there, among the multitude at Charlotte Motor Speedway Sunday night, he might've whistled and whooped and stomped his feet for Dale Earnhardt, and then sidled up beside him and said, "How'd you do that?"

As darkness settled over the countryside around the speedway, Earnhardt showed again why he's every race driver's worst nightmare.

Earnhardt, the wild one, the sliest of the sly and bravest of the brave, kept slipping out of deep trouble and somehow whipped that dreaded No. 3 through little cracks and crevices where angels fear to drive. And by the end of the Coca-Cola 600, he was out front and going away.

It must be magic.

Earnhardt was twice penalized, once for breaking the rules, once for being a bad boy. Total assessment was about a lap and a half, maybe 2 laps. Two to 3 miles.

Twice, he had to make up an entire circuit of the mile-and-a-half oval just to be up with the leaders, and twice he did it.

Earnhardt doesn't just drive, he races.

And shame on anybody who gets in his way.

Greg Sacks did. Earnhardt was in the process of trying to make up a mile or so that he had lost when he pitted under a green flag.

He was in a hurry and Sacks was in his way. Earnhardt drove up behind him and suddenly, Sacks was doing a samba, into the wall, across the track, onto the grass. This produced the caution flag Earnhardt needed to make up his lost ground but, whoa, NASCAR officials slapped a 1-lap penalty on him for rough driving.

"I was close, but I didn't hit him," said Earnhardt when it was all over. "Maybe our bumpers touched or I touched him a bit but it wasn't like I rammed the hell out of him. I don't think I nudged him." (And then, with a smile): "I might've been a-gin him."

When the green flag came out again on Lap 335, Earnhardt was a mile and a half behind and time was starting to become precious. So he did what he always does.

"I was runnin' the hell out of it," he said.

When a caution flag allowed him to close big ground, you knew what was coming. On the restart, he made some moves that chilled your blood and suddenly burst out ahead of everyone. Like magic.

Earlier, he had been leading after 221 laps but had come in for gas and tires and had gotten a 15-second penalty for exceeding the 55-mph speed limit on pit road.

"Was I going too fast on pit road?" he asked the media after the race.

Who knew? Was he?

"I don't know but No. 28 (Davey Allison) was right behind me and he was gaining on me."

Oh, Earnhardt did hit Ernie Irvan. Ran into Irvan's rear end by accident, and admitted it.

Hey, he's no angel.

> Earnhardt was twice penalized, once for breaking the rules, once for being a bad boy. ... Twice, he had to make up an entire circuit of the mile-and-a-half oval just to be up with the leaders and twice he did it.

May 31, 1993

I wanna be like Dale

by Charles Chandler

Charlotte, N.C.— Jeff Gordon is a 21-year-old NASCAR Winston Cup rookie who says and does all the things nice guys say and do.

"Awesome," Gordon said of his second-place finish Sunday in the Coca-Cola 600. "Anytime you run second to Dale Earnhardt, that's great."

Beneath his smiling, boy-next-door exterior is a terror of a driver who may someday rule his sport.

Just think of what he did Sunday.

He started the race 21st, missed one pit stop and was penalized 15 seconds by NASCAR for making a quick start at the end of a caution period on Lap 223, putting him a lap off the lead and in 15th place.

And, still, he finished second.

Rick Hendrick, Gordon's car owner, paid his driver perhaps the ultimate compliment when he said it was no coincidence Gordon and Earnhardt made up a full lap late in Sunday's race.

"He's got a lot of Dale in him," Hendrick said of Gordon. "They both smell it when it's close and they want to go for it."

Earnhardt called Gordon "a tough little driver."

"I'm glad he didn't catch me," said Earnhardt. "This was one of his better races. To run good here at Charlotte shows a lot. He's tough to handle, and he's going to be tough to handle."

June 7, 1993

WIN NO. 3: DOVER
A marathon on wheels

by Tom Higgins

**"If it means I'm going to win the races,
they can put me a lap down at the start."**
—Dale Earnhardt

Dover, Del.—Streaking Dale Earnhardt held off Dale Jarrett and won a brutal Budweiser 500 Sunday at Dover Downs, a race in which Rusty Wallace emerged unhurt from another hard crash.

Earnhardt took the checkered flag 4 car lengths ahead of fellow Chevrolet driver Jarrett in the NASCAR Winston Cup Series event, slowed by 12 wrecks and a track record-tying 14 caution periods.

"I dodged some wrecks, but thankfully they weren't that close for me," said Earnhardt, red-faced after the marathon that lasted 4 hours, 44 minutes, 6 seconds. "A lot of guys were clipping each other and spinning. I think they were a little anxious at times."

Earnhardt had a bit of misfortune Sunday, twice losing a lap because of cut tires. But his Lumina was so strong he easily made up the deficits for a third victory this season, third at Dover Downs and 56th of his career.

"If it means I'm going to win the races, they can put me a lap down at the start," Earnhardt joked.

After qualifying for a race, Dale Earnhardt helps his crew to push his car back to the garage. (Christopher A. Record/The Charlotte Observer)

Mark Martin, Dale Earnhardt, and Rusty Wallace (front to back) race in the Mello Yellow 500. (Mark Sluder/The Charlotte Observer)

July 4, 1993

WIN NO. 4: DAYTONA (SORT OF)
Last-lap winner

by Tom Higgins

Daytona Beach, Fla.—Dale Earnhardt, a master at saving race cars on the ragged edge of control, did it again Saturday on the last lap of the Pepsi 400 at Daytona International Speedway and held on to win a NASCAR Winston Cup Series thriller.

Earnhardt, whose Chevrolet led 110 of 160 laps on the 2.5-mile track, took the check- ered flag 2 car lengths ahead of Sterling Marlin's Ford for a 55th career victory. He expanded his lead toward a sixth Winston Cup championship to a com- manding 251 points over Dale Jarrett halfway through the 30-race season.

"It got pretty busy that last lap, pretty busy. I had to crack the throttle a tick and

> "I got my nose in there the last lap and Earnhardt kind of wiped it for me."
> —Kenny Schrader

pinched Kenny Schrader into the wall. We made contact. Our cars got together. That enabled Sterling Marlin to get alongside Kenny, and he was coming on but I blocked him," Earnhardt said.

"I got my nose in there the last lap and Earnhardt kind of wiped it for me," Schrader said.

It was the 20th win overall at Daytona for Earnhardt and his sec- ond victory in the 400, which he also won in 1990.

However, conspicuously missing from Earnhardt's racing resume at the circuit's most famous track is a triumph in the Daytona 500, an event he often has domi- nated only to be beaten at the very end.

WIN NO. 5: POCONO
Davey Allison and Alan Kulwicki: A tribute

by Tom Higgins

Dale Earnhardt outran Rusty Wallace for a victory Sunday in a Miller Genuine Draft 500 thriller, but it was what the two did immediately after the NASCAR Winston Cup Series race that will likely be remembered most.

On the "cool down" lap after the checkered flag, Wallace thrust a flag bearing the No. 28 out the window of his Pontiac as he circled the 2.5-mile track. Earnhardt maneuvered his Chevrolet alongside Wallace, pointing to the flag to draw it to the attention of fans.

No. 28 is the numeral borne by the Ford Davey Allison drove so brilliantly for the Robert Yates Racing team of Charlotte. Allison, 32, died Tuesday of injuries he suffered Monday in the crash of a helicopter he was piloting.

Earnhardt then pulled to the start/finish line where his Richard Childress crew awaited with an even larger No. 28 flag.

As Earnhardt stayed in the car, the crewmen knelt around the machine in prayer. Fans seemed almost frozen in the grandstands.

Earnhardt then circled the triangular track clockwise, holding the flag.

It was a "Polish Victory Lap," a combination tribute to Allison and Alan Kulwicki, the 1992 Winston Cup champion who lost his life April 1 in the crash of a private plane.

"It has been a bad year, losing both Davey and Alan," Earnhardt said after climbing from his car. "I want them back. I'd gladly have run second to them today to have them back."

Said Wallace: "We wanted to remember the Allison family today. I wish I could have done the reverse lap for Alan and brought the No. 28 flag out."

Earnhardt said, "I motioned for Rusty to go back around with me, but he didn't see me. I wish he had."

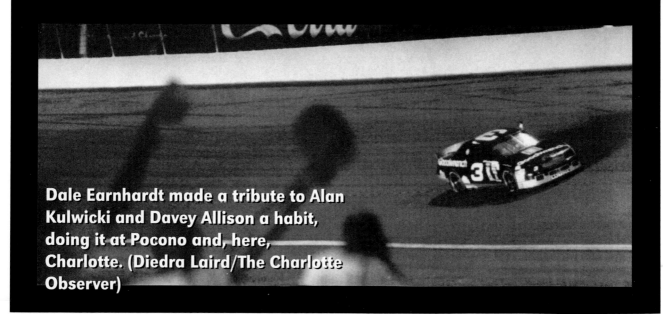

Dale Earnhardt made a tribute to Alan Kulwicki and Davey Allison a habit, doing it at Pocono and, here, Charlotte. (Diedra Laird/The Charlotte Observer)

July 26, 1993

WIN NO. 6: TALLADEGA
"Wildly violent"

by Tom Higgins

"I hated to see those crashes. But Neil, who crawled out feeling well, was doing what he wanted to do, just like Stanley Smith was doing what he enjoys."—Earnhardt, on crashes involving Neil Bonnett and Stanley Smith

Talladega, Ala.—In a NASCAR Winston Cup Series race wildly violent even by Talladega Superspeedway standards, Dale Earnhardt won a DieHard 500 thriller Sunday.

Earnhardt beat fellow Chevrolet driver Ernie Irvan to the finish line by 6 inches, with Ford's Mark Martin and Pontiac's Kyle Petty following just feet behind in two-abreast battling.

Dale Jarrett took fifth place in a Chevy, right on the bumpers of Martin and Petty.

"I didn't have a plan for the last lap,"

Earnhardt said after a race marred by airborne crashes involving Neil Bonnett and Jimmy Horton, and Stanley Smith suffering head injuries termed very critical. "I just played the game until the game ended.

Said Irvan, who narrowly missed a third straight Winston Cup victory at Talladega: "Dale and I had a heck of a drag race coming to the finish. I've got him a couple times and he's got me a few times. It was a great race. It was only inches, but I knew he beat me."

Earnhardt, a master at anticipating rivals' moves and countering them, drew on the instinct again for a sixth 500-mile victory at NASCAR's fastest speedway, two more than anyone else.

Earnhardt's 59th career victory left him with a commanding 234-point lead over Jarrett toward a sixth Winston Cup championship after 18 of 30 races.

Dale Earnhardt climbs from his car to greet crew members and well-wishers after wrapping up the Winston Cup title at Atlanta Motor Speedway. (Mark B. Sluder/The Charlotte Observer)

Dale celebrates winning the 1993 Winston Cup Championship in Atlanta with his daughter, Taylor Nicole. (Mark B. Sluder/The Charlotte Observer)

November 15, 1993

Dale takes the sixth

by Tom Higgins

Hampton, Ga.— It was a humble, close-to-tears Dale Earnhardt that emerged from Victory Lane late Sunday at Atlanta Motor Speedway to talk about his sixth NASCAR Winston Cup championship.

"It's really unbelievable to me," Earnhardt said. "I never even dreamed that I would someday be in Winston Cup racing. It's a miracle to me what we've accomplished. ... I go back home to Kannapolis and Mooresville and I'm just one of the guys. It's impressive what someone from a small town can do and accomplish.

"I'm proud of that. I'm proud to be Ralph Earnhardt's son. And I'm proud of my team ... bouncing back from a bad year like 1992, when we won only one race and finished 12th in the point standings."

Ralph Earnhardt, Dale's dad and a former NASCAR Sportsman Division champion, died in 1973 of a heart attack.

Earnhardt finished 10th Sunday and claimed the championship, worth a minimum $1.5 million, although Rusty Wallace won the race. Earnhardt finished 80 points ahead of Wallace, losing 46 points in the season finale.

"We wrapped the championship up before the race was over," said Earnhardt, who could have finished as low as 34th and still won. "We got it when at least eight cars were sidelined.

"Then, I went racing. I wanted to win the championship by taking the race. But I got a little too aggressive and too carried away with it and I got in trouble. Then I had to just ride.

"No matter whether you're a six-time champion or not, that don't make you King Kong going into the corner. It brought me back to earth."

Earnhardt, 42, was referring to a tangle with the Ford of Greg Sacks on Lap 225. The collision dented the side of Earnhardt's Chevrolet.

"In shooting for a seventh championship, which would tie Richard Petty's record, the pressure will be on from the press, our sponsor and ourselves. We've got the sixth one behind us now, and we can talk about shooting for it.

"And now, boys and girls," he said, grinning, "we can focus-s-s-s on winning the Daytona 500. Doesn't anybody want to ask when I'm going to win the Daytona 500? You want me to tell you about it now?"

Earnhardt hasn't ever won the sport's biggest race, which annually opens the season.

Races	Won	Top 5	Top 10	Poles	Earnings
31	4	20	25	2	$3,300,733

February 21, 1994

DAYTONA: Same story, different year
by Liz Clarke

Daytona Beach, Fla.—When it comes to an ill-handling race car, nobody's better than Dale Earnhardt.

But even Earnhardt, the six-time Winston Cup champion, couldn't tame his skittish Chevrolet as Sunday's Daytona 500 ground to a close.

With his car drifting farther back on the track, Earnhardt could only watch as Sterling Marlin roared over the finish line, leaving him with seventh place and one more reason for not winning his sport's greatest race in 16 tries.

"The car was just too loose today," Earnhardt said. "What can you say? I just didn't have the car to win it today."

It seemed inconceivable Earnhardt wouldn't win it this year.

He has won everything else in stock-car racing.

He has won everything else at Daytona International Speedway.

In the days leading up to Sunday's Daytona 500, he won a race a day, capturing Thursday's Twin 125 qualifying event, Friday's IROC race, and Saturday's Goody's 300—the latter in classic Earnhardt style.

Earnhardt started second Sunday and grabbed the lead from Ernie Irvan on Lap 11, never straying far from the front for the first 300 miles.

Wrecks snagged a third of the cars in the field at one point or another. Earnhardt's black No. 3 just hummed along.

He took a high line around the track, where his car seemed to work best. But with about 50 laps to go, he fell back.

Earnhardt fans waited for him to start the charge; his race car lingered, drifting higher and higher, and Mark Martin, then Morgan Shepherd zoomed underneath him and away.

Soon, he was so far back only a caution flag could help. It never fell.

"I wasn't a contender this year," Earnhardt said, climbing from his car and going straight into his team's transporter, where his legs seemed to give way. He leaned against the wall.

A reporter asked if he was all right.

"I just got out of a race car. Run 500 miles. Am I all right?" he said, before turning away.

Seven things about No. 3:

Compiled by Tom Higgins

Seven ways Dale Earnhardt is similar to Richard Petty, whose record of seven Winston Cup titles he'll try to tie this season:

1. North Carolinian from small town.
2. Has a major road named for him.
3. Second generation driver, son of a national champion.
4. Worked on own cars early in career in a backyard shop.
5. Shrewd businessman.
6. Almost always wears sunglasses and sports a mustache.
7. Devoted family man.

And seven ways he's very different:

1. More aggressive driving style.
2. Doesn't smoke cigars—or anything else.
3. Doesn't aspire to public office and hasn't formed a political action committee.
4. Hunts and fishes frequently.
5. Doesn't have a museum—yet.
6. Owns an auto dealership and actively promotes it.
7. Can't nap just anywhere.

March 28, 1994
WIN NO. 1: DARLINGTON
Dedicated to Neil Bonnett
by Tom Higgins

"We gave it our best shot. But Earnhardt wore us out."—Mark Martin

Darlington, S.C.—Dale Earnhardt intensified his love affair Sunday with Darlington Raceway, driving to victory in a TranSouth Financial 400 marked by tire wear and overheating engines.

Earnhardt's first NASCAR Winston Cup Series triumph this season was the 60th of his career and ninth at the 1.366-mile track, one short of David Pearson's record.

"You can call this ol' race track a lot of nicknames, and she deserves them," said Earnhardt, who finished a comfortable 7.4 seconds ahead of Ford's Mark Martin. "In fact, she demands them.

"If you respect her and run consistent, you'll have a chance of winning.

"David Pearson taught me that—to use my head every lap and race the track and not the other competitors."

The victory snapped a 16-race nonwinning streak for Earnhardt dating to last July and the DieHard 500 at Talladega (Ala.) Superspeedway.

"I'm never worried, but always concerned when we go that long without winning," Earnhardt said. "The first win each season is tough to get."

Earnhardt dedicated this year's first victory to his best friend, Neil Bonnett, who lost his life Feb. 11 in a crash at Daytona International Speedway.

"I miss that boy more every day," said Earnhardt. "This track, Darlington, reminds me of Neil because he liked to run here and did it so well."

Dale Earnhardt, one of the greatest drivers in NASCAR's first half century, sitting on top of his transporter. (Jeff Siner/The Chalotte Observer)

April 10, 1994

WIN NO. 2: BRISTOL
The points leader

by Tom Higgins

Bristol, Tenn.—Dale Earnhardt escaped an epidemic of trouble that struck most of his top rivals Sunday and easily won a crash-filled Food City 500 at Bristol Raceway.

Earnhardt's second straight NASCAR Winston Cup Series victory gave him the point standings lead toward a seventh championship that would tie retired Richard Petty's record.

Charging from the 24th starting position—farthest back in a field ever for a winner at the .533-mile track—Earnhardt finished a comfortable 7.63 seconds ahead of runner-up Ken Schrader.

Lake Speed placed third.

The top three were left on a lap alone when a yellow flag showed on the 323rd of 500 laps shortly after the other front-runners had pitted under green—and before Earnhardt, Schrader and Speed made scheduled stops.

Chief victim of the inopportune caution period was Geoff Bodine, who'd pitted on Lap 318 after leading impressively for 160 laps.

Bodine's stop gave first place to Earnhardt, who never relinquished it, leading the final 183 laps.

"The game plan of me and Andy Petree, my crew chief, was to stay out a little longer than the others," said Earnhardt, whose win came before a track record crowd estimated at 76,000. "That caution, which was luck, gave us track position and we went on from there.

"The story was a lot of people had trouble and we didn't. It might have looked like we had everybody covered, but we didn't outrun 'em."

Dale Earnhardt's crew celebrates a race victory. (Mark B. Sluder/The Charlotte Observer)

May 2, 1994
WIN NO. 3 TALLADEGA
Thanks, I'll pass
by Tom Higgins

"There was so much passing going on the last lap I didn't know who was passing who. Luckily we wound up in front."

—Dale Earnhardt

Talledega, Ala.—Dale Earnhardt, fending off furious last-lap challenges for the lead, won Sunday's Winston Select 500 at Talladega Superspeedway in a race marred by two multi-car wrecks.

Earnhardt's Chevrolet swept to the checkered flag just feet ahead of Ernie Irvan's Ford and Michael Waltrip's Pontiac in the NASCAR Winston Cup classic.

Waltrip and Schrader each made runs at Earnhardt in a frantic final lap around the 2.66-mile track. Waltrip went inside, Schrader outside, but neither could pull off the pass.

The scrambling enabled Irvan to charge into second place coming through Turn 4, but he stayed behind Earnhardt.

"There was so much passing going on the last lap I didn't know who was passing who," Earnhardt said. "Luckily we wound up in front. It's especially exciting to win such a competitive race."

August 27, 1994
Visiting Irvan in the hospital
by Tom Higgins

Bristol, Tenn.—Ernie Irvan and Dale Earnhardt drew the best from each other on the race track much of this NASCAR season.

Wednesday night, Earnhardt tried to do the same for Irvan in a Michigan hospital.

Earnhardt and fellow driver Mark Martin visited Irvan at St. Joseph Mercy Hospital in Ypsilanti, Mich., Wednesday night. Irvan was critically injured in a crash during practice at Michigan International Speedway last week.

"The doctor had Ernie awake when we came into his room," Martin, Irvan's best friend, said before Goody's 500 time trials at Bristol. "Dale walked to his bedside and said, 'Hey, this is Earnhardt.'

"Ernie immediately got real excited. Dale grabbed his hand and Ernie squeezed his hand. Ernie was looking right at him, trying to focus his eyes on Dale.

"I saw him last Saturday and Sunday nights and got no responses. After they started getting responses from him, I wanted to go back. I wanted to be sure that he knew I'd been there."

This nine-car pileup (above) at the Coca-Cola 600 effectively ended Dale Earnhardt's bid for his third consecutive victory in the event. (Bob Leverone/The Charlotte Observer)

Dale Earnhardt walks away from his wrecked car (left) after bouncing off Jeff Gordon's car while trying to avoid Rusty Wallace's. (Gary O'Brien/The Charlotte Observer)

October 24, 1994
WIN NO. 4: ROCKINGHAM
Seventh heaven in .06 seconds
by Tom Higgins

Rockingham, N.C.— Dale Earnhardt drove to a record-tying seventh NASCAR Winston Cup Series championship Sunday just as he'd hoped in the AC-Delco 500, charging hard for the race victory at N.C. Motor Speedway.

With the title that equaled the total of retired Richard Petty already assured when closest challenger Rusty Wallace fell out with engine trouble, Earnhardt outran Rick Mast to the checkered flag by less than a car length.

Earnhardt's Chevrolet flashed across the line .06 seconds ahead of Mast's Ford before a cheering crowd estimated at 55,000.

Members of the Richard Childress racing team, who have fielded the cars for six of Earnhardt's championships, streamed jubilantly onto pit road. Then, when Earnhardt took an extra victory lap, the crew led by Andy Petree stood atop the pit wall and bowed in salute.

Earnhardt dedicated the latest championship to the late Neil Bonnett, his best friend who was killed Feb. 11 in a crash while practicing for the season-opening Daytona 500. He dedicated Sunday's win to the late Frank Wilson, the speedway president who died in August.

"I've got so many people to remember and thank it's unbelievable," said Earnhardt after his fourth victory this season,

second at the track nicknamed "The Rock," and 63rd of his career.

Earnhardt, although holding a commanding 321-point lead over Wallace going into the 29th of the season's 31 races, had been reluctant to discuss the prospects of matching Petty's mark, once considered unapproachable.

"Now, we can talk about it all day long," said Earnhardt, who boosted his lead in the standings to an unbeatable 448 points over Wallace. The title is worth $1.25 million.

Earnhardt, who started 20th, led four times for 108 laps, including the final 77. He averaged 126.407 mph and earned $60,600.

Mark B. Sluder/The Charlotte Observer

October 24, 1994

Celebrate? Get my saddle

by Tom Higgins

> "I'm getting away. My Indian friends don't care anything about racing."
>
> —Dale Earnhardt

Rockingham, N.C.—Seven NASCAR Winston Cup Series championships and all the money and acclaim they mean hardly have changed Dale Earnhardt.

When he won his first Winston Cup championship in 1980, Earnhardt and a few friends flew to Las Vegas to celebrate.

Earnhardt, then 29, took in a show, played the slots awhile and after a few hours decided something else would be more fun and suit his tastes better.

"If I fly out now there's a tree stand in the woods in Chester County (S.C.) where I can be deer hunting by late afternoon," Earnhardt said.

And away he went.

Earnhardt clinched the championship that tied Richard Petty's once seemingly invincible record Sunday in championship style, winning the AC-Delco 500 at N.C. Motor Speedway by narrowly edging Rick Mast.

With the champion's $1.25 million share of a $3 million point fund assured, many drivers undoubtedly would go for some glamour and champagne.

Not Earnhardt.

After leaving the speedway in the Sandhills he was flying to New Mexico where he planned to mount a horse today and ride into the wilds of an Indian reservation to hunt elk.

"I'm getting away," Earnhardt said with a grin. "My Indian friends don't care anything about racing."

Maybe while he's in the remote mountains, scanning the ridges and valleys for a trophy animal, Earnhardt can grasp the significance of claiming as many crowns as Petty, NASCAR's King Richard.

"You can't sum it up in just a word or phrase," said Earnhardt. "It's going to take a long time to sink in."

By clinching the 1994 Winston Cup title, Dale Earnhardt matches Richard Petty's record of seven championships. Here's how their performances compared in each of their winning seasons:

Dale Earnhardt

Year	Races	Wins	Top 5	Top 10	Money won
1980	31	5	19	23	$588,926
1986	29	5	16	23	$1,168,100
1987	29	11	21	24	$2,069,243
1990	29	9	18	23	$3,083,056
1991	29	4	14	21	$2,396,685
1993	30	6	17	21	$3,353,789
1994	29	4	19	24	$1,453,370

Richard Petty

Year	Races	Wins	Top 5	Top 10	Money won
1964	61	9	36	41	$98,810
1967	48	27	38	39	$130,275
1971	46	21	38	41	$309,225
1972	31	8	25	27	$227,015
1974	30	10	22	23	$299,175
1975	30	13	21	24	$378,865
1979	31	5	23	27	$531,292

Dale Earnhardt takes a victory lap after wrapping up a seventh Winston Cup title to tie Richard Petty's record. (Mark B. Sluder/The Charlotte Observer)

October 30, 1994
Petty: It's hard to compare
by Tom Higgins

Phoenix, Ariz.—Dale Earnhardt's thoughts about tying Richard Petty for the most NASCAR Winston Cup Series championships, with seven, are well-known.

"In stock car racing, Richard Petty will always be the King," Earnhardt has said repeatedly. "No one will ever out-do him."

But what are the views of Petty—who won a record 200 races, 95 more than second-place David Pearson—on seeing his once seemingly invincible mark matched by Earnhardt?

"It's one of those deals where you can't compare," said Petty, 57. "It's like Hank Aaron beating Babe Ruth. They did their things in different times. Same with me and Dale.

"Right now he's the top dog going through here. I went through with Pearson, Cale Yarborough, Fred Lorenzen and Bobby Allison.

"So where would that put Earnhardt if he had run against them? He'd be up there with 'em.

"But if you go back and try to figure out

of all the drivers who's the best, there ain't no such thing."

Different approach

Fans argue about which driver, Petty or Earnhardt, faced the toughest competition for their championships. Petty says the eras are totally different.

"People didn't run for championships then (in the 1960s and early '70s, when he took titles in 1964, '67, '71, '72, '74 and '75). They ran to win races.

"When the season was over they added it up. There could have been three or four championships I could have won if I had been looking at it that way."

The title also wasn't worth nearly as much as it has been since R.J. Reynolds Tobacco Company began boosting the postseason point fund.

The minimum bonus Earnhardt clinched last week while winning the AC-Delco 500 at N.C. Motor Speedway is $1.25 million. Petty's largest championship bonus was $150,000 in 1979.

Assessing Earnhardt

When asked for his thoughts on Earnhardt as a driver, Petty shook his Stetson-covered head and replied without hesitation.

"He's really good," Petty said. "He's just got natural ability, like a Pearson. He doesn't have to work at it."

Petty said that Earnhardt staying with the same team owner for 11 years, Richard Childress, has been pivotal to his success. Earnhardt has won six of his championships in Childress team cars.

"I saw a good quote from Darrell Waltrip about that," Petty said. "Darrell said, 'Drivers win races, teams win championships.'"

Petty permitted himself a bit of what he called "horn blowing" in contrasting his 200 victories to Earnhardt's 63.

"If you compare records, the only thing he's even or above in is championships, not races. At Martinsville and North Wilkesboro we won 15 both places," Petty said. "At Daytona we won seven. I mean, he's not even in the picture."

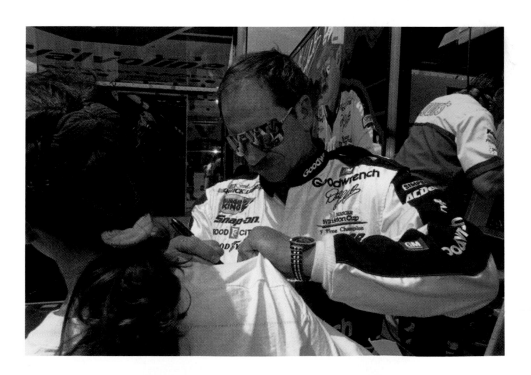

*Always a fan favorite, Dale Earnhardt signs autographs.
(Christopher A. Record/ The Charlotte Observer)*

Chapter Eighteen:
1995: Who's on my bumper?

Races	Won	Top 5	Top 10	Poles	Earnings
31	5	19	23	3	$3,154,241

February 19, 1995
Daytona 500 Jinx: 17 and counting?
by Tom Higgins

Daytona Beach, Fla.—Ordinarily a professional athlete would be honored to have his name listed in any category with Sam Snead, Arnold Palmer, Ernie Banks, Phil Niekro, Dan Marino and Patrick Ewing.

Not Dale Earnhardt.

Not in one conspicuous category.

Snead never won the U.S. Open nor Palmer the PGA Championship. Baseball greats Banks and Niekro never made it to the World Series. Prolific passer Marino doesn't have a Super Bowl championship ring. The towering Ewing has dunked everything but an NBA title.

And Dale Earnhardt never has won the Daytona 500.

Earnhardt, who would have won the season-opening NASCAR Winston Cup race several times if it covered only 499 miles, tries for the 17th year to lead the final mile today.

> "I think everybody, including all the drivers, wants to see Dale win the Daytona 500 some day. Just not this time."
>
> —Darrell Waltrip

Earnhardt, a seven-time Winston Cup champion who some rate NASCAR's greatest driver ever, starts on the front row with pole-winner Dale Jarrett.

"Ol' Neil Bonnett rode with me today and he's going to ride with me to a win in the 500. I'll be back up here (in the press box) Sunday." Earnhardt said after a 125-mile qualifying race.

Since qualifying, it has been a typical Speed Week at Daytona for Earnhardt: A sweep.

Now, only the Daytona 500, the lone NASCAR major unconquered by Earnhardt, remains.

"I haven't used up all my luck again in the preliminaries," Earnhardt insisted Saturday. "I'm going to win this time. I think I have my best chance ever.

"Even counting the times we've come so close and lost, I feel this is the best car I've ever had here."

"This is the Daytona 500, and I don't reckon I'm supposed to win the . . . thing."—Earnhardt

February 20, 1995

Maybe they should make it the Daytona 499

by Tom Higgins

Daytona Beach, Fla.—**Sterling Marlin** withstood a stirring, dramatic charge by Dale Earnhardt during the Daytona 500's final 11 laps Sunday, and claimed the NASCAR Winston Cup season-opening classic for the second straight year.

The 500 is the only Winston Cup race Marlin has won. It's the only major event Earnhardt never has won in 17 years of trying.

Gambling on a pit stop for four tires during the crash-marred event's 10th and final caution period on laps 187-189, Earnhardt was positioned 14th for the restart behind the other front-runners, who didn't pit.

Working traffic and passing cars spectacularly, seven-time Winston Cup champion Earnhardt was third by Lap 195. On Lap 197 he ran down and passed Mark Martin for second place.

Earnhardt ran down Marlin, too. But he couldn't pass him and finished runner-up for the third time. He also lists finishes of third, fourth and has been fifth four times in the 500.

"I saw Dale coming," Marlin said upon taking his Chevy to Victory Lane. "I was going to block him one way or another or I wasn't coming back the last lap. We'd have swapped some paint. Martin would probably have won the race."

"This is the Daytona 500, and I don't reckon I'm supposed to win the ... thing," Earnhardt said. "If we'd had some drafting help we might have got by Sterling, but he was awful strong. I reckon the best car won. He deserved to win it."

Earnhardt fans support their man. (Christopher A. Record/The Charlotte Observer)

Dale Earnhardt (3) encounters lapped traffic at the First Union 400, and makes contact with Derrick Cope coming out of Turn 4. (Mark B. Sluder/The Charlotte Observer)

April 10, 1995

WIN NO. 1: NORTH WILKESBORO
A race for tired tires

by Tom Higgins

North Wilkesboro, N.C.—Dale Earnhardt overwhelmed the opposition Sunday at North Wilkesboro Speedway and won the First Union 400 for his first NASCAR Winston Cup Series victory this season.

The seven-time national champion took the checkered flag 13.48 seconds ahead of runner-up Jeff Gordon for a 1-2 Chevrolet finish that pushed the Monte Carlo's record this season to 7-0.

"We've finally won one," said Earnhardt, who had driven the Richard Childress racing team's Chevy to five top-four finishes in the previous six races, a stretch in which Gordon, 23, won three

times. "It's amazing, we finally beat 'Wonder Boy.'"

Earnhardt grinned and added, "I'm just kidding. He's just another driver. A good one."

As expected, the race was marked by unusually heavy tire wear and most teams pitted approximately every 50 laps.

Earnhardt went 86 laps on his last set of tires.

"I backed off with a lot of laps left to save the tires," he said. "Even when I did that, I was still pulling away. My crew chief, Andy Petree, and the rest of the guys had the car set up perfect.

"We're looking good for now and for the future."

May 8, 1995

WIN NO. 2: SEARS POINT
Passing the road test
by Tom Higgins

Sonoma, Calif.—Dale Earnhardt passed race dominator Mark Martin on the 73rd of 74 laps Sunday at Sears Point Raceway and dramatically made the Save Mart 300 the first road course victory of his NASCAR Winston Cup career.

Martin had kept his Ford in front for all but two circuits since Lap 6 on the 2.52-mile, 11-turn track.

But running downhill through looping Turn 6, nicknamed "The Carousel," Martin drove into a patch of oil and slipped slightly. Earnhardt, who had trailed within a few feet of Martin virtually throughout, darted inside and pulled off the decisive pass in his Chevrolet.

"Mark's car kicked out just enough to open the door for me," said Earnhardt, who has been trying to win on one of NASCAR's serpentine speedways since 1979.

"We're going to send Richard back to Africa next February so we can win the Daytona 500, too," Earnhardt joked, referring to team owner Richard Childress being on safari when Earnhardt recorded his first career road course victory.

Earnhardt, making his 36th road-course start, finished .32 seconds, about a car length, in front of runner-up Martin.

"I was as careful as I could be the last lap without giving Mark a chance to get back around me," said Earnhardt, 44. "I knew I was close to getting my first win on a road course, and I didn't want to blow it after trying for so long."

Earnhardt stands atop his transporter, king of all he surveys. (Davie Hinshaw/The Charlotte Observer)

Bad night for the paint job
by Ron Green

Charlotte, N.C.—It's a good nickname for him, one that fits his daring racing style, but you may not want to mention it for a while.

He did a little more terminating Saturday night in the Winston Select race at Charlotte Motor Speedway than he would care to have brought up over his morning coffee.

In 70 laps of racing, 10 cars wrecked in accidents that he accidentally triggered. That was eight others and his twice. He must have felt like Dennis The Menace out there.

When Jeff Gordon won the Winston Select, Earnhardt was in the garage area looking at the remains of his Chevrolet.

Maybe it was the color. Earnhardt's No. 3 is ordinarily black, but he agreed to drive a silver car on this occasion to celebrate R.J. Reynolds' 25th anniversary as a sponsor of the Winston Cup program. Maybe it was like Michael Jordan wearing No. 45 and losing his jump shot.

Whatever, Earnhardt had a tough night.

It began with just a thrill. In the first of three segments of this unique race, he started fourth but quickly made a move to the front. There, he came abreast of his buddy Rusty Wallace. Suddenly, they clanged together and got a little squirrelly, which is not good when you have the entire field packed tightly behind you.

Memories of last year's Winston Select flashed to mind. They tangled in that one and wound up in smoking wreckage.

But they're good. They straightened up

> Tough night or not, Earnhardt is still the best. ... But he can see the future in his rear view mirror. It is Jeff Gordon, and it's coming on fast.

this time and hurried on off.

In the second segment, in heavy traffic, Dale Jarrett appeared to slow just a fraction to let another car tuck in, but Earnhardt, who was behind him, didn't slow. He tapped Jarrett's bumper, sending him spinning, and when the smoke cleared, five cars had run into something hard.

Asked what happened, Jarrett growled, "Got hit."

Everyone went in for pit stops. When they came out, Earnhardt was sent to the rear of the pack for having exited pit road too fast.

Told you it was a bad night.

But Earnhardt brought his beat-up silver car back near the front and finished the second segment in third place. That gave him a second-row start behind Gordon for the 10-lap shoot-out.

Now, the last 10 laps of the Winston Select is not for the faint of heart. It invites every instinct in a racer's body to express itself in some wild and crazy racing.

On the first of the 10 laps, with Darrell Waltrip coming out of the third turn, Earnhardt went under a car and Waltrip went above it. Car sandwich.

Gordon watched and said to himself, "No way are they gonna get out of the fourth turn without wrecking."

Earnhardt rarely if ever complains if someone wrecks him. And when he wrecks somebody, he admits it.

"I just got loose and lost it and got into Darrell," he said.

A thought occurred to some of us as the cars rolled toward those last 10 laps with Gordon looking at Earnhardt in his rear view mirror.

Tough night or not, Earnhardt is still the best, still running out front the way he has for years. But he can see the future. It is Jeff Gordon, and it's coming on fast.

Some of the other drivers call Gordon, The Kid.

If The Kid keeps going the way he has the past couple of years, they'll soon be calling him The Man.

The sparks fly as Dale Earnhardt and Darrell Waltrip hit the wall exiting Turn 4 on the first lap of the final segment of The Winston Select. The accident was the third involving Earnhardt of the evening, and it allowed Jeff Gordon (lower right) to slip by and cruise to a $300,000 victory. (Mark B. Sluder/The Charlotte Observer)

June 30, 1995

Changing of the Guard? Nah ...

by Leonard Laye

"I'm 44 this year. I was 43 last year. But I'm not losing my reflexes."

—Dale Earnhardt

Daytona Beach, Fla.—For all the buzz this season about the changing of the guard in Winston Cup racing, a familiar face will be looking back at the field in his rear view mirror when the flag drops Saturday for the Pepsi 400.

Dale Earnhardt roared back to the head of the pack Thursday at Daytona International Speedway, adding his own dose of heat to an already sweltering afternoon as he put his Chevrolet on the pole with a speed of 191.355 mph.

Earnhardt had not exactly been missing in action this season: He is, after all, in second place in a tight points race, has two victories and is second in money winnings.

Yet he has not won on a superspeedway, claiming his wins at North Wilkesboro and Sears Point, Calif., and his chances have been cut by three accidents this season. He is coming off his worst finish of the season, 35th at Michigan.

Thursday, though, Earnhardt, 44, was back, leading a Chevrolet sweep of the first five positions.

"We unfortunately had some bad luck and got in some wrecks," said

Earnhardt, who suffered a bruised esophagus in the Michigan crash. "That's the way racing goes, though."

"Am I slowing down? Am I getting old? Am I losing my reflexes? Is that what you're asking?

"I'm 44 this year. I was 43 last year. But I'm not losing my reflexes."

August 5, 1995
WIN NO. 3: INDIANAPOLIS
Big day at the Brickyard
by Tom Higgins

Indianapolis, Ind. — Dale Earnhardt held off Rusty Wallace and Dale Jarrett to win a Brickyard 400 thriller Saturday that appeared destined to be postponed by rain at Indianapolis Motor Speedway.

Thousands of the 300,000 fans who bought tickets had headed home and came rushing back to the grandstands when NASCAR officials finally got the Winston Cup cars on the historic 2.5-mile track 4 hours later than planned. The show was worth sprinting for, especially the final 25 laps following the event's only caution flag as Ford drivers Wallace and Jarrett tried to run down Earnhardt's Chevrolet.

Earnhardt flashed across the yard-wide strip of bricks forming the start/finish line .37 seconds ahead of runner-up Wallace and .904 seconds ahead of the third-place Jarrett.

"To win this race is great," said a breathless Earnhardt, who averaged 131.999 mph, a record for the two-year-old race. "This Richard Childress racing team is hard to beat when we're right.

"I've never won the Daytona 500, our biggest race. The Brickyard is next to it, and we'll sure take it.

"I heard a lot of talk this week that we're out of (the points race). I think winning at a place as big as Indy shows we aren't dead yet."

James Johnson, CEO of RJR, introduces Winston Cup Champion Dale Earnhardt to the crowd at the inaugural running of the Brickyard 400 at Indianapolis Motor Speedway. (Mark B. Sluder/The Charlotte Observer)

August 29, 1995

Take aspirin, throw Perrier, and call me . . .

by Ron Green

> "I ain't forgetting
> this and I ain't
> forgetting
> Talladega."
> —Rusty Wallace

Bristol, Tenn.— Dale Earnhardt can be so aggravating, he could make Mother Teresa want to slap his face.

It's no surprise, then, that the black-clad, steely-eyed pedal pusher finally made one of his best friends in stock car racing throw something at him and warn Earnhardt more was coming.

Always in the past, pals Earnhardt and Rusty Wallace, the Butch Cassidy and Sundance Kid of stock car racing, have pushed each other aside to take the blame when they've tangled on the race track. But after the race Saturday night, all that nice stopped and nasty started.

In the aftermath of a rain-delayed and grueling race that ended well past midnight, a furious Wallace threw a plastic water bottle at Earnhardt and told him he would see him at Darlington Sunday—and he didn't mean, "Let's do lunch." Although Earnhardt did say, "Call me."

There were undoubtedly some people whose cars have felt the wrath of Earnhardt's bumper over the years who wished Wallace had thrown an anvil instead of a bottle. They don't call Earnhardt the Intimidator and the Terminator for nothing.

Earnhardt had run up behind Wallace in the Goody's 500 at Bristol Raceway and rammed him, knocking Wallace into a wall. NASCAR officials deemed it "rough driving" and penalized Earnhardt by placing him at the rear of the field, not the first time they've banished him to the back.

That's throwing the rabbit into the briar patch. Earnhardt can work his way through a field like water running through rocks. The fans love it, he loves it and NASCAR should love it. Although, along the way, he does tend to bump into people.

He races closer than anyone else, which is why he has won seven points titles and also why he bumps into people.

Wallace made no apparent attempt at revenge, but hours later he was still fuming, and in the garage area he threw the bottle at Earnhardt. Eyewitness reports say the bottle hit Earnhardt's car, then his nose.

And then Wallace said, "I ain't forgetting this and I ain't forgetting Talladega." That was probably not a sentiment like, "We'll always have Paris."

Dale Earnhardt and Rusty Wallace, who were involved in a bumping incident and, later, a shouting match at Bristol, raced close and clean at Darlington. (Mark B. Sluder/The Charlotte Observer)

September 25, 1995

WIN NO. 4: MARTINSVILLE
A flicker of hope
by Tom Higgins

Martinsville, Va.—Dale Earnhardt grabbed the lead from longtime rival Rusty Wallace with 9 laps to go Sunday in the Goody's 500, then pulled away to win at Martinsville Speedway, keeping his hopes for an eighth NASCAR Winston Cup Series championship flickering.

Earnhardt's fourth victory this season, and sixth of his career at the .526-mile track, cut Jeff Gordon's lead toward the $1.3 million title from 309 points to 275 with five of 31 races remaining. Gordon, whose car didn't handle well, finished seventh.

> **"We're still trying, but it's going to be tough to catch Gordon in the points."**
>
> **—Dale Earnhardt**

"We're still trying, but it's going to be tough to catch Gordon in the points," Earnhardt said. Earnhardt flashed to the checkered flag 1.3 seconds ahead of fellow Chevrolet driver Terry Labonte.

"I didn't beat Rusty as a driver," Earnhardt said. "It was the tires more than anything. I think he made a good gamble. He was back there fourth or fifth before the rest of us pitted, so he improved himself.

"I think Terry probably had the best car. But he had trouble on a restart (on Lap 480, after the final caution period). That put him back in bad position."

November 13, 1995

WIN NO. 5: ATLANTA
It's a win; It's a loss
by Tom Higgins

"It's good to end a season so clean. But don't ask what it's like finishing second in points. Everybody knows what I think of second."

—Dale Earnhardt

"Gordon is so young they're going to serve his team milk at the banquet in New York instead of champagne."

—Dale Earnhardt

Hampton, Ga.—Dale Earnhardt scored a dominating victory Sunday in the NAPA 500 at Atlanta Motor Speedway, but it wasn't enough to overtake Jeff Gordon for the NASCAR Winston Cup championship.

Gordon clinched a first title for himself and Hendrick Motorsports when he led the 61st of the race's 328 laps for five bonus points. That gave Gordon, who started the season finale 147 points ahead of defending champion Earnhardt, the cushion he needed for the title worth a minimum $1.3 million.

After a strong early run, Gordon's Chevrolet developed handling problems and he finished 32nd, 14 laps down, winning the championship by 34 points.

"We didn't have a great day, but we had a great year," said Gordon.

Earnhardt started his black Chevrolet in the 11th position on the 1.522-mile track. He swept into first place on Lap 18 and stayed ahead the rest of the way except during or shortly after pit stops.

"It's good to end a season so clean. But don't ask what it's like finishing second in points. Everybody knows what I think of second," Earnhardt said.

Earnhardt led six times for 268 laps, including the final 59, in averaging a track-record 163.632 mph, breaking his mark of 156.849 set in March of 1990. The victory was his seventh at the speedway, tying the retired Cale Yarborough for the most.

"This ended a good year for us," Earnhardt said after his fifth victory of 1995 and 68th of his career.

On Friday, Earnhardt, known for his all-out driving style, told reporters he was going to start "running on the careful side of the ragged edge."

However, on Lap 82 Earnhardt made a daring dive to the inside in Turn 3 and by the time he emerged from Turn 4 he had passed Gordon and Ford foes Ricky Rudd and Mark Martin in a stirring surge that had the crowd estimated at 135,000 screaming.

That's careful?

"I got up this morning feeling cocky," explained Earnhardt. "I love kicking fanny, and that's what the black car did today.

"I sort of filled you reporters full of bull Friday."

Earnhardt congratulated Gordon. However, Earnhardt, 44, couldn't resist teasing the youthful new champion.

"Gordon is so young they're going to serve his team milk at the banquet in New York instead of champagne," Earnhardt said of the series' Dec. 1 awards banquet.

November 14, 1995

Pass the torch?
I don't think so

by Tom Higgins

Charlotte, N.C.—A rousing rivalry undoubtedly has been forged between Jeff Gordon and Dale Earnhardt for at least the next five NASCAR Winston Cup Series seasons.

Both predicted as much Sunday at Atlanta Motor Speedway after Gordon, 24, edged Earnhardt, 44, by 34 points for the circuit's championship, worth a minimum $1.3 million.

"We know Earnhardt isn't going away just because we won this year," said Gordon, who gave himself and team owner Rick Hendrick of Charlotte the treasured title for the first time despite finishing 32nd to Earnhardt's first in the NAPA 500.

"Earnhardt is incredible, the way he drove the last races of the season. He did what he needed to do, but we'd put a total season-long package together and he couldn't bring us down," Gordon added.

"Dale and I get along good. He jokes and gouges on me in the garage, but that's his personality. I think we have some exciting racing ahead of us."

In the last 10 races Earnhardt and his

Richard Childress team finished first twice, second three times, third twice, fifth, seventh and ninth. The surge steadily cut a Gordon lead that once hovered around 300 points.

"Dale thumped us pretty good," said Ray Evernham, Gordon's crew chief. "He's a great champion, a great guy, and you know he's the type that's going to come back tough. I'm sure we're going to have some more good points races with him."

"I think an upstart-old guard rivalry is good for the sport," Earnhardt said. "Darrell Waltrip had one with Richard Petty and Bobby Allison for championships. I had one with Cale Yarborough. And now me and Jeff have got one.

"I get along with Jeff, but we don't travel in the same circles. He plays video games, I go big-game hunting. He wears athletic shoes, I wear boots. What we have in common is that we love to race."

Jeff Gordon talks with Dale Earnhardt and Richard Childress in the garage area at Charlotte Motor Speedway. (Christopher A. Record/The Charlotte Observer)

Chapter Nineteen:
1996: Speed bumps

Races	Won	Top 5	Top 10	Poles	Earnings
31	2	13	17	2	$2,285,926

February 18, 1996
If it's February, it must be . . .
by Tom Higgins

Daytona Beach, Fla.—Get the large headline type ready:

Dale Does it in Daytona 500!

Today, in his 18th try, the seven-time NASCAR Winston Cup Series champion will win his sport's biggest show for the first time.

That's the widespread prediction. Chevrolet driver Earnhardt is the favorite of Las Vegas oddsmakers at 2-1.

He is heavily favored among members of the motorsports media covering the classic race at Daytona International Speedway, gaining six times more votes in a poll than anyone else, including mine.

Why?

Here are 10 reasons I think Earnhardt will take the only major superspeedway event to elude him and make it his 69th career win:

10. Earnhardt's Richard Childress team is the best prepared ever for the 500.

Not only did Earnhardt test during the offseason for the Welcome-based Childress operation, but drivers Dave Marcis and Mike Skinner took part in a research and development program as well.

"We spent more time testing here than probably 10 other tracks together," Earnhardt said.

"This car was developed strictly for Daytona and nowhere else."

9. The Childress team has made a smooth transition in the promotions of David Smith to crew chief and Bobby Hutchens to team manager/chief engineer.

Smith, a veteran of 14 years with Childress as a jackman and a mechanic, succeeds Andy Petree, who returned to owner Leo Jackson's team. Hutchens' spot is newly created.

8. Earnhardt proved the power of his car by winning the pole for the 500 for the first time on Feb. 10 with a lap of 189.510 mph. He drove the same car to victory Thursday in a 125-mile qualifying race.

7. Earnhardt hasn't won everything he's entered this week, his pattern in recent years

only to misfire in the 500. He finished third in the Busch Clash.

6. Earnhardt won't run out of fuel late in the race as he did in 1986, finishing 14th after dominating.

5. Earnhardt won't run over a "chicken bone" as he did in 1990 on the last lap while leading, cutting a tire and winding up fifth after dominating the 500.

4. This time, Earnhardt won't be involved in a late-race tangle as he was in 1991 with the late Davey Allison, just when it appeared they were on the verge of running down leader Ernie Irvan.

3. Today, Earnhardt will have the power to fend off the late race charges of rivals, like the one Jarrett made to wrest the lead, and victory, from Earnhardt on the 199th of the race's 200 laps in 1993.

"Seems like I've won the Daytona 499 a dozen times," Earnhardt said with a smile Thursday after posting his third straight International Race Of Champions victory. It was his 28th win overall at the track, an incredible record. "Someday we're going to lead that final mile, and I've got a good feeling this is that time."

2. Earnhardt wants to eliminate the question he constantly hears from the press and fans, mostly the press, "When are you going to win the Daytona 500?"

1. And, finally, the guaranteed No. 1 reason that Dale Earnhardt, rated by many as NASCAR's top driver ever, and the law of averages finally merge for the checkered flag in the Daytona 500.

I did not draw him in the press box pool.

February 19, 1996

Dale wins!
No, not that Dale!

by Tom Higgins

"I was doing all I could, but every move I made, he moved over to block. We tried to get a run on him, but he was too stout. We finished second again, and that's not a problem. We'll go on."

—Dale Earnhardt,
on Dale Jarrett's Daytona 500 victory

For the second time in four years, Dale Jarrett denied NASCAR rival Dale Earnhardt a first victory Sunday in the Daytona 500.

Jarrett, driving a Ford, did it this time at Daytona International Speedway by holding off Earnhardt's Chevrolet over a tension-packed final 24 laps at the 2.5-mile track.

Brilliantly blocking Earnhardt's darting moves to pass during the last lap, Jarrett got the checkered flag .12 seconds ahead of the race's four-time runner-up, whose record in the season-opening Winston Cup classic is 0-for-18.

"I was doing all I could, but every move I made, he moved over to block. We tried to get a run on him, but he was too stout," Earnhardt said. "We finished second again, and that's not a problem. We'll go on."

Jarrett took a different route to his previous Daytona 500 victory in 1993, when he passed Earnhardt on the next-to-last lap and held on to win by .16 seconds.

"I knew I had a really strong engine, and that was the key today," said Jarrett, 39, who also won the Busch Clash at Daytona on Feb. 11. "I didn't beat Dale Earnhardt, my Robert Yates team's engine beat him. I'm not a better driver, I just had a better engine.

"The last lap seemed like it was 500 miles. I'd rather see anything than that black No. 3 in my mirror."

February 26, 1996

WIN NO. 1: ROCKINGHAM
A bumpy win, just like old times
by Ron Green

Rockingham, N.C.—Dale Earnhardt polished up his image as "the Intimidator" Sunday. Just when he was starting to look like a choirboy.

Even he has spoken, albeit briefly, about driving with a bit more caution now at age 44 than he did in his earlier days when he was earning his reputation as the nightmare in every racer's rear view mirror. But caution ran quivering for the exits Sunday when Earnhardt hooked up with Bobby Hamilton in a breathtaking, lead-swapping battle around North Carolina Motor Speedway.

With the Goodwrench 400 starting to wind down, Hamilton drove the red-and-blue No. 43 that Richard Petty made famous around Earnhardt's black racer into the lead. That lasted one lap. Earnhardt swept back around him.

So Hamilton swept back around Earnhardt. Then suddenly, Hamilton was sliding sideways, tagged by the Intimidator. Hamilton gathered his car up enough to keep it from wrecking, but it scraped the wall and when he opened his eyes, he was back in fifth place.

Earnhardt went on to win. It was his 69th Winston Cup victory. Hamilton, who has never won a Winston Cup race, spun out trying to make up his lost ground, hit the wall and finished 24th.

> "You saw a lot of hard racing all day. There was nothing we saw about that move to create a penalty box situation."
> —NASCAR official at Rockingham, on the Dale Earnhardt-Bobby Hamilton incident.

Earnhardt dismissed the incident as just a racing accident.

"We were coming through the (fourth) corner and there are some bumps down there," he said. "We were bumping and we just bumped together."

Did you bump him or did he bump you?

"I didn't turn the steering wheel to bump him. When we got together, I tried to get off him as fast as he tried to get off me," he said, his hawk-like features showing nothing in the way of emotion.

Hamilton saw it differently.

"I haven't won seven championships (as Earnhardt has) and I haven't won 80-something races but I'm smart enough to know you don't do stuff like that this early in the season," he said. "That's an end-of-the-season move (when positions in the points race are at stake.) He plain hit me. It wasn't close at all."

A NASCAR spokesman testified in Earnhardt's behalf. He said, "We have a penalty box for certain situations. We use it when we're much more sure of an intentional move to advance a position or to create a caution period than we were today.

"You saw a lot of hard racing all day. There was nothing we saw about that move to create a penalty box situation."

Earnhardt is an easy target in a situation such as this. His car is black, his racing uniform is black, therefore his heart must be black. He could have been as blameless as a baby Sunday but when you move the guy in front of you out of the way with a good whack at 100-plus mph, you're going to enhance that Intimidator image, no way around it.

It didn't help that the man he bumped was trying for his first Winston Cup victory and was driving a car owned by Petty, the King himself. And that Earnhardt was driving a Goodwrench-sponsored car in a Goodwrench-sponsored race.

Earnhardt looked down the road apiece, at what he called "the big picture," and said, "I'm just going to race whoever is there racing.

"We'll just see who's next to come up there and race, and see who wins."

He didn't mean it to sound like a threat but it did, like bring 'em on and I'll kick their tailpipes. When the Intimidator says it, it sounds, well, intimidating.

Seven-time Winston Cup champion Dale Earnhardt looks pleased as he leans on the roof of his Chevrolet Monte Carlo. (Mark B. Sluder/The Charlotte Observer)

March 11, 1996

WIN NO. 2: ATLANTA
This prize is the pits

by Tom Higgins

Hampton, Ga. — Dale Earnhardt had a sizzling final pit stop Sunday and converted it into a Purolator 500 triumph that made him the all-time victory leader at Atlanta Motor Speedway.

The win was Earnhardt's eighth at the 1.522-mile track, breaking his tie with retired Cale Yarborough, and boosting his NASCAR Winston Cup career total to 70 victories.

Earnhardt was in second place, 1.47 seconds behind fellow Chevrolet driver Terry Labonte, just before the two made final stops for four tires and fuel. Earnhardt came in on the 291st of the race's 328 laps and the crew got him out in a splendid 19.72 seconds.

"I've got to hand it to my crew again," said a grinning Earnhardt, who took the checkered flag 4.17 seconds ahead of Labonte. "They did it

for me. When I came down the front straight and saw Terry just rolling off of Turn 3, I knew I was in good shape."

Earnhardt averaged 161.298 mph and earned $91,050.

It's the second-fastest NASCAR event in the Atlanta track's 37-year history. The quickest was Earnhardt's victory last November in the season finale NAPA 500, achieved at 163.633 mph.

"We used the same car as last fall," said Earnhardt, who moved into second place in the standings toward an eighth title, 50 points behind leader Dale Jarrett.

Rusty Wallace led 36 laps in his Ford but was sidelined on Lap 178 with a burned piston.

"I had a great time racing Rusty," said Earnhardt. "I thought it might be his day until he had the engine problem."

There were an unusual number of engine failures, with 10 teams listing that as the reason their car was sidelined.

"They sucked the guts out of the engines trying to keep up with Labonte, Rusty and me," said Earnhardt.

Dale Earnhardt's crew races through a pit stop. (Davie Hinshaw/The Charlotte Observer)

The crash at Talladega
by Tom Higgins

"Thank God everyone was able to walk away."—Dale Jarrett

Talladega, Ala.—Jeff Gordon dodged a horrifying crash Sunday that hospitalized Dale Earnhardt and won a DieHard 500 at Talladega Superspeedway that was so wild it had many drivers thanking God to be safe.

Seven-time NASCAR Winston Cup champion Earnhardt was taken to a Birmingham hospital complaining of chest pains and suffering fractures of the sternum and left collarbone.

Doctors said there is a possibility Earnhardt also has a bruised heart, but that can't be determined until today.

"Dale is going to be all right," said Richard Childress, Earnhardt's teamowner. "He's tough."

The victory in the rain-delayed, darkness-shortened race enabled Gordon to overtake Hendrick Motorsports teammate Terry Labonte and Earnhardt for the lead toward the $1.5-million Winston Cup championship.

Earnhardt's ghastly crash occurred as he battled fellow Chevrolet driver Sterling Marlin for the lead going into Turn 1. There was contact between Marlin and Ford rival Ernie Irvan, third at the time, and Marlin tagged Earnhardt in the right rear, turning him hard into the wall. Marlin also hit the wall.

Earnhardt's car flipped on its side and was hit in the roof by the following Ford of Derrike Cope, then by the Chevys of Robert Pressley and Ken Schrader as the machine got back upright. With a crowd estimated at 100,000 watching somberly, it took safety crewmen several minutes to get Earnhardt out of his mangled Monte Carlo. He walked to an ambulance under his own power, clutching his left shoulder.

Dale Earnhardt and Terry Labonte race for position. (Jeff Siner/ The Charlotte Observer)

August 1, 1996

The wreck, in detail

by Tom Higgins

Indianapolis, Ind.—Dale Earnhardt realized he was facing a grim certainty Sunday when contact from a rival turned his leading Chevrolet sideways during the DieHard 500 at Talladega (Ala.) Superspeedway, NASCAR's fastest track.

"I knew I was going to hit the wall and I knew it was going to hurt," Earnhardt, in pain from fractures of the collarbone and sternum, said Wednesday at Indianapolis Motor Speedway.

Despite his injuries, Earnhardt is planning to drive in today's time trials for Saturday's Brickyard 400.

Although obviously in discomfort, Earnhardt managed to smile during a news conference in which he was joined by team owner Childress.

After expressing thanks to well-wishers, Earnhardt discussed the violent accident that produced his injuries.

"As we came through the tri-oval (homestretch) I looked in the mirror and saw the No. 4 car (Sterling Marlin) to my right rear and the No. 28 (Ernie Irvan) behind me," Earnhardt said. "Then, going toward Turn 1, I felt contact in the right rear and around I went.

"That's when I knew what was coming.

"I remember everything.

"When I turned abruptly into the wall is when I broke my sternum. Then the car got up on its side and slid along and I could see the asphalt pavement through the window net.

"I hunkered down as much as I could and I was gripping the steering wheel with both hands to keep from being thrown around in the cockpit, 'cause I knew following cars were going to hit me.

"I saw Derrike Cope coming and he hit me in the roof, mashing the front of the roof down toward the dash. Then Robert Pressley hit me, and I think this collision broke my left collarbone. As my car got back on its wheels, Kenny Schrader hit me."

Earnhardt grinned.

"Kenny told me, 'I seen you and I aimed for you,'" Earnhardt said.

"Smoke was rolling out from under the dash because a lot of wires were burning. I was hurting, but I was able to reach out and switch the battery off.

"I could hear Richard calling me on the radio. And I could hear Richard talking with my wife, Teresa, who had a radio. My radio wouldn't transmit, and I couldn't talk back.

"I remember the rescue crew getting to my car. Also a couple NASCAR guys. I told them not to cut the roof off, 'cause I thought I could get out with a little help.

"I did get out, and I wanted to lay down, but couldn't because of the pain. That's why I walked to the ambulance rather than getting on a stretcher."

August 10, 1996

Winning a pole, one-handed

by Rick Bonnell

Watkins Glen, N.Y.— **Dale Earnhardt fans probably always thought their driver could top the field with one hand tied behind his back.**

That's roughly what Earnhardt accomplished Friday.

A broken sternum and collarbone, suffered in a wreck at Talladega, Ala., two weeks ago, made Earnhardt a virtual one-armed driver. It didn't stop him from winning the pole at the Bud at the Glen with a track-record speed of 120.733 mph.

Earnhardt will start at the front of Sunday's race alongside Dale Jarrett (120.375 mph) and Ricky Rudd (120.322).

"When you're going after something like we were in qualifying, you're focused on that. You don't feel the pain as much," said Earnhardt. "As I went across that (finish) line and relaxed, the pain was there.

"It's hard to breathe. I'm short of breath ... It feels good to relax, but it hurts. It's a good hurt."

August 12, 1996

It's iron . . . what?

by Rick Bonnell

Watkins Glen, N.Y.— **Dale Earnhardt and owner Richard Childress thought they had a deal; Earnhardt would get out of his pole-sitting Chevrolet at the first caution flag.**

Then Earnhardt lived up to one of his nicknames—"Ironhead"—and kept on driving when caution was declared on the fourth lap of Sunday's Bud at the Glen.

"I feel too good!" Earnhardt radioed to Childress as he veered away from the pits.

He knew what he was doing. Despite a broken collarbone and injured sternum, Earnhardt led 51 of the first 54 laps Sunday and finished sixth to stay within 76 points of Terry Labonte in the Winston Cup points race.

"What's his name? Ironhead? Guess he was Ironchest today," Geoff Bodine said.

Earnhardt never did give up his seat to relief driver David Green, though he'd maintained all weekend he would at some point in the 90-lap race.

"I got a little soft on brakes there at the end. I had used them pretty hard all day. I think the driver gave out a little bit too," Earnhardt said of his performance.

"I had David Green's seat in there and I held on. If I get over this soreness this week, I'll be OK next week at Michigan."

Christopher A. Record/The Charlotte Observer

October 2, 1996

Seven and seven forever?

by Tom Higgins

Charlotte, N.C.—Mathematically, Dale Earnhardt still has a chance this season to win the eighth NASCAR Winston Cup Series championship he craves.

Realistically, he probably has no chance.

As tonight's qualifying opens Race Week for Sunday's UAW-GM Quality 500 at Charlotte Motor Speedway, Earnhardt is fourth in the standings, trailing leader Jeff Gordon by 351 points.

> "Earnhardt is the type of guy who'll have a fire burning in him as long as he's in racing in any capacity. But just because the will is there, it doesn't mean the way is."
>
> **—A NASCAR driver**

Earnhardt has only four races to erase the deficit—CMS, Rockingham, Phoenix and Atlanta.

Earnhardt's hopes would be more substantial if it were only he and Gordon in the tussle for a title worth a minimum $1.5 million. But it isn't.

Between the two are Terry Labonte and Dale Jarrett. Earnhardt is 240 points down to Labonte and 169 behind Jarrett.

All three drivers are unlikely to experience enough trouble before the checkered flag Nov. 10 at Atlanta to enable Earnhardt to become the first eight-time champion.

Earnhardt shares the record for titles with Richard Petty, now a team owner. The two are marketing "Seven and Seven" souvenirs.

Is it destined to forever be "Seven and Seven?"

A rival team owner, one of NASCAR's most respected figures, thinks this is the case.

"Dale is 45 years old now, and when you get to that age a long season like the 32 races NASCAR will run in 1997 wears on you," said the competitor, who asked that his name not be used. "Earnhardt is the type of guy who'll have a fire burning in him as long as he's in racing in any capacity.

"But just because the will is there, it doesn't mean the way is."

I feel the opposite.

I think Earnhardt and his Richard Childress racing team will mount a furious run next season and win.

After what has happened to Earnhardt during this year's tour, it won't simply be a fire burning within him. It'll be an inferno.

I've known Earnhardt since he started his first Winston Cup race in 1975, and he isn't the sort of driver to take this standing up.

He'll take it by sitting down determinedly in his race car next season.

"The Man In Black" will be back.

Chapter Twenty:
1997: Season-long struggle

Races	Won	Top 5	Top 10	Poles	Earnings
32	0	7	16	0	$2,151,909

"Unless I am very, very wrong, it's going to be a great year for us."

—Dale Earnhardt

February 13, 1997
He does, and he does . . . and he doesn't
by David Poole

Daytona Beach, Fla.—For all Dale Earnhardt has done at Daytona International Speedway, what he hasn't done is that much more amazing.

"I have won more races at Daytona than any driver, living or dead," Earnhardt said.

That's not bragging, that's fact.

But unless and until Earnhardt wins the Daytona 500, he will still have what football announcer John Madden calls a "yeah, but" hanging over his career. As in yeah, Earnhardt has had an incredible career, but he never won Winston Cup racing's biggest

event.

Today, he'll take to the track in the second of this afternoon's 125-mile qualifying races. And if Earnhardt has been cursed on the final Sunday of Speedweeks, on Thursday he has been bulletproof.

Earnhardt has won his 125-miler nine times overall and he has not lost one since he finished third in 1989.

"Maybe we won't win anything up until the 500 this week," said Earnhardt, who finished third in last Sunday's Busch Clash, an event he has won a record six times. "Maybe we will just save it all for the 500 this year."

February 17, 1997

Daytona just gets weirder

by Ron Green

Daytona Beach, Fla.—At some point while he was wrecking, perhaps while he was upside down going about 190 mph, or maybe when he landed on top of Ernie Irvan's car, or when he was spinning wildly through traffic, Dale Earnhardt thought, well, so far, so good.

One moment, the man called the Intimidator had been in second place in the Daytona 500 as the last laps of a wild and wonderful race wound down. The next moment, he was sideways and airborne and upside down and against the wall and spinning and generally in a fix.

The thousands watching from the grandstands held their breaths. This could be bad. Just Thursday, he had said, "I feel like I'm bulletproof," but his black Chevy looked like it had been hit by cannon fire.

But then Earnhardt climbed out of the wreckage. "I didn't hear no loud bangs and didn't feel any hard crashes so I figured I must be OK so far," he said. "And then it stopped and I got out.

"I got in the ambulance and looked back over there and I said, 'Man, the wheels ain't knocked off that car yet.' I went back over there and looked at the wheels and I told the guy in the car (who was preparing to haul it away) to flip the switch, and it fired up.

"I said, 'Get out. I gotta go.'"

And he went. He climbed back into the remains of his car and drove it around the track to his pit. His crew went to work on it, ripping stuff off, taping stuff down, and Earnhardt took what was left back out to finish what he had started.

He's 45 years old, rich as an oil baron and has nothing left to prove to anybody, but as long as that ol' car would run, he was gonna drive it. Anybody else—anybody else—would have taken a seat in the ambulance and ridden off, and let the wreckers put that heap on a hook. But not ol' Ironhead.

It wasn't the triumphant ride for which he had hoped. He has won 70 Winston Cup races, has won 29 races of various types on this track and has been the Winston Cup champion seven times, and has won more than $28 million but he has never won the Daytona 500.

He thought Sunday might be the day. You could tell he liked his chances of finally ending the jinx. And there he was in second place with 11 laps to go, sitting there just waiting for the right time to make his move, and then suddenly the world was spinning every which way and pieces of his car were flying around like the sea gulls that hang around the speedway.

Jeff Gordon, who would go on to win the race, had started to pass him when the accident happened. The young champion said, "I saw his car push up (toward the wall) and give me an opening so I went. When he came back down off the wall, he hit me

> "After the race (on the cool-down lap), I saw this mangled black No. 3 coming up behind me and I thought, 'Uh oh,' but he pulled up beside me and gave me a thumbs-up sign and I knew he understood I was just trying to do what he was trying to do, win the Daytona 500."
>
> **—Jeff Gordon**

square in the door, which was lucky. If he'd hit me a little farther back, I would have been caught up in the wreck.

"After the race (on the cool-down lap), I saw this mangled black No. 3 coming up behind me and I thought, 'Uh oh,' but he pulled up beside me and gave me a thumbs-up sign and I knew he understood I was just trying to do what he was trying to do, win the Daytona 500."

Earnhardt says he can get along fine without ever winning this race, but he can't. He's done everything else. He wants this one, because he's a racer.

His ride around those last laps in that piece of junk might have looked funny to some. But to some, it looked noble.

Dale Earnhardt drives his battered car down pit road after being involved in an accident with Ernie Irvan in the backstretch of Daytona International Speedway. Earnhardt did finish the 1997 race after his crew taped his car together. (Jeff Siner/The Charlotte Observer)

Shifting to a lower gear
by Ron Green

Charlotte, N.C.—Dale Earnhardt has made a career of driving on the ragged edge—a lead-footed legend, all tire smoke, horsepower and bravado.

Where Richard Petty ended, Earnhardt began. But Earnhardt has arrived at the inevitable moment in his career when there is more racing glory behind him than ahead. Winston Cup wins—he has 70—are now elusive.

"Hell, I know it," says Earnhardt. "You don't have to tell me."

When he starts today's Coca-Cola 600 at Charlotte Motor Speedway, it will mark 14 months since he last notched a Winston Cup victory. Earnhardt hasn't won in 37 starts, his longest winless streak since 1984.

He's 46 years old with just one top-five finish this season. A record-setting eighth season points championship appears increasingly unlikely. People wonder if they're witnessing his decline even as they cheer their lungs raw for him.

Has time softened the driver widely known as "the Intimidator"?

"Everybody has their time. I'm still having mine, and I'm enjoying it," Earnhardt says. "Maybe I'm not right at the peak of it as much as I was but I'm still there.

"I'm still a factor and a contender and by no means ready to throw in the towel and give up. Or hand over the flag. (They're) going to have to take it from me."

He spends many dawns prowling his Mooresville farm, watching the world wake up. Alone with his thoughts, he ponders his career.

Other than his family, nothing—not his farm, his Chevrolet dealership, his Learjet, his fishing boats or his hunting expeditions—consumes Earnhardt like racing.

He wants an eighth points championship. He looks at Jeff Gordon and sees racing's future. But Earnhardt isn't ready for racing to go there without him.

"You could be content with seven championships because you tied the King (Petty). But that eighth one would make the difference," he says.

Of more immediate concern, Earnhardt would like to win another race. He's won at least one in each of the last 15 years.

"When you listen on television, it's like they're saying he's a loser. It's ridiculous," says Earnhardt's wife, Teresa.

His list of finishes in the past year is littered with 29ths, 16ths and 12ths. Earnhardt may never win 11 races in a season again like he did in 1987, but it's been a sudden drop.

"If you get just a little behind, you go from winning to wondering what happened," says Richard Childress, Earnhardt's car owner.

What has happened?

A key moment came July 28 at Talladega, Ala., last year. Earnhardt entered the race 12 points behind first-place Terry Labonte in the Winston Cup points chase. In a horrifying instant, Earnhardt's car was bumped by Sterling Marlin's and thrown into the air at more than 200 mph.

When his car finally landed with its sheet metal twisted and torn, Earnhardt had a broken sternum and collarbone. He was fortunate to be alive.

"In your dark moments of thought, you think (what happened to Earnhardt) could be a one-way ticket out of here," says H.A. "Humpy" Wheeler, CMS president.

Instead, three days later, Earnhardt

qualified 12th at Indianapolis for the Brick-yard 400. He hurt too badly to raise one arm over his shoulder, but he drove 6 laps in the race anyway. When he pulled himself from the car during a caution period, he was in tears from pain and disappointment.

"I didn't want to give up," Earnhardt says now.

Earnhardt's team also had problems. A once-promising year fizzled out and, eventually, crew chief David Smith was replaced with Larry McReynolds. This year, pit-stop problems at Daytona led to a massive reshuffling of the race crew and the learning process between driver and team began again.

After early frustrations, Earnhardt can feel the team starting to gel.

Now, Earnhardt is trying to become the oldest driver to win a championship. If he does so, it would be with his undeniable flair for the dramatic.

Earnhardt has always been gifted physically.

When other drivers' heart rates were measured at more than 100 beats per minute prior to a race, Earnhardt's was ticking along at 53 beats a minute. Where others got excited, he was relaxed.

"I'm more calculating," Earnhardt says. "You don't panic. You concern yourself more with the long term of the race.

"As far as the aggressiveness, it's still there. Watch the last lap if I'm in there. If I've got a smell of the front, watch what happens."

His three grown children—Kerry, Kelley and Dale Jr.—live near Earnhardt's farm. Earnhardt, Teresa and their 8-year-old daughter, Taylor, live on the farm. Earnhardt cherishes the moments when he and Taylor work the farm and ride horses together.

"You're always learning how to be a better dad," he says.

Dale and Teresa Earnhardt were married Nov. 14, 1982. The date is etched into his wedding ring, and they sound like sweethearts. When he calls her at home during a break from practice at the track, Earnhardt says a quick "I love you" before turning off the cell phone.

On Monday, a rare day off, Earnhardt checked out cushions Teresa bought for their outdoor furniture, hung wind chimes, put in a horseshoe pit and installed hitching posts for their horses.

He likes being at home. When he wants to be alone, he'll climb into his tractor with an enclosed cab and cut hay.

In the evenings, he'll watch the Atlanta Braves on TV. If they're not playing, he'll check out CNN or the Weather Channel, often with headphones so he doesn't disturb Teresa.

"I feel 30. I haven't changed in that respect," Earnhardt says. "My body tells me two beers is enough now. Two glasses of wine at dinner are OK. Drink any more than that and your body will tell on you. That's just life."

Earnhardt is awake by 5:30 most mornings, listening to the geese at his fishing pond. He's out of the house and on his farm by 6:30.

"You see so much more than you used to see," Earnhardt says. "I reckon age does that to you."

But it always comes back to racing. He wants to win again badly and believes he will.

"His desire is still there," Teresa says. "I think he's comfortable but I don't think he's content."

Earnhardt says he's not ready to retire.

"This is what I'm thinking," he says. "In five or six years, if Dale Jr.'s starting to make it (as a race car driver) and if I'm involved with that, then it may be easier to retire.

"I surely don't want to race too long. I think A.J. Foyt raced too long. I think Richard Petty raced too long out of necessity. I think Richard would have liked to have retired earlier. But I bet Richard still has the fire inside.

"That's the part I worry about ... when I do think it's time or, when time says it's time, that inside I can accept it."

June 15, 1997

Will someone boo me, please?

by David Poole

Charlotte, N.C.—Dale Earnhardt hears the boos cascading from the stands when Jeff Gordon is introduced these days.

Those used to be Earnhardt's boos.

"I wish they were booing me," Earnhardt said Saturday at Michigan Speedway. "If they boo you on Sunday, you go to the bank on Monday.

"I don't want to be the guy who's not the hero, but I want to be the winner."

That's something Earnhardt hasn't been in the past 40 races, tying the longest nonwinning streak of his career. He's sixth in the Winston Cup standings, but he has only one top-five finish this season—a second in the Winston 500 at Talladega.

"We're going to win," Earnhardt said. "It's not a question of whether we'll ever win again, it's a question of when it's going to be. It could be this Sunday or next Sunday.

"I'm flattered you're worried about me," Earnhardt told reporters. "That makes me feel like we're not out of the picture, and we're not."

*Jeff Siner/
The Charlotte
Observer*

September 1, 1997

What's wrong with Dale?

by David Poole

Darlington, S.C.—All of a sudden, the question "What's wrong with Dale Earnhardt?" took a more serious tone Sunday.

Earnhardt spent the night at McLeod Regional Medical Center in Florence, S.C., after an odd first-lap incident in Sunday's Southern 500.

Earnhardt, who started 36th, hit the outside wall on the first turn of the first lap at Darlington Raceway.

His car brushed the wall in Turn 1, then smacked it hard in Turn 2. Earnhardt slowed and tried to drive around to his pit stall on the backstretch.

He missed the turn-in, however, and had to take the car all the way around again. He got onto pit road this time, and was helped out of the car by his crew.

He was taken to the infield care center and then to the hospital for tests.

"They checked Dale out pretty good," said Don Hawk, president of Dale Earnhardt Inc. "They checked for heat exhaustion and potassium levels and carbon monoxide. They're checking everything they can possibly check. It was none of the above.

"We've just got to wait and see what happens. More tests are coming. There's no answer."

Team owner Richard Childress said Earnhardt was "a little groggy" before the race.

"We were going to try to get him in (the pits) before the race ever started, but he didn't hear us," Childress said.

After Earnhardt hit the wall and then missed the entrance to pit road, his crew called him on the radio but he did not respond immediately. At one point, a crew member told Earnhardt to "just park the car on the backstretch" rather than try to bring it around again. But Earnhardt continued.

"We don't know what it is. He just can't remember what happened," Hawk said.

Racing legend and seven-time Winston Cup champion, Dale Earnhardt. (Christopher A. Record/The Charlotte Observer)

DALE'S SUNDAY

11 a.m.: Dale Earnhardt and the other 42 drivers in the Southern 500 gather for the drivers meeting in the garage area at Darlington Raceway.

12:30 p.m.: Earnhardt goes to the stage for driver introductions.

12:45 p.m.: Earnhardt gets into his No. 3 Chevrolet, which is on the outside of the 18th row of the starting grid.

12:55 p.m.: Members of his crew notice that Earnhardt, who often dozes in his car while it is being worked on or during race delays, seems to be sleeping. As the command to start engines approaches, a crew member wakes him up. But when Earnhardt seems to nod off again, crew members begin to sense a problem.

1 p.m.: The command is given to fire the engines. The field rolls off pit road and begins taking 3 pace laps.

1:05 p.m.: Earnhardt's crew grows more concerned. Don Hawk, president of Dale Earnhardt Inc., monitors radio transmission during the pace laps. "His voice was very unclear," Hawk said. "It just didn't sound like Dale."

1:10 p.m.: As the field comes up to speed, Earnhardt's car lags back. It brushes the Turn 1 wall, then hits the wall hard in Turn 2. Earnhardt drives slowly around the track, but misses the entrance to pit road. He goes around again, ignoring team owner Richard Childress' radio command to park the car where it is.

1:12 p.m.: Earnhardt gets his car onto pit road, but his crew has to get in front of it to bring it to a stop. The crew helps him from the car, sits him down against the pit wall and begins giving him oxygen. Medical crews arrive and Earnhardt, his body hanging limp, is carried to the infield care center.

1:30 p.m.: Earnhardt is taken to McLeod Regional Medical Center in Florence for tests. Over the next several hours, he is checked for heart and neurological problems, heat exhaustion, carbon monoxide inhalation, dehydration and a myriad of other possible problems.

Cleared to race
by David Poole

Richmond, Va.—Dale Earnhardt said Friday doctors did everything "other than taking me apart" in their search for the cause of last Sunday's blackout at Darlington.

"They dug and prodded and did everything they could do," Earnhardt said. "They worked awful hard on me and looked awful deep and found nothing, which is a great relief."

Dr. Charles Branch, a neurosurgeon at Bowman Gray Medical Center in Winston-Salem, said Earnhardt "had an episode that probably remains somewhat unexplained."

Branch said Earnhardt was cleared to race in tonight's Exide 400 at Richmond International Raceway after doctors reviewed an extensive battery of tests "to determine whether or not there was any medical condition that we could identify that ... would put him at any further risk at continuing ... as a race car driver, and we could find none."

Branch offered two possible explanations for the blackout, or what he called "a temporary dysfunction of the brain," which led to Earnhardt hitting the wall twice on the first

Racer Dale Earnhardt sits in his car before a qualifying race. (Christopher A. Record/The Charlotte Observer)

lap and then missing pit road the first time he tried to find the entrance.

The first is that it was a migraine-like episode in which a blood vessel went into a spasm or contracted to restrict blood flow to Earnhardt's brain stem just long enough to create the dysfunction.

"This is not something you can treat or identify once it's gone," Branch said.

The second possible explanation Branch offered was a "short circuit" of the brain caused by an injury Earnhardt suffered years ago.

"Any contusion or bruise of the brain ... can leave a little scar in the brain," Branch said. "Stress or heat, or getting too tired, might precipitate a little event where the brain short-circuits temporarily."

Branch said he could not tell Earnhardt the same thing won't happen again.

"The brain-wave testing and all the other testing we did were normal," the doctor said. "So whatever this was, was temporary and it's impossible to say if this will or won't happen again. But it doesn't appear likely."

October 6, 1997

Back to the front

by Ron Green

For all those years, Dale Earnhardt was the star of the show, taking all the Oscars for best in a leading role.

They could have handed him the trophy before the Winston Cup racing season began.

Sunday at Charlotte Motor Speedway, he was best in a supporting role, reprising some of his best work from his seven Winston Cup championship seasons, the key element of which is simple—racing, real racing, door-to-door, nerve-to-nerve.

And Sunday he made us understand what he never doubted, that 46 years of living and 54 races without a victory don't mean he can't play the leading role again.

Dale Jarrett won the UAW-GM 500, his sixth victory of the year, and Bobby Labonte finished second, but it was Earnhardt who kept the pot boiling. He raced Jarrett side-by-side and Labonte side-by-side and anybody else who wanted to try him.

His crew chief, Larry McReynolds, loved it.

"For everyone who was second-guessing him, he showed from Lap 160 to 210 that he's as good as he ever was," said McReynolds.

That was the period when Earnhardt and Jarrett were frequently racing close enough to have a conversation at 180 mph.

"If they'd done that much longer," said McReynolds, "there probably wouldn't have been no more seats in the grandstands because they'd have torn 'em out and thrown 'em."

At one point, car owner Richard Childress told McReynolds he had better calm Earnhardt down, and McReynolds replied, "No way. That's the guy I came to work for. That's the guy I used to sit and watch and try to outrun every Sunday."

That was the guy, the great racer who had won 70 times, the man in black with the cold stare, the chilling smile and the skill to make 3,600 pounds of steel dance a waltz. The Intimidator.

This is the third race in a row Earnhardt has threatened to win. He has finished 2-2-3 and is tasting it.

He climbed out of his black Chevy at day's end and said, "It was fun getting up there and doing it again. We're getting it back. It's just a matter of time."

Jeff Siner/The Charlotte Observer

May 22, 1998

The son also rises

By Ron Green Jr

Mooresville, N.C.—It's lunchtime at Dale Earnhardt, Inc. and the man whose name is on the sprawling building is trying to eat spaghetti in his office while talking to a visitor.

A throbbing bass line from a car stereo thumps through Dale Earnhardt's office, providing an unwanted soundtrack to dinner hour.

Exasperated by the low-slung sound that beats, beats, beats its way inside the office walls, Earnhardt excuses himself, opens the front door and gives his 23-year-old son, Dale Jr., whose black Chevy Impala has become a rolling concert hall, a warning.

"Turn the music down or turn it off ... now," Earnhardt barks at his son.

Kids.

Dale Earnhardt Jr. is still a kid in so many ways.

He lives rent-free in a double-wide trailer on property his father owns. He's got a set of drums he loves to bang on, he's always got a buddy or two hanging around his home, and if he's not driving his Grand National race car like he'll be doing Saturday in the Carquest Auto Parts 300 at Charlotte Motor Speedway, he's probably listening to music (he favors alternative bands) or playing on his computer.

"He still gets to be himself," says sister Kelley, who's three years older than Dale Jr.

But he's becoming a star.

In his first full season on the Grand National circuit, Dale Jr. has already won one race, finished second in two others and, keeping with Earnhardt tradition, flipped his car on the back straight at Daytona and then walked away from it.

He has already begun to live up to the enormous expectations that come with having a name framed by tire smoke and trophies.

He's so popular, industry insiders say sales of Dale Jr. merchandise already rank among the top 10 for all drivers—Winston Cup included.

"There ain't no pressure," Dale Jr. says, sitting below a framed photograph of his grandfather, Ralph, the inspiration of the Earnhardt racing family.

"I use it to my advantage. That's the only way this deal's going to work—if everything that could be a negative gets made into a positive."

It's not easy being the son of a legend.

In Dale Jr.'s case, it meant a childhood in which he rarely lacked for anything except the constant presence of his father. Dale Sr. has won seven Winston Cup points championships, 71 races and the hearts of thousands of fans.

But it came with a cost.

Dover. Daytona. Talladega. Bristol. Earnhardt was always somewhere else when Dale Jr. was growing up.

"There was an absence," Dale Jr. says. "We had good schooling and good opportunities because of him. But when you're a kid, you don't realize all of that.

"The family suffers but it's part of the job."

They had their moments together.

Like the summer afternoon when Earnhardt tried to teach his son to get up on water skis. To make it easier, Earnhardt put Dale Jr. on skis in shallow water behind a pickup truck then drove him through the boat house.

"They drug me up on that concrete and skinned my rear all up," Dale Jr. says.

Then there was the time when Dale Jr. climbed into a go-kart for the first time. He hardly knew the brake from the accelerator and when he put his foot down, the go-kart climbed several feet up a guide wire holding a power line in place.

And there was always racing.

Earnhardt learned the sport by watching his father, a local hero. He hung around the garage, he tinkered with engines and he let racing become his oxygen.

Dale Jr. was the same way. He did odd jobs around the shop for his dad, gradually taking on more responsibility as he grew older.

After graduating from Mooresville High School in 1992, Dale Jr. attended a trade school for two years, then worked in his dad's Chevrolet dealership in Newton. He did oil changes, body work, whatever was necessary, learning his way into the business. Nothing was given to him.

He began racing street stock cars at Concord Motor Speedway when he was 17, building his own car while getting a hands-on feel for what his father did.

"If you pay attention, that's where you get good at what you do," Dale Jr. says.

Parked behind a maintenance building behind Earnhardt's race shop is the rusting shell of Dale Jr.'s first race car. Dead leaves litter the interior and the faded red paint is peeling off. It's an old Monte Carlo that Dale Jr. built, feeling his way into the sport.

"We've come a long way from that," Dale Jr. says, looking at his training wheels.

Now, in addition to being father and son, Dale and Dale Jr. are mentor and student, car owner (though stepmother Teresa Earnhardt officially owns Dale Jr.'s car) and driver.

It's difficult to separate the professional relationship from the paternal one.

When Earnhardt talks about Dale Jr.'s progress, you sense the pride. He keeps mentioning how well he's doing and how, at age 23, Dale Jr. is doing all the right things.

"He's an Earnhardt," the father says, referring to the aggressive driving style that has defined his career.

Earnhardt has guided Dale Jr. in racing without forcing his knowledge on his son. Earnhardt believes in his kids earning what they have.

"It's totally up to him," Earnhardt says. "Everything they (the kids) have done, apart from education, I've tried to let them decide about their life and how they live it."

Sometimes, Dale Jr. has strained at the leash. It led to a two-year stint at Oak Ridge Military Academy in Greensboro when Dale Jr. was in the seventh and eighth grades. Talking in class and running wild at times were all part of Dale Jr.'s personality for a time.

"I was always kept in a box, so to speak, under strict adult supervision," he says. "Anytime they opened it, I came out of that box."

Does Dale Jr. listen better now?

"Do they ever?'" his father says with a laugh.

"I'm proud of him growing up the way he has. I feel he turned out pretty nice."

Like most sons, Dale Jr. seeks his father's approval above all others.

"It's like a never-ending process earning his respect," Dale Jr. says. "It's bottomless. I get worn out by it at times. But it's something you always want. Sometimes it becomes more important than the job at hand."

It's Dale Jr.'s greatest incentive.

"What other reason do you race for?" Dale Jr. asks.

"You race for thousands of dollars. That's good. You race to win. That's good. Those are good reasons. But there's nothing wrong with wanting to make my dad happy."

When Dale Jr. won his first Grand National race at Texas last month, father and son flew home together.

Two months earlier, the Earnhardt family and close friends had gathered at 3 a.m. to welcome Dale Sr. home after his Daytona 500 victory.

In April, Dale Sr. called ahead to make sure family and friends did the same for his son.

"Dad brought him inside and told him congratulations," Kelley says.

It's after lunch now and Dale Jr. is on his way to being a star again.

He's got to hit the road for an autograph session in Salem, Va., and he's making sure he's got everything. Autograph cards he'll sign. Directions.

He's on his way.

"I'll see you later," Dale Jr. tells his dad as he turns to go.

"You be careful," Earnhardt, the father, says.

As the Impala pulls away, the music thumps to life.

Chapter Twenty-one:
1998: Dale-tona 500

"Dale Earnhardt comes out smokin' and wins the Daytona 500, the Intimidator intimidating again."

—Ron Green, in a column published Dec. 30, 1997, on things he'd like to see happen in 1998.

February 6, 1998
The real Dale Earnhardt?
by David Poole

Daytona Beach, Fla.—Dale Earnhardt is exactly what he appears to be. He's also nothing like what he appears to be.

He appears, for example, to have a simple approach to racing. When the green flag falls, he runs as hard as his car will let him for as long as it will let him. They pay the most money for winning, so that's what he wants to do.

On the other hand, he was one of the first Winston Cup drivers to fully appreciate and capitalize on the off-track business opportunities his on-track success made possible.

He appears, also, to be gruff, surly and unapproachable. His image is "the Intimidator," and his no-nonsense demeanor backs that up.

It's just as true, however, that there's hardly anybody in racing who enjoys himself more when he's at the track. At times, he's as playful as his young daughter, Taylor Nicole, who can often be seen riding her bicycle around the drivers' motor home area at the tracks.

One thing, though, is exactly what it appears to be. Dale Earnhardt can flat drive a race car. ...

Earnhardt enters the final year of the fifth decade on a nonwinning streak that goes back to March of 1996. And although he has won six Busch Clashes, two Pepsi 400s and nine 125-mile qualifying races at Daytona, he has never won the Daytona 500. ...

As NASCAR turns 50, it appears Earnhardt's days as a dominant force in the sport could be ending.

Just remember, though, when it comes to Earnhardt, things might not be always exactly as they appear.

February 13, 1998

Thursday money
by David Poole

Daytona Beach, Fla.—On Dale Earnhardt's Daytona calendar, every day should be Thursday.

For the ninth straight year, Earnhardt won a 125-mile qualifying race Thursday at Daytona International Speedway, joining Sterling Marlin in giving Chevrolet a pair of victories as the field for Sunday's Daytona 500 was set.

Earnhardt's domination—he led all 50 laps in the second race—provided another page in his Daytona saga.

The seven-time Winston Cup champion has 30 wins at the 2.5-mile speedway, but never the Daytona 500 in 19 starts.

"It's about time we got in the winner's circle again," said Earnhardt, whose victory in last year's 125-miler was his only trip there in 1997. In addition to his much-discussed Daytona 500 jinx, Earnhardt hasn't won in 59 Winston Cup starts in almost two full seasons.

"We're going to start our winning streak here at Daytona and go on from that," Earnhardt said. "I'm ready to start. I don't want those other guys to have any time to practice and get their cars better."

> "It's about time we got in the winner's circle again."
> —Earnhardt, after winning a 125-mile qualifying race at Daytona

Jeff Siner/The Charlotte Observer

February 15, 1998

Vintage Earnhardt returns

by Ron Green

"You could write a big book on everything that has happened to me the last 19 years in the Daytona 500. I'm sure we're going to write another chapter into it and hopefully it's a great chapter."—Dale Earnhardt, before the 1998 Daytona 500

Dale Earnhardt went winless last year for the first time since 1981. That suggests that at age 46, with all those millions in the bank, he may be losing some of the skill and daring that have won him 70 NASCAR Winston Cup races, seven Winston Cup championships and the nickname of the Intimidator.

But he gives that notion the back of his hand, fixing you with those Intimidator eyes and telling you he has lost none of his confidence. And if you doubt it, how about that move he made Thursday in a 125-mile race when his car got sideways in the third turn? Instead of checking up, he drove on through and came out of the turn leading the race.

"I don't know if that's craziness or determination," he said.

Vintage Earnhardt is what it was.

History says, nevertheless, that he will lose at least one more race before he wins again. He's in the Daytona 500 today. He has won 30 races on this track, all kinds of races but one. He has never won the 500. He has run it 19 times and always, someone else has driven into the winner's circle.

But John Elway finally won his Super Bowl, maybe this year Earnhardt finally wins his Daytona 500.

"Remember that look in Elway's eyes?" said Earnhardt. "Look in my eyes. We're going to be after it."

Dale Earnhardt (with glasses) stands with other NASCAR drivers (L-R) Jimmy Spencer, Michael Waltrip, Dale Jarrett, Sterling Martin and Terry Labonte during driver introductions for the Daytona 500. (Jeff Siner/The Charlotte Observer)

February 16, 1998

DALE-TONA 500

by David Poole

"It was my time. I have been passed on the last lap, I have run out of gas and I have cut a tire. I knew we were coming back to the checkered."—Earnhardt

Daytona Beach, Fla.—At last.

Dale Earnhardt ended two decades of frustration in the Daytona 500 Sunday, scoring a heart-pounding victory to stop the two most maddening streaks of his racing career.

Earnhardt had won 30 races at the 2.5-mile mother church of stock car racing, but never Winston Cup racing's biggest event, the season-opening 500. He also had gone 59 races, almost two full seasons, without winning anywhere.

Both streaks were washed away in his 20th start in a race he had led four times before with 10 laps to go, only to lose in heart-rending fashion.

"All right!" Earnhardt said as he popped his head out of the black No. 3 Chevrolet in Victory Lane. "Yes! Yes! Yes!"

Earnhardt's average speed for winning the race was 172.712 mph, making this the third fastest Daytona 500.

His average speed for his trip down pit road to Victory Lane, though, was one handshake per second. In a remarkable show of respect, members of virtually every team lined up to congratulate the seven-time Winston Cup champion on his 71st career victory.

"I cried a little bit in the race car on the way to the checkered flag," Earnhardt said. "Well, maybe not cried, but at least my eyes watered up.

"Everybody over the last week has said this is your year. Man, they were just so adamant about it. They knew something I didn't, I reckon."

Earnhardt's victory, worth a Winston Cup record $1,059,105, was assured one lap early.

He took the lead by passing Richard Childress teammate Mike Skinner in Turn 4 of Lap 140, and held it after stopping for fuel and right-side tires under yellow with less than 30 laps to go.

After the green flag flew on Lap 178, Earnhardt was chased like the rabbit at a dog track by a swarming nest of challengers determined to deny him this long-awaited moment.

On Lap 199 of 200, Jimmy Spencer's Ford smacked into John Andretti's Pontiac coming out of Turn 2. Andretti spun, collecting Lake Speed's Ford as it did, and brought out the third caution of the day.

Earnhardt just needed to win the race back to the caution and white flags. Coming out of Turn 4, he saw Rick Mast's lapped Ford rolling in the inside lane and used it as a blocker. That left Bobby Labonte to squeeze past a strong Jeremy Mayfield for second, and popped the cork on a celebration Earnhardt fans have been awaiting for 20 years. ...

When he saw the yellow and white flags flying together, Earnhardt knew the victory was his. Unless, of course, his car quit on him as he made the final lap under yellow.

Hey, stranger things have happened to him here.

"It was my time," Earnhardt said. "I have been passed on the last lap, I have run out of gas and I have cut a tire.

"I knew we were coming back to the checkered. I started going slow, but then I decided I would go fast because I wanted to get on back around there. I don't care how we won it, but we won it."

Finally.

(Above) Dale Earnhardt leads Bobby Labonte down the front stretch in the closing moments as the crowd stands to cheer Earnhardt's first win in the Daytona 500. (Below) Dale Earnhardt crosses the finish line as the flagman drops the checkered and yellow caution flag. (Jeff Siner/The Charlotte Observer)

DALE IN THE DAYTONA 500

Year	Car	Start	Fin.	Laps	Earnings
1979	Buick No.2	10	8	199	22,845
1980	Oldsmobile No. 2	32	4	199	36,350
1981	Pontiac No. 2	7	5	200	37,365
1982	Ford No. 15	10	36	44	14,700
1983	Ford No. 15	3	35	63	37,011
1984	Chevrolet No. 3	29	2	200	81,825
1985	Chevrolet No. 3	18	32	84	17,150
1986	Chevrolet No. 3	4	14	197	61,655
1987	Chevrolet No. 3	13	5	200	64,925
1988	Chevrolet No. 3	6	10	200	2,540
1989	Chevrolet No. 3	8	3	200	95,550
1990	Chevrolet No. 3	2	5	200	109,325
1991	Chevrolet No. 3	4	5	200	113,850
1992	Chevrolet No. 3	3	9	199	87,000
1993	Chevrolet No. 3	4	2	200	181,825
1994	Chevrolet No. 3	2	7	200	110,340
1995	Chevrolet No. 3	2	2	200	212,250
1996	Chevrolet No. 3	1	2	200	215,065
1997	Chevrolet No. 3	4	31	195	72,545
1998	Chevrolet No. 3	2	1	200	$1,059,105

Dale Earnhardt with his wife, Teresa, and his crew celebrate his victory in the Daytona 500. (Jeff Siner/The Charlotte Observer)

February 16, 1998
Beating the jinx
by Ron Green

Daytona Beach, Fla.—The racing had gone from hard to fierce, the laps winding down under threatening skies, men with millions of dollars at stake driving 190 mph and taking chances that would scare the devil himself.

Dale Earnhardt was leading, as he had much of the afternoon, but you wondered what would happen this time to defeat him. This was the Daytona 500, and he doesn't win this race. He had won 70 NASCAR Winston Cup races and seven season championships and 30 other Daytona International Speedway races, but not the 500. Something always happened to keep him from winning his sport's biggest race. He cut a tire or ran out of gas or broke something or just got beat.

What would happen this time?

Everybody in the crowd of 180,000 was standing. On the next-to-last lap, there was a wreck on the backstretch, far behind the leaders, which meant the last lap would be run under caution and whoever crossed the finish line first on this 199th of 200 laps would win.

Cars gathered up in a growling cluster behind Earnhardt, banging into each other, clawing to get to the front. But they couldn't make it. Not this time.

The Great American Racer had won the Great American Race.

It may have been the most popular victory in the 50 years since NASCAR racing was born in this place, or certainly one rivaled only by Richard Petty's 200th win, in 1984.

It came out of the blue. Earnhardt, 46, hadn't won in his past 59 races. Questions arose. Would he ever win anything again, let alone the Daytona 500? Had he lost his daring, his reflexes, his desire?

He answered those questions Sunday, and the sport of racing smiled.

As Earnhardt drove down pit road toward Victory Lane, hundreds of crewmen from other teams came out to congratulate him and to touch his hand as he drove by. Then, the man they call the Intimidator acted like a kid with a new toy. He drove into the infield grass and did a couple of doughnuts.

And either because he's a heckuva driver or he was just lucky, when he had done his spins in the grass, the tracks were shaped like a 3, the number on his car.

Fans went out there and picked up some of the grass he had knocked loose and put it in their coolers, saving a piece of this moment. Some lay down in the tire tracks, to feel the place where Earnhardt had driven. And some stood in the tracks and had their pictures taken.

Mike Skinner, Earnhardt's teammate in the Richard Childress stable and one of his toughest competitors Sunday, yelled, "You're the man. You're a baaad man!"

In Victory Lane, Earnhardt said,

> **"In the press box, he pulled a toy monkey out of his uniform shirt, threw it to the floor and shouted, "I'm here, I'm here, I'm here and I got that . . . monkey off my back!"**
> **—Dale Earnhardt**

"Daytona is ours! We won it, we won it, we won it!"

In the press box, he pulled a toy monkey out of his uniform shirt, threw it to the floor and shouted, "I'm here, I'm here, I'm here and I got that . . . monkey off my back!"

History would have been out of kilter if Earnhardt hadn't ever won the Daytona 500, the premier event in NASCAR Winston Cup racing. He has won everything else and in doing so has become the foremost figure in his sport. But this one was, of course, special, and as tough as he is, he had tears in his eyes

on the last lap.

The past didn't haunt him on the closing laps.

"I wasn't thinking about what could happen," he said. "I was just doing what I had to do. I was working to keep my car in front until somebody turned me over or we got to the finish line."

During his post-race news conference, Earnhardt looked down to the infield and saw several dozen fans lined up to form a 3.

"Race fans are awesome," he said.

"Gosh, it was a great day."

February 18, 1998
The "Late Show" Top Ten

"Reasons It Took Me 20 Years to Win the Daytona 500." As presented by Daytona 500 winner Dale Earnhardt on the Monday broadcast of the "Late Show" with David Letterman.

10. It took me 19 years to realize I had the emergency brake on.
9. Finally rotated and balanced my mustache.
8. Quit training with the Canadian snowboarding team.
7. Stopped letting my 300-pound cousin, Ricky, ride shotgun.
6. New strategy: Pretend I'm Dave driving home on the Merritt Parkway.

5. Who cares that it took me 20 years—at least my name isn't Dick Trickle.
4. Just figured out that if you mash the gas pedal all the way down, the car takes off like a SOB.
3. My new pit crew—the Spice Girls.
2. This year, whenever I passed somebody, I gave them the (obscene gesture).
1. My secret to success: one can of motor oil in my engine, one can of motor oil in my pants!

The checkered floor of Victory Lane is reflected in Dale Earnhardt's sunglasses. (Jeff Siner/The Charlotte Observer)

"Yes! Yes! Yes!" in Victory Lane, Dale Earnhardt celebrates the end of two decades of frustration at Daytona. (Jeff Siner/The Charlotte Oberver)

Chapter Twenty-two:
1999: No slowing down

Races	Won	Top 5	Top 10	Poles	Earnings
34	3	7	21	0	$2,682,089

August 28, 1999
Bristol dishes out more than some could take
by David Poole

BRISTOL, Tenn.—Cantankerous, aggressive and exciting.

Dale Earnhardt used those words to describe Bristol Motor Speedway Saturday night after his controversial victory in the Goody's 500.

The same words, of course, could also be used to describe the man who uttered them. He was certainly all three on a wild night that will keep Winston Cup race fans talking for weeks to come.

Terry Labonte had the lead with a half-lap to go until Earnhardt's Chevrolet hit Labonte's in the left rear and sent Labonte spinning on the backstretch. Earnhardt dove low around Labonte and beat Jimmy Spencer back to the checkered flag to win for the second time this season and the 73rd time in his Winston Cup career.

It was his first short-track win since a victory at Martinsville in 1995 and his first win at a non-restrictor-plate track since Atlanta in March of 1996.

"Terry caught me coming to the white flag in (turns) three and four and bumped me a little," Earnhardt said. "When we went back to Turn 1, I went back in there to get with him and get under him. Whether he checked up or I got in deeper or what, I bumped him too hard and turned him loose. It spun him.

"I didn't mean to do it intentionally. I meant to get in there and race with him, but I know he's not going to see it that way. I know he's upset. He has a right to be."

Labonte was doubly upset, actually. He took the lead from Earnhardt on Lap 439 and was on his way to victory until he slowed for a caution on Lap 491 and got hit from behind by Darrell Waltrip. That spun him in Turn 4, but he got new tires and the green flag with five laps to go. He sliced back toward the front and had grabbed the lead back as he and Earnhardt got the white flag. But he never made it back to the start-finish line and wound up eighth with a wrecked Chevrolet.

"Dale gave me a shot and turned me around," Labonte said. "That's the way it goes, I guess."

Earnhardt maintains that all he intended to do was to race with everything he had to take the victory away on the final lap.

"When you go into the corner after someone on the last lap and he checks up or you get into the corner harder or whatever, you've got no control of the speeds of the race car when you get together," he said. "I definitely didn't mean to go down there and turn him around. I was getting after it. I knew I was going to have to race him hard to get in the corner and try to get back under him."

The controversy added another chapter to Bristol's history of eventful finishes. Labonte's last win in 1995, in fact, came when he took the checkered flag going sideways after a bump from Earnhardt in Turn 2. In the spring race in 1997, Jeff Gordon tapped Rusty Wallace loose in the final two turns and took away the victory.

The major development in the first half of the race was points leader Dale Jarrett's trouble. He spun on Lap 77 and then got hit from

behind by Jerry Nadeau on Lap 99. The damage from those two wrecks put him behind the wall for more than 150 laps, and Jarrett wound up 38th. He lost 101 points from his lead over Mark Martin but still has a 213-point edge.

"We knew sooner or later it was going to happen," said Jarrett, who hadn't finished worse than 11th since the season-opening Daytona 500. "You can't ride without all the trouble all the time. We'll just take our lumps here and go on."

That's a sentiment several drivers might have shared after another typically wild evening at Bristol.

2000 Race-by-Race Results

Event	Location	Start	Finish	Points	Money Won
Daytona 500	Daytona	4	2	170	$613,659
Dura Lube/Big K 400	Rockingham	18	41	40	$36,725
Las Vegas 400	Las Vegas	38	7	146	$91,350
Cracker Barrel 500	Atlanta	33	40	43	$41,625
TranSouth Financial 400	Darlington	30	25	88	$37,020
PRIMESTAR 500	Texas	38	8	142	$97,775
Food City 500	Bristol	43	10	124	$48,630
Goody's Body Pain 500	Martinsville	39	19	106	$39,150
DieHard 500	Talladega	17	1	185	$147,795
California 500 presented by NAPA	California	9	12	132	$55,425
Pontiac Excitement 400	Richmond	37	8	142	$48,540
Coca-Cola 600	Charlotte	15	6	150	$70,225
MBNA Platinum 400	Dover	34	11	130	$49,510
Kmart 400	Michigan	15	16	115	$39,825
Pocono 500	Pocono	25	7	146	$57,190
Save Mart/Kragen 350	Sears Point	23	9	138	$46,165
Pepsi 400	Daytona	10	2	175	$92,175
Jiffy Lube 300	New Hampshire	14	8	142	$56,675
Pennsylvania 500	Pocono	11	9	143	$48,765
Brickyard 400	Indianapolis	18	10	134	$135,525
Frontier @ the Glen	Watkins Glen	14	20	103	$41,525
Pepsi 400 presented by Meijer	Michigan	38	5	160	$51,005
Goody's Headache Powder 500	Bristol	26	1	180	$89,880
The 50th Pepsi Southern 500	Darlington	25	22	97	$42,470
Exide NASCAR Select Batteries 400	Richmond	33	6	150	$47,055
Dura Lube/Kmart 300	New Hampshire	16	13	124	$55,125
MBNA Gold 400	Dover	37	8	142	$52,065
NAPA AutoCare 500	Martinsville	38	2	175	$70,225
UAW-GM Quality 500	Charlotte	17	12	127	$44,450
Winston 500	Talladega	27	1	180	$120,290
Pop Secret Microwave Popcorn 400	Rockingham	37	40	43	$36,900
Checker Auto Parts/Dura Lube 500	Phoenix	14	11	130	$57,225
Pennzoil 400 presented by Kmart	Homestead	23	8	142	$65,575
NAPA 500	Atlanta	36	9	138	$54,550
					$2,682,089

Chapter Twenty-three:
2000: Still the master

Races	Won	Top 5	Top 10	Poles	Earnings
34	2	13	24	0	$2,605,677

October 15, 2000

Earnhardt charges from 18th to front, wins

by David Poole

TALLADEGA, Ala.—Nobody can do what Dale Earnhardt did to win the Winston 500 at Talladega Superspeedway. Not even Earnhardt.

Forget what you saw. Forget what the official results show.

Nobody can be 18th with five laps to go and then have to spend the final lap worrying about being passed to have a win taken away. Nobody can run up the middle of a three-wide pack of screaming race cars and draft his way from oblivion to Victory Lane.

Nobody can do that. Not even Earnhardt.

And yet, it happened.

Earnhardt added a chapter to his legend on Sunday, roaring through traffic over the final laps in incredible fashion to win for the second time this season, the third time in four races at Talladega and the 10th time in his career at the 2.66-mile speedway.

Even Earnhardt had trouble conceiving it.

"To think anybody could come from as far back in the field as we were and win this race is beyond me," he said. "You saw it. I couldn't believe it."

How can you describe what you can't believe?

Well, for starters, the day's third caution flag came out on Lap 168 and brought the lead-pack cars in for final pit stops. Jeff Gordon had been on pit road when the yellow came after Mark Martin and Bobby Hamilton made contact behind him as they started in, too. Gordon got his tank of gas before the rest of the leaders and was up front when the green flew with 15 laps to go.

Earnhardt, meanwhile, took fuel and two tires and was 15th on the restart. He tried to start back toward the front using an outside line, but within two laps that move had punted him to 23rd. He had only improved five spots after 183 laps in the 188-lap event.

And then along came Kenny Wallace, who had four new tires on his Chevrolet and was looking for a drafting partner. When Earnhardt pulled down in front of Wallace, Joe Nemechek, Wallace's teammate on Andy Petree's team, lined up behind him, then things started happening.

"It was like I had turbos," Wallace said.

Those turbos were also pushing Earnhardt toward the front.

"I finally got on the outside of the inside line and kept working," Earnhardt said. "Kenny got in there with me along with Nemechek, and we just kept working and they pushed me to the front."

Earnhardt went from 16th to eighth on Lap 185. Coming off Turn 4 on the next lap, his car popped out in front of the middle lane and he suddenly was in fourth, behind only Dale Earnhardt Jr., John Andretti and Mike Skinner.

Andretti led Lap 185. Skinner led 186. But Earnhardt was coming, and with the push from Wallace and Nemechek he was open for business. Earnhardt passed Skinner, his teammate at Richard Childress Racing, on the way to the white flag.

Earnhardt, Wallace and Nemechek were moving so fast that they pushed ahead of the pack, which bunched up racing three-wide behind them. Now, it was a matter of whether Earnhardt could hold the lead he had so miraculously attained.

"I knew they didn't want to sit behind me and run," Earnhardt said.

The fact that the front three broke clear of the rest of the traffic, however, worked against any kind of a last-lap pass by Wallace that would have been a 50th lead change and given the spine-tingling race its 22nd different leader.

"Joe and I knew what we had to do," Wallace said. "But when the three of us broke away there on the last lap it was over because we didn't have any help."

Earnhardt did his part, of course, weaving his car down the backstretch on the final lap to break the draft and keep the teammates

behind him from getting a run off the final corner. The front three raced single-file to the checkered flag, with Wallace matching his career-best finish with a second and Nemechek third after starting from the pole.

"I personally won the race for him," Wallace said of Earnhardt. "And he owes me. You're at Talladega, thinking you've got a shot to win the race, and he's just the master."

Behind the front three came Gordon, Terry Labonte and Skinner as Chevrolet swept the top six spots. As the rest of the lead pack crossed the finish line four- and even five-wide, several cars began to spin and some crashed into the wall at the end of the front-stretch. It was the only major altercation in a race that drivers had feared would be a crash-fest because of new aerodynamic rules and Saturday's last-minute NASCAR decision to reduce the size of the restrictor-plate openings from one inch to fifteen-sixteenths of an inch.

**With victories at the Cracker Barrel 500 in Atlanta (right) and the Winston 500 at Talladega, along with 11 other top-five showings in 2000, Earnhardt finished behind only Winston Cup champion Dale Jarrett in the season's final point standings.
(Ric Feld, AP/Wide World Photos)**

The new rules certainly had the desired effect. The 49 lead changes told only part of the story. Cars swapped positions in the running order the way 13-year-olds swap sweethearts all day long.

Nemechek started from the pole. At the end of Lap 1, he was 16th.

Gordon, who damaged his Chevrolet in Saturday's final practice and had to start from the back of the field in his backup car, had the lead on Lap 13.

With five laps remaining in the race, Earnhardt Jr. was in the lead. When the race ended he was third—third, that is, among rookies in the field. Overall, he was 14th.

Winston Cup points leader Bobby Labonte was second after Lap 184. He finished 12th and lost 48 points to Earnhardt, who moved back into second in the standings ahead of Jeff Burton. Labonte's lead is now 210 points with four races remaining.

"It's the wildest race I've been in in a long time," Nemechek said. "We were running four inches apart going around the corner three-wide all the way down to the bottom of the race track."

That was before everybody really started racing after the final yellow. The final 15 laps looked like rush hour on a four-lane highway, except that the traffic jam was moving at 190 mph. In spite of that and in spite of the wreck after the checkered flag, there was a general sense that things went about as well as could be expected.

Earnhardt leads Kenny Wallace (center) and Joe Nemechek on his way to victory at the 2000 Winston 500 at Talladega Superspeedway. (Jay LaPrete, AP/ Wide World Photos)

"I've got to hand it to the race drivers," Earnhardt said. "They all worked good together. It was a pretty good day, seeing that kind of racing side-by-side and three- and four-wide and nobody got in trouble. It was good, hard racing, but I still don't like restrictor-plate racing. I'm not that good at it."

He's right. Nobody's that good at it, not good enough to do what Earnhardt did.

And yet, it happened.

2000 Race-by-Race Results

Event	Location	Start	Finish	Points	Money Won
Daytona 500	Daytona	21	21	100	$116,107
Dura Lube/Kmart 400	Rockingham	4	2	175	$78,610
CarsDirect.com 400	Las Vegas	33	8	142	$94,900
Cracker Barrel 500	Atlanta	35	1	180	$123,100
Mall.com 400	Darlington	4	3	165	$68,590
Food City 500	Bristol	11	39	51	$26,225
DIRECTV 500	Texas	17	7	146	$108,750
Goody's Body Pain 500	Martinsville	17	9	143	$48,550
DieHard 500	Talladega	4	3	170	$92,630
NAPA Auto Parts 500	California	35	17	112	$59,075
Pontiac Excitement 400	Richmond	31	10	139	$52,800
Coca-Cola 600	Charlotte	15	3	170	$103,250
MBNA Platinum 400	Dover	30	6	155	$75,455
Kmart 400	Michigan	9	2	170	$80,575
Pocono 400	Pocono	16	4	165	$87,495
Save Mart/Kragen 350	Sears Point	29	6	150	$65,165
Pepsi 400	Daytona	18	8	142	$64,375
thatlook.com 300	New Hampshire	24	6	150	$69,425
Pennsylvania 500	Pocono	25	25	93	$48,915
Brickyard 400	Indianapolis	8	8	142	$143,510
Global Crossing @ the Glen	Watkins Glen	3	25	88	$45,180
Pepsi 400 presented by Meijer	Michigan	37	6	150	$51,190
goracing.com 500	Bristol	17	4	165	$62,980
Pepsi Southern 500	Darlington	6	3	170	$82,745
Chevrolet Monte Carlo 400	Richmond	22	2	170	$81,190
Dura Lube 300	New Hampshire	37	12	127	$62,550
MBNA.com 400	Dover	37	17	112	$63,390
NAPA AutoCare 500	Martinsville	12	2	170	$77,925
UAW/GM Quality 500	Charlotte	37	11	135	$58,750
Winston 500	Talladega	20	1	180	$135,900
Pop Secret Microwave Popcorn 400	Rockingham	27	17	117	$49,025
Checker Auto Parts/Dura Lube 500	Phoenix	31	9	143	$65,490
Pennzoil 400 presented by Kmart	Homestead	37	20	103	$60,700
NAPA 500	Atlanta	8	2	175	$99,750
					$2,605,677

Chapter Twenty-four:
2001: Goodbye, No. 3

February 18, 2001
Dale Earnhardt dies at Daytona
by David Poole

DAYTONA BEACH, Fla. - Stock-car racing legend Dale Earnhardt died Sunday afternoon from injuries he suffered in a crash on the final lap of the Daytona 500.

Earnhardt's black No. 3 Chevrolet, which had become a NASCAR icon during his remarkable career, slammed head-on into the outside concrete wall in Turn 4 of the 2.5-mile Daytona International Speedway.

Earnhardt, a Kannapolis native, was unconscious and unresponsive when emergency workers reached him in his car, which came to rest about 300 yards short of the start-finish line. He was cut from his car and taken to nearby Halifax Medical Center, where efforts to revive him failed.

The seven-time Winston Cup champion, tied with Richard Petty for the most all time, was pronounced dead at 5:16 p.m. He was 49.

NASCAR president Mike Helton announced the news at 7 p.m.

"This is undoubtedly one of the most difficult announcements I've ever had to make," Helton said. "But after the accident in Turn 4 at the end of the Daytona 500, we've lost Dale Earnhardt."

Helton, his voice breaking, also read a statement from Bill France Jr., chairman of NASCAR's board of directors, that Helton said summed up the sport's reaction:

"Today NASCAR lost its greatest driver in the history of the sport," France's statement said.

Dr. Steve Bohannon, an emergency room physician at Halifax Medical Center and director of the track's emergency medical services, said the likely cause of Earnhardt's death was a basal skull fracture. That is the same injury that caused the on-track deaths of NASCAR drivers Adam Petty, Kenny Irwin and Tony Roper last year.

In response to those deaths, some drivers began using what's called a HANS device, a head-and-neck restraint system designed to help prevent such injuries.

Earnhardt didn't use the device, and in fact didn't like it, calling it "a noose." Earnhardt still drove with an open-faced helmet, too.

"I know a full-face helmet would not have made any difference whatsoever," Bohannon said of Sunday's crash. "He had no evidence of facial injuries. I don't know if the HANS device would have helped or not. I suspect not."

Bohannon said Earnhardt had blood in his airway and in his ears, injuries that would be consistent with basal skull fractures, but no other external evidence of trauma.

Earnhardt was racing side by side with Sterling Marlin for third place on the final lap of the season's first race. Earnhardt lost control after their cars made contact as they exited the third turn, and his Chevrolet shot up the track in front of Ken Schrader's Pontiac.

The No. 3 Chevrolet slid back down across the track and came to rest in the infield grass with Schrader's Pontiac up against it as the first- and second-place cars, driven by Michael Waltrip and Dale Earnhardt Jr., the oldest of Earnhardt's four children, crossed the finish line. Earnhardt was the car owner of both of those Chevrolets.

Schrader climbed out of his car and ran to check on Earnhardt. He immediately urged emergency workers to come to the injured driver's aid.

Bohannon said he was on the third or fourth ambulance to reach the scene.

One paramedic had an oxygen mask on Earnhardt from the right-side window, while another doctor was administering cardio-pulmonary resuscitation through the driver's-side window as a second paramedic held Earnhardt's head. Other rescue workers were removing the roof from the car, a process that Bohannon said took five to six minutes.

Earnhardt was taken immediately to Halifax Medical Center, a few blocks down

During a break in practice the week before the 2001 Daytona 500, the Earnhardts survey the situation at NASCAR's most famous speedway.
(Paul Kizzle, AP/Wide World Photos)

International Speedway Boulevard from the track. A trauma team including a neurosurgeon and several other doctors was waiting when Earnhardt arrived at 4:54 p.m.

Resuscitation efforts continued for about 20 minutes, but Earnhardt never showed any signs of life. His wife, Teresa, was at his bedside when the doctors pronounced him dead.

"We all did everything we could for him," Bohannon said. "He had what I consider to be life-ending injuries at the time of impact. There was really nothing that could be done for him."

Earnhardt's final career victory came on Oct. 15 of last season at Talladega, Ala., on the day Tony Roper died from injuries he'd suffered in a truck series crash at Texas Motor Speedway the night before.

Earnhardt came from 18th to first in the final laps of that race to score a remarkable victory that will now resonate as a final great memory in a career that included seven championships, tying him with Richard Petty for the all-time record, and 76 victories, sixth best in history.

Sunday's race was the 53rd Winston Cup race at Daytona or Talladega in which restrictor plates had been used. Earnhardt had raced in all of them, winning 11 and finishing in the top 10 in 32 of them. Nobody else was even close to those records, but Earnhardt still openly despised the use of restrictor plates.

The morning of the ill-fated race, Earnhardt walks down pit road at Daytona while holding hands with his wife, Teresa. (Bruce Ackerman, AP/ Wide World Photos)

When Earnhardt made a narrow escape from the 19-car pileup on Lap 173 that sent Tony Stewart's car (20) airborne into a spectacular barrel-roll crash, it appeared that Earnhardt had avoided trouble for the day.
(Chuck McQuinn, AP/Wide World Photos)

While battling for third place on the final lap of the race, Earnhardt and Sterling Marlin bumped, sending Earnhardt crashing into Ken Schrader (36) and head-on into the Turn 4 wall at Daytona. (Glenn Smith, AP/Wide World Photos)

"A race driver hates a restrictor plate," Earnhardt said last year when NASCAR ordered their use for the return race to New Hampshire after the Petty and Irwin tragedies there. "I think the same thing about restrictor plates that I've always thought about restrictor plates. It's not racing. Racing is going out there and trying to be the fastest guy on the race track."

Sunday afternoon, as rescue workers were scrambling toward Earnhardt's wrecked car, Michael Waltrip was driving across the infield grass to begin celebrating his Daytona 500 victory with his crew.

Waltrip knew his car owner had been in a wreck, but he didn't know Earnhardt was hurt until Schrader came to Victory Lane to tell him. When he came to the press box for his winner's interview, Waltrip still did not know how badly Earnhardt was hurt.

But almost as if he instinctively knew the worst, though, the newly crowned Daytona 500 champion was already talking in the past tense about the man who'd made that possible.

"I was so looking forward to doing well for him," Waltrip said. "He wasn't there in Victory Lane and I didn't know he was hurt.

The day after Earnhardt's fatal crash, a memorial outside the Daytona International Speedway drew fans from all over the country. (Layne Bailey/The Charlotte Observer)

That's where my mind is. Racing is our job and he's my owner, but he's also my friend."

About a dozen family and close friends gathered Sunday evening at Earnhardt's childhood home in Kannapolis, where his 70-year-old mother, Martha, still lives.

Two local police officers quietly shooed away fans so the family could have time together at the white bungalow home on Sedan Avenue.

Earnhardt's two older sisters—he was the third of five children—were watching Daytona Sunday afternoon with their mother, who always watches Earnhardt's races. Usually, at least one of the children is there with her because she gets nervous, said Kaye Snipes, the oldest sister.

Snipes said the fear of a fatal wreck is always there, but she said, "You don't think about that, or it drives you crazy."

The last time the family was all together was at Christmas, although Earnhardt talked to his mother once a week, the sisters said.

"Everybody thought he would grow old, like Richard Petty," said Snipes.

Earnhardt is survived by his wife, Teresa; two sons, Dale Jr. and Kerry; and two daughters, Kelly and Taylor Nicole.

Medical doctor Steve Bohannon (center) describes the condition of Dale Earnhardt as NASCAR president Mike Helton (far left) listens to the devastating news. (Layne Bailey/The Charlotte Observer)

Dale Earnhardt's final wave to the crowd before the start of the 2001 Daytona 500. (Russell Williams, AP/Wide World Photos)

NE   1/02